THE NIGHT THE DEFEOS DIED

THE NIGHT THE DEFEOS DIED

RIC OSUNA

Noble Kai Media
Nevada - U.S.A.

Noble Kai Media
Nevada, United States

© Copyright 2002, 2003 by Ric Osuna

All Rights Reserved. No part of this book may be reproduced or transmitted in any form without written permission from the copyright owner.

Noble Kai Media First Edition: 2003

Designed by Ric Osuna
Design Consultant: Eric Hirshfeld
Printed in the United States

Library of Congress Number: 2002090272
ISBN: 1-59109-586-7

To Chie

My best friend and wife,
whose love, patience, and support allowed for the truth to be
uncovered.

CONTENTS

FOREWORD ix

INTRODUCTION xi
Searching for the Truth

PART ONE: MISTAKEN PERCEPTIONS
ONE—Murder on Ocean Avenue 24
TWO—An Open and Shut Case 33

PART TWO: THE UNTOLD STORY
THREE—Life as a DeFeo 41
FOUR—On the Road to Disaster 68
FIVE—In the Sweat of an Autumn Night 97

PART THREE: CORRUPTION IN SUFFOLK COUNTY
SIX—Exposing Police Brutality 120
SEVEN—Dissecting the Facts 146
EIGHT—Guilty Until Proven Innocent 171

Contents

PART FOUR: A MOCKERY OF JUSTICE
NINE—A Losing Strategy   205
TEN—Impeaching the DeFeo Trial   215

PART FIVE: ALTERNATIVE PATHWAYS TO FREEDOM
ELEVEN—Capitalizing on a Tragedy   251
TWELVE—In the Pursuit of Justice   301
THIRTEEN—Life Incarcerated   328

AFTERWORD   349

ACKNOWLEDGMENTS   353

ENDNOTES   355

ABOUT THE AUTHOR   369

FOREWORD

IN 1974, I was not only the wife of Ronald Joseph "Butch" DeFeo Jr., but also the mother of his child. I knew his family and loved them as my own. Part of my life ended when the DeFeos were murdered and my husband was accused of committing this unspeakable crime.

Since then, society has labeled Butch an antisocial, devil incarnate and often compared him to the likes of Jack the Ripper and Charles Manson. Butch may not have been a saint or a choirboy, but he definitely was not all the things he has been made out to be.

After the DeFeo murders, I have had to remain silent and hidden, partly out of fear for my children and partly out of respect for those who went to such great lengths to make sure I was not unjustly implicated in the crime. The ones closest to the DeFeos suffered greatly from the tragic murders of their loved ones and from the ridicule following a cruel hoax.

Until July 2000, nothing could be said or done about all the lies told about Butch DeFeo, his family and their house; rich, powerful family members made sure of that. But now that they are dead and my children are grown, it is time to set the record straight. But I have been asked, why bother after all of these years?

Well, you bother when you have wondered if the man you have watched being a loving and adoring son and brother could have murdered his entire family. You bother when you are aware that the police were looking for two other people because it was a fact that Butch DeFeo could not have committed the crime alone. You bother when you watch a corrupt police force distort, fabricate and destroy evidence. You bother when it is said that nobody heard a high-powered rifle in the dead of the night.

You bother when you get physically sick wondering how and why this happened. You bother when you hear people condemn the DeFeo family even though they really do not know what it was like to be a DeFeo. You bother to set the record straight when, in fact, Butch DeFeo did have a lot of girlfriends, but *never* committed incest with his sister. You bother when you no longer have to tolerate watching people capitalize on a pack of lies that destroyed the small shreds of humanity and respect the family has left.

Facts were distorted, and lies were told even in so-called "true" books written by supposedly reputable individuals. You bother when you would like to see something truthful written about the people you once loved, and not solely for the reason of greed and self-gratification. To quote the words of Michael Brigante Sr., Butch's grandfather, "The truth shall set you free."

The truth that Ric Osuna uncovered in his investigation will, indeed, set all of us free. Unfortunately, some truths about the family are not so pleasant, but telling the truth means telling the bad with the good. Ric Osuna bothered to sort out fact from fiction and bothered to care about a family perpetually immortalized in books that portray lie after lie. He took numerous research trips and asked personal questions about a family's life even though they are remembered only for their sensational deaths. He bothered to care enough to defend the memories of the DeFeo children, who are not here to defend themselves against all the lies that were told.

Why bother? Because nobody ever bothered to seek the truth like Ric Osuna. This book finally will answer all the questions and set the DeFeo family free, at last. **--Geraldine DeFeo**

INTRODUCTION
Searching for the Truth

LOCATED ON LONG Island's South Shore is the Village of Amityville, a quaint, sleepy community proud of its Colonial roots. Celebrities like Will Rogers, Annie Oakley and even the notorious Al Capone had vacation homes there in the early part of the 20th century. Yet ever since the mid-70s, hordes of tourists have flocked to the picturesque village for far more macabre reasons.

Amityville's sensational identity began to take root in the early morning hours of November 13, 1974, when six members of the DeFeo family were brutally killed at 112 Ocean Avenue. Thirteen months afterward, the Lutz family moved into the vacant house. But 28 days later, George and Kathy Lutz and their three children abandoned 112 Ocean Avenue and all of their belongings to an unnatural evil, or so they claimed.

The next year, author Jay Anson chronicled their 28-day account in *The Amityville Horror*. The story went on to become a worldwide sensation, inspiring a hit motion picture, a series of books, seven sequels and several TV documentaries. The results have made the name Amityville synonymous with horror and turned the DeFeo house into an icon of American supernatural lore.

* * *

At age six, I was drawn to Jay Anson's *The Amityville Horror* after witnessing my mother and sister's fascination with it. Although I was intrigued by their frightening reactions to the book, I was interested more in the red image of the Dutch Colonial home on the book's cover. As I held the book in my small hand, I had the eerie feeling that the house was staring back at me with its eye-like windows.

Twenty years later, my interest was rekindled, and I established *The Amityville Murders* Web site, www.amityvillemurders.com. Since its inception in January 1999, it unexpectedly has grown into the leading authority for the Amityville story on the Internet. Although I never intended my Web site to be more than a hobby, it grew into a launching point for a whole new investigation into the case.

Wanting to display as much documentation on my Web site as I could, I filed several Freedom of Information Act requests with the appropriate law-enforcement departments in Suffolk County, where Amityville is located. In these requests, I sought crime-scene photos, autopsy reports, police investigative reports and court records.

After an entire year of waiting patiently and filing repeated requests, I was informed by the supervising assistant district attorney of the appeals bureau that the only way I would ever get the information I sought was through a court order. The bottom line was that the Freedom of Information Act did not seem to apply in the DeFeo case.

Regardless, I moved forward and was contacted by some TV producers to assist with their documentary about the Amityville "horrors." I eventually rose to the status of co-producer as the documentary was picked up by The History Channel. It was through my connections with the documentary that I got to meet several of the original cast of characters of the Amityville stories, including

William Weber, Roxanne Kaplan, Hans Holzer, Ed and Lorraine Warren, and even George and Kathy Lutz.

Fate would have it that I lived only 10 minutes from George Lutz, who by this time was divorced from Kathy. This close proximity led me to begin a business relationship with him, which included a planned movie sequel and a follow-on book to his purported "true" story. Since I had grown up believing George and Kathy Lutz had actually battled a supernatural force, I was honored to work with them. Sadly, I was misled.

This became apparent when George told me that setting any record straight was not as important as getting another fictional movie made. Nevertheless, the relationship soured after I discovered the truth about the Lutzes and their claims.

The inspirational figure behind *The Night the DeFeos Died* was Geraldine DeFeo. In June 2000, I was contacted by Mrs. DeFeo, who told me a remarkable story. I must admit that, in the beginning, I was skeptical of her claims that she was married to Butch DeFeo before his family was killed. She had even insisted that their daughter was born only a few months before the murders.

Despite my skepticism, I found Mrs. DeFeo to be highly knowledgeable about the DeFeos, the murders, and their house. Maybe it was impolite, but for the first few weeks, I constantly tested her to see if I could catch her in any lies. She passed with flying colors.

After weeks of talking on the phone, I finally decided that it was time to meet her face to face. So at the end of July 2000, I ventured to New York.

To help alleviate any concerns about her authenticity, she immediately showed me a sheriff's identification card once I arrived. Mrs. DeFeo claimed she had obtained the ID through fingerprinting and a valid marriage license. Even though the card seemed genuine, I still took it to the Cayuga County Sheriff's Office, where it had been issued in 1985, to have it verified.

After I asked for a written verification of the card's legitimacy, the sheriff's clerk wrote, "The enclosed personal identification card is true and original from the Cayuga County Sheriff's Department,

SWORN AFFIDAVIT

STATE OF FLORIDA)
) ss.:
COUNTY OF ALACHUA)

I CHUCK TEWKSBURY, being duly and sworn deposes and says:

1) I am affiant and make this affidavit voluntarily and freely regarding Ronald DeFeo and his wife Geraldine Romondoe.

2) I am 36 years of age, I reside at

3) That I met Geraldine Romondoe early in the year 1974.

4) That Geraldine Romondoe is the mother of Ronald DeFeo's daughter, who was born in August of 1974.

5) That I have knowledge of the fact that in October 1974, Ronald DeFeo married Geraldine Romondoe in the State of New Jersey.

WHEREFORE, the above is true and correct to the best of this affiants personal knowledge.

CHUCK TEWKSBURY

Sworn to before me this 30th day of May 19 89

NOTARY PUBLIC
State of Florida at Large
My Commission Expires May 10, 1992

Pictured above and on the next page are two affidavits that have been submitted to the courts attesting to the fact that Geraldine DeFeo is authentic. To preserve privacy, all private information has been blackened.

State of New York)
County of Suffolk)

I, BARRY SPRINGER, being duly and sworn deposes and says:

1) I am affiant and make this affidavit voluntarily and freely regarding Ronald DeFeo and his wife Geraldine Romondoe.

2) I am 38 years of age. I reside at ▉▉▉▉▉▉▉
▉▉▉▉▉▉▉

3) That I met Geraldine Romondoe early in the year 1974.

4) That Geraldine Romondoe is the mother of Ronald Defeo's daughter ▉▉▉▉▉ who was born in August of 1974.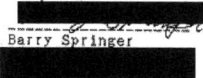

5) That I have knowledge of the fact that in October 1974, Ronald DeFeo married Geraldine Romondoe in the State of New Jersey.

WHEREFORE, the above is true and correct to the best of this affiants personal knowledge.

Barry Springer

RONALD JOSEPH DeFeo Jr.
being duly sworn deposes and says:

1) That Geraldine Rullo is my lawfull and legal wife;

2) That ▉▉▉▉ DeFeo, who was born on August 21, 1974 is my legitmate daughter, conceived from Geraldine Rullo.

3) That the above paragraphs 1) and 2) are factual and true

I, Ronald J. DeFeo Jr , declares under the penalty of perjury that the forgoing is true and correct.

Signed this 18 Day of June 1987

Ronald J. DeFeo Jr.

which was issued on July 16, 1985."

So was this a case of a woman marrying a convicted mass murderer while he was in prison for his notoriety? Not so. It was not until 1989 that a federal judge reversed a New York law prohibiting inmates with life sentences, like Butch DeFeo, the right to marry. Her ID card, on the other hand, was issued in 1985.

In addition, the New York Department of Corrections had to approve who could write or visit Butch DeFeo. I also uncovered several affidavits that were presented in court in support of her marriage to Butch DeFeo. Besides, seeing the genuine pain and tears Mrs. DeFeo displayed every time she visited the DeFeo grave convinced me, beyond a reasonable doubt, that she was telling the truth.

Although I assured The History Channel that Mrs. DeFeo was a legitimate relative with an incredible story to tell, the network executives refused to listen or view the documentation she had. Rather, they were interested only in the photographs she had of the DeFeo family and their house. I was told by the executive producer that their show was entertaining and perfect for the Halloween air date it was scheduled for. Feeling betrayed, I resigned from the documentary and continued with my own investigation.

I should mention that Mrs. DeFeo has voluntarily waived all of her rights to profit from her story in *The Night the DeFeos Died*. She does not seek to be famous. In fact, she refused to go on camera during the 2001 production of A&E's "City Confidential" series on the DeFeo murders, even in silhouette form. And by no means is Geraldine DeFeo simply looking to free Butch DeFeo. So with no apparent motive to lie, it becomes increasingly difficult to disregard this woman's testimony simply because she remained silent all of these years.

After being convinced that Mrs. DeFeo was authentic, I began to listen intently to her story. It was during this time that she convinced me of the need for further research to set the record straight. Moreover, she had just as many unanswered questions about the DeFeo murders as I had.

Although I thought highly of Mrs. DeFeo, and her refusal to

profit from the deaths of the DeFeos, I still viewed Butch DeFeo in a negative light. Nevertheless, on November 30, 2000, Mrs. DeFeo and I visited Green Haven Correctional Facility in Stormville, New York, Butch DeFeo's current residence. It was the first time that I ever visited a prison, so the 50-foot concrete walls and massive guard towers were somewhat intimidating.

Already nervous enough to be in a maximum security prison, I was also leery about meeting the famed Amityville murderer. After all, I only knew Butch DeFeo as a devil incarnate, a sociopath, and an insane maniac. Yet those descriptions did not fit the man Mrs. DeFeo described to me. I could not picture Mrs. DeFeo, a no-nonsense woman, with a barbaric lug who was capable of killing his entire family.

After entering the facility's visiting room, we handed our request forms to a female corrections officer seated at a tall desk. Upon seeing Butch DeFeo's name, she commented to us that he was her favorite inmate because he was so polite.

Wait a minute, I thought; *this did not sound like the convicted killer I heard so many negative things about.* Regardless, we sat down at a little table to wait for Butch.

The visiting room reminded me of a high-school cafeteria. All kinds of vending machines lined either side of the large area. And round tables, which sat four, were scattered throughout the room. Although security was tight, the atmosphere was relaxed enough for families to enjoy their visits.

While we waited for Butch, we passed the time by drinking a cup of stale coffee from one of the vending machines and staring at the falling snow outside. During this time, Mrs. DeFeo reminisced out loud about what could have been and how the murders devastated her life.

Suddenly, a group of inmates walked through the door. Seeing Butch DeFeo among them, Mrs. DeFeo walked over to him. They greeted each other with an affectionate kiss and hug. Although they were divorced, it was clear they still cared deeply for each other.

Everything that Mrs. DeFeo had described to me about Butch's appearance was true. His pants were neatly creased, his shirt was wrinkle-free, his fingernails and hair were immaculately groomed. I was slightly embarrassed because my own pants had a wrinkled, stuffed-in-a-suitcase look to them.

Nevertheless, Butch gave me a large smile and friendly handshake before he sat down at the table. We spent the next six hours discussing his case and the Amityville stories. I found Butch to be very frank and open, even though he seemed nervous at the constant gawks and stares he received from other visitors. Even after all this time, people still recognized him as the Amityville murderer.

During one point, I was half expecting him to get angry at Mrs. DeFeo, who had spilt coffee all over the paperwork he had brought with him. Instead of overreacting, he calmly said, "You have to relax." Butch then proceeded to clean up the spill until there was not a drop left on the table. Mrs. DeFeo's claims that Butch DeFeo was a cleanliness freak were proving true.

I left that day with the knowledge that Butch DeFeo had never granted a similar interview to anyone in the past. The story he told me was incredible. And I was thankful when he expressed his confidence in my ability to prove it true, even though I was not sure he had been completely truthful with me.

I vowed to him to remain objective in order to report the total, unbiased truth. Mrs. DeFeo agreed with this statement and said, "If Butch did it all, then report it. If Butch did not do it all, then report that, too. Ric, report only the truth."

She may have loved Butch, but she was not on a crusade to get him out of prison. Rather, she was on a quest to find the truth, just as I was. According to Mrs. DeFeo, the story that Butch told me fit with what he had told her immediately after his arraignment in 1974. But since Butch DeFeo has told countless lies over the years, it was hard to take this habitual liar at his word. Since age was creeping up on Butch DeFeo, not to mention his failing health, he seemed as if he finally wanted the truth to come out. Months later, however, I would find out that Butch DeFeo had an ulterior motive for speaking with me.

For the next 15 months, I worked day and night to uncover anything and everything related to Amityville. All too often, however, I encountered roadblocks. In fact, on many occasions, Mrs. DeFeo took matters into her own hands to make sure I got all the materials I needed. One example of this was when she contacted Federal Judge Jack B. Weinstein to unseal certain court records that I felt were beneficial. Although I had tried a year before to get Judge Weinstein to unseal these same records, only a legitimate DeFeo relative was able to convince him that it was time to unseal documents pertaining to the Lutz hoax.

Mrs. DeFeo also put me in contact with the current owner of the famed Amityville house, who, after talking to me, realized I was a legitimate researcher. Our conversations eventually led to an invitation for a guided tour of the house, something he has never granted to people outside of family and friends.

The interior of the house was much smaller than I imagined, but nothing short of remarkable. The alleged negative feelings the Lutzes described were nowhere to be sensed. All that existed was the feeling of a loving, happy home. And I found the owner and his family to be quite friendly and receptive. In fact, two hours into my visit, I completely forgot I was in the Amityville house. After touring the house, I could see why the current owners would get sick of all the negative media attention.

My investigation, however, was not always filled with such positive developments. In November 2000, a Suffolk County homicide detective contacted Mrs. DeFeo. He had gotten word from a supervisor at the medical examiner's office that we wanted to obtain a new set of autopsy reports. According to Mrs. DeFeo, the officer was quite rude and adamant that no information about the DeFeo case would be released.

I found this odd and decided to contact the detective myself. Sure enough, the detective told me that short of a court order, nothing pertaining to the DeFeo case would ever be released, regardless of what the law said. Indifferent to his attitude, I discussed certain specifics of the case with the detective, whose only reply was that Butch DeFeo was guilty and the story had already been told.

But I thought that if the story already has been told, then why treat the documents as if they were classified information? Despite my failings to convince the detective to change his mind, I did get an unexpected bonus: He provided further corroboration that Geraldine was married to Butch prior to the DeFeo murders in 1974.

Unbeknownst to the detective, his tactics did not deter me from wanting to get to the bottom of the truth. In fact, it inspired me even more, leaving me feeling the Suffolk County justice system was hiding something.

But what Suffolk County failed to understand was that we already had most of the reports relating to the DeFeo investigation. So additional copies of the reports would simply be an added bonus. However, my goal was to confirm or refute Butch and Geraldine DeFeo's assertions that the authorities in Suffolk County would do anything to prevent the true story from coming out.

A few months after our conversation with the homicide detective, both Mrs. DeFeo and I traveled to the Suffolk County Medical Examiner's office to obtain copies of the autopsy reports.

Lo and behold, I finally got to see firsthand the bureaucracy of Suffolk County in action. The same supervisor who informed the homicide detective that we wanted the DeFeo autopsies in November again reminded us that they would not be released until the homicide squad signed off on them.

By this time, I knew that the only way to get anything was make a scene and shout, "Coverup!" It worked, but not the way I expected. The assistant director of the medical examiner's office approached us in the lobby wanting to know what the problem was. After informing him of the situation, he confirmed the fact that the homicide squad had no power to dictate what the medical examiner's office could or should release. Of course, he would not put this in writing for me, but suggested we get approval from the county attorney.

After days of waiting, the county attorney finally sided with the homicide department. So once again we were denied the reports. But that was not the best part of it.

Just hours after my little outburst at the medical examiner's office, a stolen car was placed in front of my house, thousands of miles away, and set ablaze. Coincidence? Possibly. But coincidence could not explain the death threats we began receiving or the bullet fired into Geraldine DeFeo's home.

Incredibly, toward the completion of this book, the Suffolk County Police Department finally changed its attitudes toward releasing information. To my surprise, in September 2001, after filing another Freedom of Information Act request, I was finally granted access to the documentation and photographs I had originally sought. To this day, I am not sure what caused the change in attitude. However, the change seemed to occur after my participation in a radio interview where I discussed Suffolk County's coverup.

Nevertheless, there were also those who took it upon themselves to help me. These "deep throats" met with me in the oddest places to explain the coverup in the DeFeo case. They were invaluable sources for discovering the truth. And they are a testament to the honorable men and women in Suffolk County law enforcement who believe in upholding the law.

I have to admit that at times I felt like the lone, dissenting voice of juror #8 played by Henry Fonda in "12 Angry Men." Juror #8 was interested only in finding out the truth, no matter what that was.

Let me assure you that the story you are about to read is true and has never been made public. I have done everything humanly possible to cite, verify and reference everything contained in the upcoming pages. Additionally, in the rear of the book, there are several end notes to assist you. In this edition, there also are several graphic photos of the DeFeo crime scene. In the past, I have vehemently opposed the use of photos showing the DeFeo bodies if their use was merely for "shock" value. Their inclusion in this edition, however, has become necessary not only to prove some of the facts presented in this book, but also to expose an unprecedented coverup. With regards to any documentation, the signatures and addresses, along with any other confidential information, has been blackened-out to ensure privacy.

Chapter Six, titled "Exposing Police Brutality," is one of the most important chapters in this book. Although it may seem as if it detracts from the Amityville case, its inclusion was imperative to prepare the reader for many of Butch DeFeo's allegations regarding the Suffolk County Police Department and District Attorney's office.

So, for those who think they already know the Amityville story, get ready for a mind-blowing, roller-coaster ride.

Letter from Butch DeFeo.
Pictured above is a letter from Butch DeFeo proclaiming his love to Geraldine DeFeo and requesting a visit from author Ric Osuna, so that the true Amityville story could be finally told.

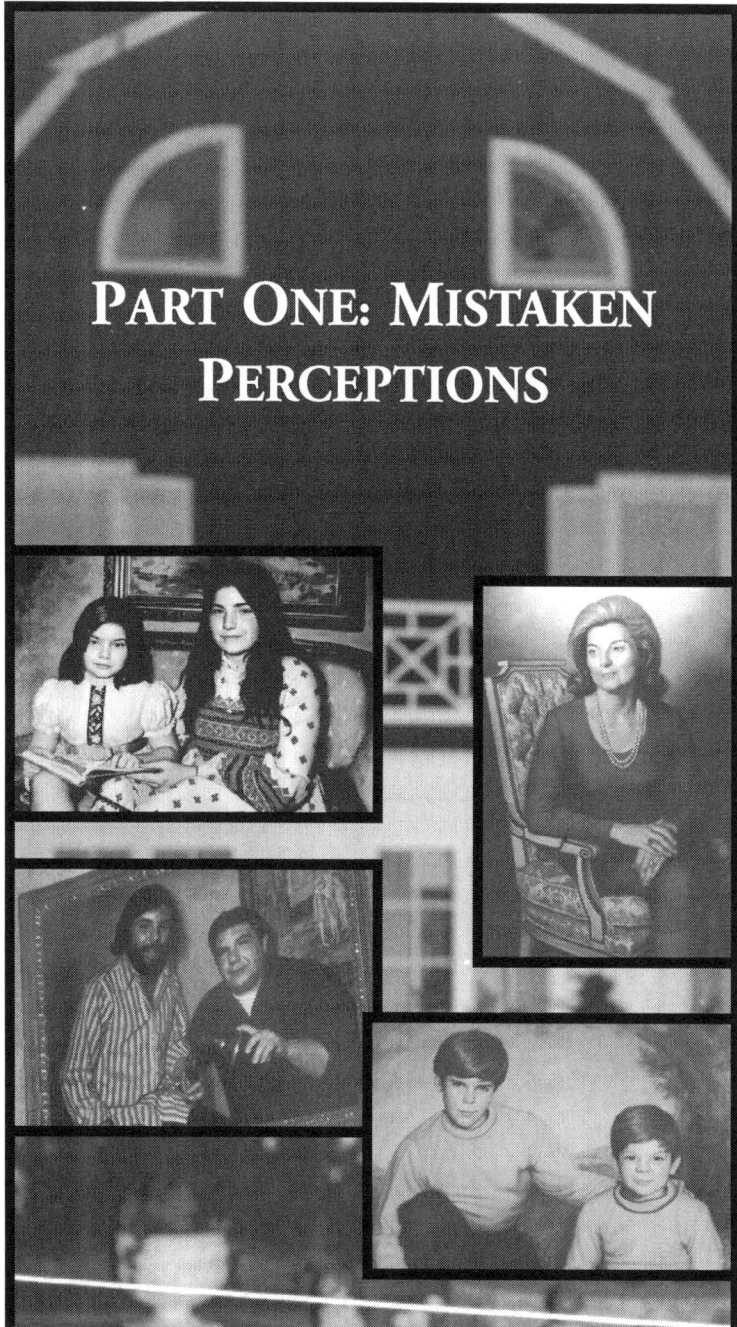

CHAPTER ONE
Murder on Ocean Avenue

IN THE EARLY evening hours of November 13, 1974, the patrons of Henry's Bar, a tavern located at the corner of Merrick Road and Ocean Avenue in Amityville, chatted while sipping their beers and cocktails. To them, the start of the evening seemed just like a typical one in Amityville: calm and uneventful. By night's end, however, life in Amityville would never again be the same.

At 6:30 p.m., Ronald DeFeo Jr., known by the locals as "Butch," opened the door to the bar and yelled, "You got to help me! I think my mother and father are shot."

One of the patrons seated at the bar was Robert "Bobby" Kelske, an out-of-work brick mason and Butch's best friend. Bobby raced to his friend, who had fallen to his knees. Crying hysterically, Butch again pleaded for help, "Bobby, you got to help me. Somebody shot my mother and father."

"Are you sure they're not asleep?" Bobby offered.

"No, I saw them up there."

Chapter One

"Come on then; let's go."

Butch got to his feet and called for others at the bar to follow Bobby and him back to the house. Answering Butch's call was John Altieri, Joey Yeswoit, Al Saxton and William Scordamaglia, owner of Henry's Bar. The six men piled into Butch's 1970 blue Buick Electra 225. Butch climbed in the back while Bobby took the wheel.

Although the DeFeo house was only a block away, Bobby drove frantically down the street. One of the men yelled out for him to slow down, but Bobby ignored the comment, arriving at 112 Ocean Avenue in a matter of seconds.

The DeFeo residence was a large, rambling, three-story Dutch Colonial home built in 1925. Because the property was long and narrow, the dark-shingled house sat sideways with the front door facing the elongated driveway. At the end of the DeFeos' 237-foot-long lot sat their boathouse, right at the edge of the Amityville Creek.

But the most distinguishable characteristic of 112 Ocean Avenue was its dramatic front yard. Overlooking the street were two quarter-moon windows that looked like eyes, a feature common in Dutch Colonial homes. On the front lawn stood a lamp post with a sign attached that read "High Hopes," a symbolic title of the family's life in suburbia. Kneeling behind the sign were three figurines of children praying to a larger statue of St. Joseph holding the baby Jesus.

Bobby pulled the car to a quick halt and climbed out. As he climbed up the front-porch steps, one of the other men cautioned, "Be careful! Somebody might be in there!"

"I don't care," Bobby yelled as he opened the unlocked door to the DeFeo home.

The house was quiet, except for the barking of Shaggy, the DeFeos' sheepdog, who was tied up to the inside of the kitchen's back door. Because the dog was not totally housebroken, the family routinely tied the animal there.

The interior of the DeFeo home was just as impressive as the exterior. To the right of the marble-covered foyer was the formal dining room with red, velvet-textured wallpaper lining the walls. In

112 Ocean Avenue on November 13, 1974.
As the bar patrons approached 112 Ocean Avenue, the headlights of Butch's blue Buick Electra illuminated the religious statues outside the home, which seemed to be holding their own private vigil. This crime-scene photo, courtesy of the Suffolk County Police Department, was taken soon after the DeFeos were discovered shot and killed.

Chapter One

the center of the room, over the Dutch-style table seating six, hung a crystal chandelier. A textbook belonging to one of Butch's younger siblings sat, unopened, on the table next to a bouquet of wilting red roses.

Across the foyer was the living room, which contained a baby grand piano. Fronting the large fireplace was a pair of white satin-cushioned chairs. Lavish paintings and statues were scattered throughout the room. It was evident that Butch's parents insisted on the most expensive items for their house.

With Bobby Kelske in the lead, the five men hurried up the stairs to the second floor. Bobby, a regular visitor to the DeFeo household, knew exactly where the master bedroom was located. As they reached the second floor, they were overwhelmed with the stench of death.

Bobby stopped at the doorway to the master bedroom and hit the light switch. Before him lay Ronald Joseph DeFeo Sr., 43, and his wife Louise DeFeo, 42. A hole in the center of DeFeo Sr.'s bare back was the first indication the couple was not sleeping. Dried blood had trickled out of the wound, disappearing beneath the obese man's blue boxer shorts.

In contrast, Louise DeFeo's wounds were not clearly ascertainable because her body was buried beneath an orange blanket as if she were protecting herself against the evening chill. Behind the bed was a mirrored wall, which eerily reflected the macabre scene.

Seeing that Bobby was ready to pass out, the other men led him downstairs, past the life-size portraits of family members that hung on the staircase wall.

John Altieri remained on the second floor and checked out the northeast bedroom. Clipper ships, cannons and eagles dotted the room's wallpaper. On the dresser, to the left of the door, lay several statues and figurines that one would expect to find in a devout Catholic home. Strewn across the floor were athletic shoes and toys signaling that the bedroom belonged to a boy, two boys to be exact.

On opposite sides of the room lay the bodies of two young boys, face down like their parents. In the bed on the left lay the body of John DeFeo, nine. Altieri could not pinpoint the bullet hole

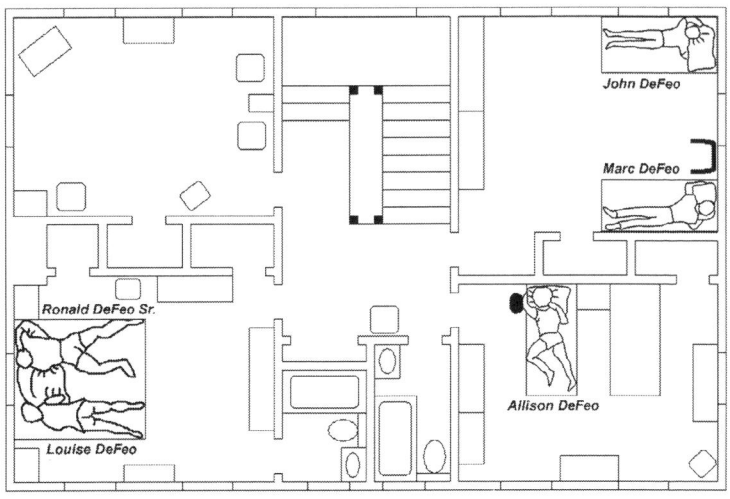

Crime-scene diagrams of 112 Ocean Avenue
(Courtesy of Rip Holly).

On the second floor of the DeFeo home, the lifeless bodies of Ronald Sr., Louise, Allison, Marc and John Matthew DeFeo, who had all been shot at close range, were discovered at approximately 6:30 p.m. However, it was not until police arrived that the men learned the fate of Dawn DeFeo on the third floor.

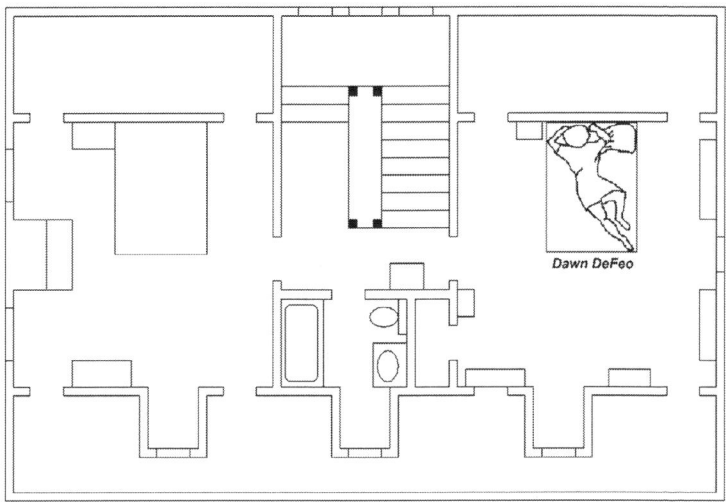

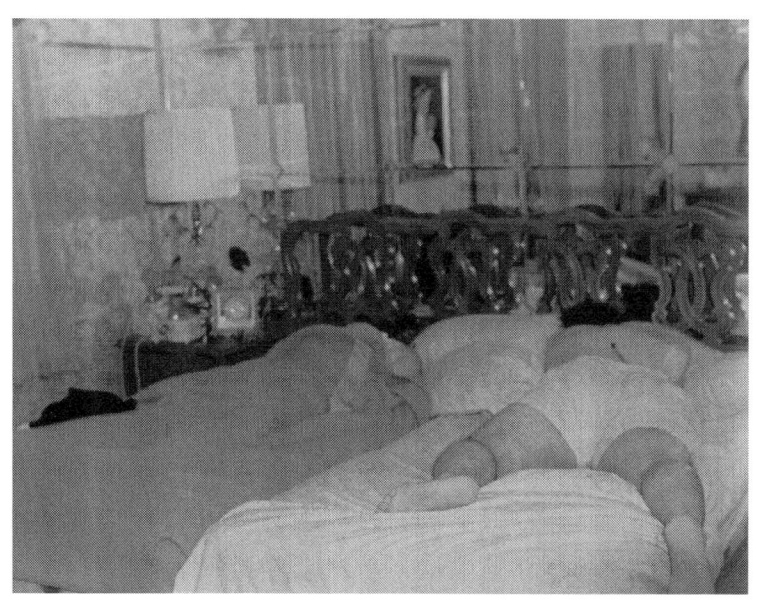

The grisly discovery.
Above: Before the men, lay the bodies of Ronald Sr. and his wife Louise. Below: Like her sister on the second floor, Dawn lay on her stomach as if nestled beneath the covers of her bed. In reality, she had suffered a fatal shot to the head.

in John's back since the "Knicks" sweatshirt he was wearing was covered in blood.

In the other bed lay John's brother, Marc DeFeo, 12. Next to Marc's bed was a pair of crutches and a plain, gray wheel chair. The boy had recently suffered a football injury and needed their assistance to get around. At the foot of his bed lay a crumpled-up green and yellow bedspread and an orange blanket. This time, Altieri could make out the wound: a single bullet hole in the center of the boy's back.

Seeing more than he had wanted, Altieri left the room and rejoined the others on the ground floor. There, Joe Yeswoit called 911, giving details to an emergency operator. The operator seemed to be more concerned with the spelling of Yeswoit's name than with the reason for the call. Unsure of the address, Yeswoit went outside during the middle of the conversation to get the house number.

By this time, Bobby had rejoined his friend in the driveway. Butch repeatedly pounded the hood of his car, screaming, "I am not going back into that house!"

"Who in your family do you want me to call?" Bobby asked.

"Call Rocco." Rocco DeFeo was Butch's paternal grandfather, who lived about 10 miles away in West Islip.

After Yeswoit finished with the 911 call, Bobby went back inside and dialed Rocco DeFeo's number. Vincent Procita, Rocco's son-in-law, answered. Bobby simply told the man that there had been trouble and that he was to get everyone down to Amityville as soon as possible.

* * *

At around 6:40 p.m., the Amityville Police Department dispatched Officer Kenneth Greguski, shield #123, to investigate the shooting report on Ocean Avenue. Officer Greguski, who had just gotten a sandwich from a deli in the village, acknowledged the call and proceeded to 112 Ocean Avenue to investigate. A minute later, the wail of Greguski's siren could be heard coming down Ocean Avenue.

Upon arrival, Greguski met with Butch and his friends in the

Chapter One

driveway. Greguski asked, "What is the problem?"

"My parents are dead," Butch replied.

Greguski entered the DeFeo home with Butch and Bobby in tow. While the cop went upstairs, the two men sat at the kitchen nook awaiting his return. Behind the nook was a mural depicting an Italian villa, but the bright and majestic setting had little impact on the inconsolable mood. When Greguski returned, he used the dining room phone to call headquarters to inform them that he had found four deceased persons and that he needed homicide detectives from Suffolk County's First Squad. Because Amityville is a small village, homicides are typically left to the county detectives while lesser infractions are left to the village police force.

Overhearing the cop's conversation, Butch informed Greguski that he also had two sisters. Upon hearing this, Greguski put down the phone and raced back upstairs. By this time, Amityville Police Officer Edwin Tyndall, shield #125, arrived to assist Greguski.

On the second floor, the officers approached the closed door of the southeast bedroom. What lay behind the door was a horrifying sight. In bed, underneath a pink blanket, lying on her stomach with her arm beneath her pillow, was Allison DeFeo, 13. It was apparent from the amount of blood that had dripped from the sheets and onto the floor that little could be done for the girl.

Originally believing the staircase to his left led to an attic, Greguski had ignored the third floor in his initial sweep of the house. Now, both Greguski and Tyndall ascended the staircase.

At the east end of the floor, the two cops entered another bedroom, which had a window overlooking the pool in the backyard. A gold-colored, flowery wallpaper print decorated the entire room. In the room's corner, eyeing the cops, was a stuffed monkey with a silly grin seated in a red chair.

Like her sister on the floor below, Dawn DeFeo, 18, lay on her stomach as if nestled beneath the covers of her bed. Closer examination, however, revealed the girl had suffered a traumatic head injury. Her pillow had hair, blood and brain matter embedded in it, even though her white headboard was suspiciously clean.

Both officers returned to the first floor, and Greguski called his headquarters again to advise them he now had a total of six bodies in the house. After Greguski hung up the phone, he sympathetically put his hand on Butch's shoulder, telling him to "take it easy."

Over the next few hours, the neighborhood turned chaotic. Neighbors and other residents of Amityville started to gather in front of the house, behind the police barricades. It was an eerie scene. The only thing that penetrated the dark street on this pitch-black night was the flashing lights from the multitude of squad cars parked on Ocean Avenue. The crowds got so big that the police had to close down access to the street. Regardless, journalists still got through.

One journalist was Doug Spero, who was then working as a reporter for WNBC radio. Initially receiving a report of a double homicide, Spero recalled that "it seemed much larger than a double homicide because of the amount of police and emergency vehicles present at the scene." Like many other reporters, Spero stood watch and waited for the police to release any details because "nobody knew the magnitude of the crime."

People in the neighborhood could not believe that such a thing could happen on Ocean Avenue, the most affluent street in the village. In their minds, it was the last place on earth that they would have suspected such a thing. From talk of a homicidal maniac loose in the streets to a Mafia hit, rumors went unchecked, and people seemed afraid to stay in their homes or go to sleep that night.

CHAPTER TWO
An Open and Shut Case

O N NOVEMBER 15, 1974, a headline in the New York *Daily News* read, "Son charged in slaying of six." For Long Islanders, the thought that a son killed his entire family was as frightful as the thought of a mass murderer loose in Amityville.

Grace Fagan, friend and classmate of Dawn DeFeo, commented about Butch's arrest, saying, "He loved those kids; he could never do it. He was a lamb." But this was one of the few positive things the papers would report about Butch.

Almost overnight, in people's minds, Butch went from the poor victimized sole survivor to a monster of unspeakable proportions. His trial had yet to begin, but the public had already found Butch guilty of murder.

Rumors circulated in the newspapers that Butch had drugged his family at dinner and then killed them so he could collect the $200,000 life insurance policy his father had purportedly taken out on the family. Although the police still maintained that money was the motive, toxicology reports from the autopsies indicated that the DeFeos had not been drugged.

According to the Suffolk County homicide detectives, Butch DeFeo was extremely helpful and cooperative, even volunteering to spend the night of November 13, 1974 at the precinct so he could stay close to the investigation. The next morning, however, Butch DeFeo awoke to learn that he had become the chief suspect in the murder of his family.

Veteran Suffolk County Detective Dennis Rafferty, shield #417, accompanied by Detective Lieutenant Robert Dunn, took over the interrogation later in the morning. Detective Rafferty would later testify how Butch had offered several different, if not ludicrous, versions of what had occurred. By that afternoon, Butch supposedly broke down, crying on Detective Rafferty's shoulder, saying, "Once I started, I just couldn't stop. It went so fast."

Purportedly, over the next few hours, Butch admitted to the police he had done the unthinkable: killed all six members of his family while they slept soundly. The homicide detectives claimed Butch further cooperated by revealing where he had discarded certain pieces of incriminating evidence, including the murder weapon.

On November 17, 1974, three days after Butch DeFeo had reportedly confessed to killing his entire family, a memorial service was held for the six DeFeos at the Boyd Funeral Home in Deer Park. "Upon entering the chapel, you became weak at the knees from seeing the six coffins in front of you," Geraldine DeFeo recalled.

Each of the DeFeos was propped up on a satiny pillow, surrounded by scores of flowers. According to Geraldine, the funeral home successfully hid the two girls' head wounds, "but it was a sickening sight to approach the six opened caskets and see the pale faces of our loved ones."

The next day, funeral services were held at St. Martin of Tours in Amityville. St. Martin's school was located directly across the street, and dozens of school children stared out of the large second-floor windows of the school to watch the six coffins being carried

Photo by Ric Osuna

The tragedy hits home.
Just three days after the murders, a memorial service was held at Amityville's St. Martin of Tours (pictured above and below). Father McNamara, who presided over the service, said, "I shall not attempt to give any explanation of the tragedy..."

Photo by Ric Osuna

into the red brick church. Because Allison, Marc and John DeFeo had attended school at St. Martin's, many of the students knew the children.

During the service, Father James McNamara, an assistant pastor at St. Martin of Tours in Amityville, said, with a heavy heart, "I shall not attempt to give any explanation of the tragedy that has gathered us here together."

According to friends and relatives, no amount of explanations or reasoning could take away the pain they would have to endure the rest of their lives. The why and the how were the hardest questions to answer.

As part of an old Italian tradition, part of the funeral procession slowly drove down Ocean Avenue and past the Dutch Colonial home with the jack-o'-lantern eyes. The "High Hopes" sign, placed in the front yard by Mr. DeFeo soon after moving there from Brooklyn in 1965, was a sickening reminder of shattered hopes.

Interment came at St. Charles Cemetery later that day, and more than 300 mourners, with red carnations in hand, attended. At the end of graveside services, Michael and Angela Brigante, Louise DeFeo's parents, had to be led away because they were too grief-stricken. Rocco DeFeo stayed sitting in the back of a black limousine just staring at the grave, even after the services were complete and the mourners had gone.

THE "OFFICIAL" ACCOUNT OF THE MURDERS

Allegedly, at 3 a.m., on November 13, 1974, Butch DeFeo awoke in the second floor's TV room. Earlier, he had fallen asleep after finishing the World War Two thriller "Castle Keep." Butch got up, went to his own room on the third floor, grabbed his .35-caliber Marlin rifle, loaded it and proceeded back to the second floor where his parents' bedroom was.

A small votive candle burning on his father's dresser, a makeshift shrine with several Catholic statues and pictures, and the second-floor hallway's bathroom light were his only light source. Butch stood in the doorway and fired two expert shots into each of

Chapter Two

his slumbering parents.

Forensic evidence indicated Butch's parents had awoken from the gunfire. The fact, however, that their bodies were found in bed, in an execution pose, later inspired the wild and absurd claims that a supernatural presence prevented the rifle from making a sound and the DeFeos from moving.

After shooting his parents, Butch DeFeo then went across the hallway into his brothers' bedroom. He took aim as he stood in between their beds, only two feet away from their sleeping forms. Suffolk County Homicide Detective Dennis Rafferty would later testify that after firing two shots into their backs, Butch stood there callously and watched his youngest brother's foot twitch.

Butch then proceed to the adjacent bedroom. As the bedroom door swung open, Allison DeFeo lifted up her head to see a dark shadow standing there. As she stared into the rifle's muzzle, the killer fired. Allison never knew what hit her as the bullet tore threw her left cheek and exited out her right ear, finally coming to rest underneath her bed. Death was instantaneous.

Afterward, Butch reloaded the rifle as he climbed the staircase to the third floor. Dawn DeFeo had awakened and had asked if everything was all right. Butch informed his other sister that everything was fine and that she should return to bed.

As Dawn settled back underneath the covers, Butch stood at the foot of her bed and took aim. The bullet struck the back of her neck, causing the left portion of her head to implode.

Although the deed was done, Butch still had to discard the evidence that would tie him to the crime. He grabbed two pillowcases, putting one into the other. Next, he went from room to room picking up every bit of incriminating evidence, including the spent rifle casings.

Seeing a rifle casing had landed in a pool of Allison's blood, Butch retrieved it anyway. And even though this mass-murderer had the foresight to get rid of incriminating evidence, he decided that it was all right to wipe the blood that he had gotten on his hand onto his clothing.

Realizing his mistake, Butch took a shower, and then deposited his bloody garments and the towel he used to dry himself into the pillowcase.

Although the one pillowcase was already brimming with his clothes, towel, eight shell casings and the other empty pillowcase, he managed to fit in a rifle scabbard, a pistol holster, one full box of .35-caliber Marlin ammunition and one empty box. What he forget to discard, however, was the Marlin rifle box that his .35-caliber rifle had come in. Before leaving, Butch grabbed the Marlin rifle, which still had two live rounds inside it.

After leaving home, Butch proceeded to the end of Ocean Avenue and dumped the rifle into the water. Fearing that the pillowcase would float, Butch decided to take it with him to Brooklyn.

After arriving near Sea View Avenue and 96th Street in Brooklyn, Butch discarded the pillowcase into a sewer, which the police insist was in a remote location despite the row of houses and delicatessen fronting it. Butch, nonetheless, proceeded to work and began establishing his alibi.

That evening, after the police had arrived at the crime scene, Butch, who before had such a disdain for policemen, decided to volunteer to go down to the precinct to give a statement. And later, even though he was free to go, he decided to spend the night on a police cot in a file room in the homicide department.

At 9:00 a.m. on November 14, 1974, the homicide detectives decided to awaken Butch to inform him that he was their sole suspect because they felt a .35-caliber Marlin, which they knew Butch had owned from the empty Marlin box in his room, was the murder weapon.

At 10:30 a.m., Detective Dennis Rafferty, accompanied by Detective Lieutenant Robert Dunn, began to interrogate Butch DeFeo. Interestingly enough, Detective Rafferty commented in *High Hopes*, co-authored by the prosecutor in Butch's murder trial, saying, "I think when I walk in that the guy's guilty and that it's my job to do the best I can to get him to give us direct evidence."

By evening of the 14th, Butch DeFeo had allegedly confessed to the crime. This was in addition to pointing out for the detectives the location of the evidence he had been so careful to discard. Detective

Chapter Two

Rafferty had not only solved the case in record time, but he had also elicited a confession.

* * *

In October 1975, a jury was sworn in, and Butch DeFeo's trial got underway. After several weeks of testimony, Butch was found guilty of killing his father, mother, two brothers and two sisters. On December 4, 1975, Justice Thomas Stark said that the crimes were "the most heinous and abhorrent" and sentenced Butch to 25 years to life.

Today, Butch sits incarcerated at Green Haven Correctional Facility in Stormville, New York. On September 21, 1999, Butch DeFeo went before the New York State Parole Board for the first time. After offering a different account from what was presented at his trial, Butch contended that he was innocent of the crimes he was charged with. After deliberation, the board denied Butch's request for parole.

In spite of the fact that Butch's trial ended with a guilty verdict, many unanswered questions remained. For instance, why would a son kill his entire family when he showed every indication of an enduring love for them? Why were all of the victims found in the same position? And didn't any of the victims get out of bed to put up a struggle for their lives?

Herman Race, a former New York City police detective, was hired by Michael Brigante Sr. to investigate the murders. Brigante had testified at trial that he did not feel that his grandson acted alone in the commission of the crime. Since Brigante did not feel that his grandson had done all that he was accused of, he wanted Race, a licensed investigator and friend, either to prove or disprove the case against Butch.

Like Brigante, it was Race's opinion that these murders were not committed by Butch alone and that there were accomplices who went undetected and unpunished because the Suffolk County justice system wanted an open-and-shut case. If, indeed, these conclusions have any merit, then the question that remains to be answered is: What *really* happened the night the DeFeos died?

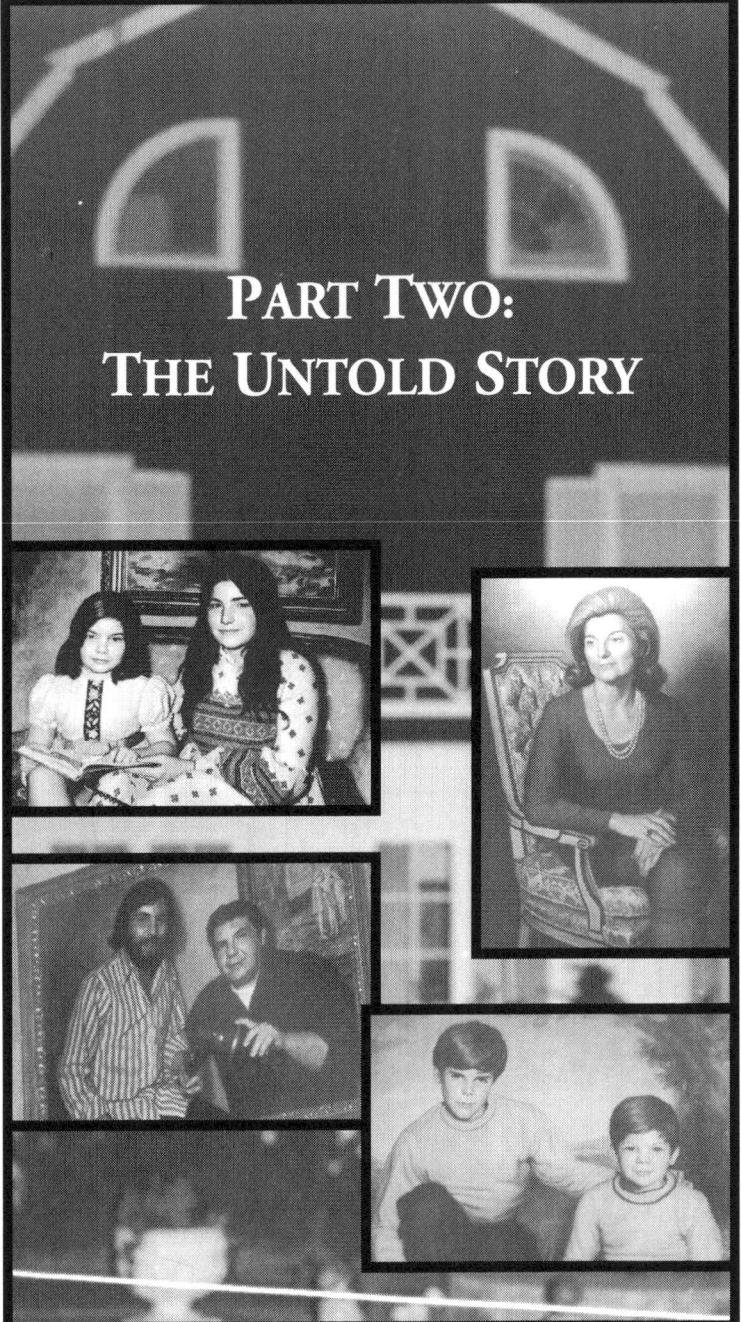

CHAPTER THREE
Life as a DeFeo

IN 1969, GERALDINE Romondoe had a promising singing career that kept her on the road travelling between bars and nightclubs along the East Coast. Even though she was only 21 years old, she was a divorcée with two daughters.

In May of that year, she was singing at the popular New York City bar called The Ninth Circle. "One night while I was singing there, a group of kids came in," Geraldine said. "They were loud and obnoxious, and obviously too young to drink."

Geraldine continued, "After I had finished my set, the biggest braggart of them all came over. He introduced himself as Butch Black. I started laughing when he told me his name. So he asked, 'What's so funny?' I asked him, 'Butch Black is your name?' He said, 'Yeah, what about it?' I let it go and asked him what he wanted. He said he wanted to buy me a drink. I passed and left the bar."

Later that summer, Geraldine and Butch Black would meet again. Singing at The Ebb Tide, a bar near Long Branch, New Jersey, Geraldine had left the stage to take a break.

Geraldine recalled, "I sat down on my seat to rest and sat right on what felt like a stack of hot needles. The whole bar turned and looked at me as I jumped out of my seat, hollering in pain. I turned around to see what I had sat on and saw a dozen red roses on the seat. I hadn't noticed them as I sat down on the thorny stems. I then yelled, 'Who the hell put these here?' That was when I noticed Butch Black sitting at the bar shrinking in embarrassment."

After calming Geraldine down, Butch was able to coax her into a drink. "I have to admit," Geraldine recalled, "he looked good in the tight-fitting, black bell-bottoms he was wearing."

But Butch was not satisfied with just a drink. He wanted to take Geraldine out on a date and persisted until he got his way. Eventually, she accepted the offer.

It was on their first date that Geraldine learned Butch Black's real name was Ronald Joseph DeFeo Jr. When he was very young, he had acquired the nickname "Butch" from his grandfather Rocco DeFeo because it was a manly name. Butch Black was his alias.

Although it was only their first date, Butch had expected to have sex with Geraldine. He was in for a rude awakening because Geraldine was from a traditional Italian family. Sex on the first date was something that was out of the question. Yet, instead of losing interest, Butch was fascinated with her strong will and stubbornness.

Although Geraldine enjoyed herself enough on their first date to keep seeing Butch, it would be several months later, when he turned 18, that Geraldine found out she had been dating a minor. Geraldine said, "Butch really swooped me off my feet. I felt so comfortable being around him that I didn't figure he was only 17. He was romantic, understanding, and he had a really good sense of humor. There was something really genuine about his character that the older guys I went out with didn't have."

In August 1969, Butch invited Geraldine to his home in Amityville, New York. He had wanted to show off his older girlfriend to his family. "Butch constantly bragged about his home, saying it was a mansion. Since the DeFeos had come from a Brooklyn apartment, I suppose to him it was a mansion," Geraldine said.

Chapter Three

Originally from Brooklyn, Ronald DeFeo Sr. and his wife Louise wanted to move their growing family away from the city. They eventually settled on the quaint Village of Amityville, a picturesque Long Island South Shore community. And on June 28, 1965, they closed escrow on the Dutch Colonial style home at 112 Ocean Avenue, which they had purchased for $30,000. At the time of the move, Louise was already pregnant with her fifth child.

Coming from an apartment, the DeFeos took some time getting used to the spacious home and large yard. Not everyone in Amityville welcomed the DeFeos with open arms. Many in the close-knit community viewed the DeFeos as outsiders who should have stayed in Brooklyn.

In spite of the lukewarm reception from the community, the DeFeos looked at the move as a chance for a new beginning. To symbolize this, Big Ronnie, the name Mr. DeFeo had acquired because he weighed nearly 300 pounds, hung a sign on a lamp post in the front yard that read: "High Hopes."

Right away, Big Ronnie knew he had to redecorate the home to fit his tastes. Geraldine said, "There was no two ways about it. Big Ronnie's tastes were gaudy. And in order to build himself up, Big Ronnie would make it a point to tell you how much something had cost."

Despite the large and expensive home, Butch was not happy to move away from his grandfather, Michael Brigante Sr., who still resided in Brooklyn. In an effort to live with his grandparents, Butch faked his own kidnapping. A few days later, he was found and forced to return to Amityville.

During the renovation of the house, Butch was asked what color of wallpaper he wanted for his bedroom. Butch sarcastically told his father he did not care if he put up polka dots. Out of spite, his father did just that and covered the room with baby blue, orange and dark blue polka-dotted wallpaper.

By 1969, the DeFeos had begun building a pool and a permanent brick patio. But there were delays because Big Ronnie and Louise's parents battled over the details. Since the early days of their marriage, both sets of in-laws competed to outdo each other. When one side of the family bought an expensive piece of furniture for the Amityville house, the other side would try to top it.

It was early afternoon when Geraldine arrived for the pool party Butch had planned. It was a hot, muggy day, perfect for swimming.

The first person Butch introduced Geraldine to was his mother. "At first, Louise probably just viewed me as another one of Butch's floozies," Geraldine said. "She was polite, but not overly receptive. What I found odd was that she was dressed from head to toe: slacks, heels, long-sleeve shirt and dark sunglasses."

Months later, Geraldine discovered that Louise was wearing the uncomfortable ensemble to hide the bruises on her body. Ever since the early days of her marriage, Louise was brutally beaten by her husband. It was a regular occurrence because Big Ronnie would fly into tirades for the slightest infraction of his rules.

After giving Geraldine a cursory tour of the house, Butch and his girlfriend joined his other friends in the pool. Unbeknownst to the swimmers, Big Ronnie had come out of the house with a lit cherry bomb in his hands. Without warning, he tossed it in the pool, near them.

"All of a sudden," Geraldine said, "there was this big bang, followed by a splash. Everyone just about had a heart attack. After the smoke cleared, we looked up to see a big oaf standing there in his boxer shorts. Butch yelled, 'Dad!' That was how I was introduced to Big Ronnie."

Angered over the prank, Geraldine dried off, got into her car, and drove home, ignoring Butch's pleas to stop. Butch, nonetheless, gave pursuit.

"I was so mad," Geraldine said, "that I must have been doing 90 the whole way back to New Jersey. It didn't matter because Butch stuck right behind me the whole way. He kept flashing his lights trying to get me to pull over."

It was only after Geraldine pulled in her driveway at her home in Elberon, New Jersey, that Butch got his chance to proclaim his total love for her. Although she refused to return to Amityville that day, over the coming months, Geraldine would spend much of her time at the DeFeo house. And it would not be the last time that she

The DeFeo residence.
A large, rambling, three-story Dutch Colonial home built in 1925, the DeFeo house had two quarter-moon windows that looked like eyes, a feature common in Dutch Colonial homes. The backyard area contained a pool and boathouse.

and Big Ronnie did not see eye to eye on things.

Since his father's prank almost cost him his girlfriend, Butch sought his revenge. While his father was floating on his back in the pool, Butch threw in a cherry bomb just as his father had done. This time, however, Big Ronnie failed to find any humor in the situation. He was so enraged that he got into his car and chased his son throughout all of Amityville before finally giving up.

For more reasons than one, Big Ronnie frowned on his son's courtship. Nevertheless, in October 1970, Butch and Geraldine eloped in New Jersey. Geraldine had felt she had found a great husband. Not only was Butch a good father to her children, but he constantly displayed his affection for her.

Commenting on her stepfather, Stacy, Geraldine's oldest daughter from her previous marriage, said, "Butch was a good stepdad. When he was around, he used to tell my mother to let us do this or that, or whatever we wanted. I had the happiest times on Butch's boat when we packed food and stayed on it most of the day. Butch was always so happy then and always made sure we had a lot of fun."

Big Ronnie, however, did not share his son's enthusiasm for his new family. Geraldine recalled, "Big Ronnie disapproved of our relationship because I had already been married and had two daughters. Every time he wanted to remind me of this fact, he would sing the song, 'Secondhand Rose.' He told Butch I was used garbage, a secondhand woman.

"After we had eloped, Butch called his parents and told them he was moving in with me. Upon hearing this, Big Ronnie demanded that Butch return. Butch refused, so his father told him he was taking back everything he had given him: his car, clothes, everything. But it didn't end there.

"Big Ronnie stormed into my home in New Jersey and physically dragged Butch out. It was an unbelievable sight. It was like Butch was a 10-year-old. I demanded Big Ronnie to let go of Butch and jumped in front of him. I should have known that Big Ronnie had no qualms about pushing a woman to the ground. That was when Butch finally spoke up, telling his father that we had just gotten married."

Despite being a married man, Butch was required to live part-time with his family in Amityville. Otherwise, Big Ronnie would make good on his threat and take away Butch's car and anything else he had given him.

Butch also knew that his mother and younger brothers and sisters would suffer for his absence if he did not return. The DeFeo household was ran like a dictatorship, and its absolute ruler was Big Ronnie.

Linnea Nonnewitz, the DeFeo housekeeper and Louise's best friend, summed it up best when she said, "Ronald DeFeo Sr. was the devil."

THE BEGINNINGS OF THE FAMILY

Ronald Joseph DeFeo was born on November 16, 1930, to parents Rocco and Antoinette DeFeo. Eighteen years later, Big Ronnie graduated from Saint Francis Preparatory High School in Fresh Meadows, New York. At best, his grades were slightly above average, accompanied by an occasional high mark.

Starting in his sophomore year, Big Ronnie participated in the sports program at his school. He played basketball, volleyball and, in his senior year, football.

When he was younger, Big Ronnie was slender, handsome, and had a powerful gaze reminiscent of Rudolph Valentino's. Reportedly, Big Ronnie enjoyed football enough to consider making it a career. But for reasons unknown, he chose not to pursue it. However, with his suave looks, he was able to attract the attention of Louise Marie Brigante.

Born on November 3, 1931 to Michael and Angela Brigante, Louise had wanted to pursue a modeling career. She was beautiful enough to hobnob with the best, including legendary singer Mel Torme.

After a brief courtship, Big Ronnie and Louise got married. Since the Brigantes disapproved of Big Ronnie, they cut all ties with the newlyweds. This isolation remained in effect until September 26, 1951, when Big Ronnie and Louise DeFeo became the proud

Ronald "Big Ronnie" DeFeo Sr.
When he was younger, Big Ronnie was slender, handsome, and had a powerful gaze reminiscent of Rudolph Valentino's.

parents of Ronald Joseph DeFeo Jr. It was only after the birth of their grandson that Michael and Angela Brigante rebuilt their relationship with their daughter and new son-in-law.

Growing up, Butch DeFeo had it hard. Because he was first born and a boy, his father expected more from him. And Big Ronnie was not afraid to discipline Butch in the cruelest fashion. One minute, he would hug his son; the next minute, he would throw him across the room.

Louise's brother, Michael Brigante Jr., would later testify at the DeFeo trial about an incident he witnessed when Butch was two years old. He said, "We were all sitting down in the basement watching TV, and, I don't know, the boy had done something. All of a sudden, he stood up, the father, and just pushed the boy this way into the wall. The boy banged his head or part of his shoulder or something."

As a child, Butch was extremely overweight, and would remain so until his later teenage years when he began using amphetamines. Butch's school life suffered because of his weight problem. Bigger kids would often make fun of him, calling him names like, "the blob," "Bucky Beaver," and "porkchop." The only way Butch could release this frustration was to run around in circles until he finally dropped from exhaustion.

Big Ronnie and Louise felt Butch's behavior warranted taking him to a psychiatrist. After examining Butch, the doctor told Big Ronnie that he was to blame for Butch's condition. Geraldine said, "Louise told me that Big Ronnie wanted to shoot the psychiatrist right then and there. He thought that it was perfectly normal to hit his child."

Butch was not an only child for long. On July 29, 1956, Louise gave birth to a daughter, Dawn Theresa DeFeo. A few years later, on August 16, 1961, Louise gave birth to Allison Louise DeFeo, and then again on September 4, 1962 to Marc Gregory DeFeo.

Sometime after the birth of Marc, Louise decided to leave her husband for reasons that remain unclear. Friends and family theorize that she could no longer tolerate her husband's abusive behavior.

To get his wife back, Big Ronnie decided to put his writing talents to good use. He had once written a short story about the mythical donkey that carried the pregnant Virgin Mary.

Needing to express his love for his wife, Big Ronnie co-wrote a song called "The Real Thing." And in 1963, Jazz great Joe Williams recorded the song for his album titled "One Is a Lonesome Number." An excerpt of the lyrics read:

> *If you are going with her*
> *And you can't win*
> *And you're constantly in a spin*
> *If the winter time*
> *Feels like spring*
> *It's not puppy love*
> *It's the real thing...*
>
> *So now you know what love is*
> *It comes to everyone*
> *Love is that certain feeling*
> *When it comes your life has begun*
> *When you fall in love*
> *Go all the way*
> *And thank your lucky stars*
> *For the day*
> *When you can be sure*
> *It's not a fling*
> *Then your heart will know*
> *It is the real thing...*

Friends and family are unsure if it was Big Ronnie's song or Dawn's constant cries for her daddy, but Louise gave in and finally returned home.

On October 24, 1965, Big Ronnie was blessed with a third son, John Matthew DeFeo. By this time, the family had moved from their Brooklyn apartment to the affluent Long Island South Shore community of Amityville. Only for many, it was a mystery how Big Ronnie could afford such a lavish home on a car dealer's service manager's salary.

THE DEALERSHIP

Out of love for his daughter, Michael Brigante Sr. gave his son-in-law the service manager's position at the Brigante-Karl Buick dealership. Since his dealership was in the heart of Brooklyn, both he and his son-in-law established close ties to many New York City police benevolent societies. Any cop who bought a car from the dealership received a discount.

Selling and repairing cars, however, were the legitimate sides of the dealership. In addition to having close ties to the police, the dealership also established close ties to organized crime. And, evidence exists to connect some police officers to this illegal operation. In fact, it is purported that the "Karl" in Brigante-Karl stood for Carlo Gambino. When they were young, Gambino and Brigante had allegedly worked together, also becoming fast friends. In later years, Brigante made it a point to celebrate each Thanksgiving with the Gambinos.

In the 1960s, after a shakeup of power, Joseph Colombo Sr. assumed control of the Profaci crime family, later to be known as the Colombo crime family. Since the late 1950s, the Profacis had been at war with the Gallo brothers over disputed Brooklyn territories and the Gallos' need to become a recognized crime family. It would last well into the 1970s with the death of infamous mobster Joey Gallo and the near-assassination of Colombo at one of his own Italian Anti-defamation League rallies.

Earlier, Colombo had been rewarded with heading the Profaci family by the "boss of bosses," Carlo Gambino. It was a reward for Colombo's ratting out Joseph Bonnano and Joseph Magliocco's plans to knock off the then-two most powerful Mafia figures: Gaetano Lucchese and Carlo Gambino.

In his book, *Racket Squad*, former Brooklyn assistant district attorney John Christopher Fine, who was part of the notorious

Brooklyn Racket Squad, described that the investigation of Colombo revealed how the crime boss posed as a legitimate business man. He not only used his New York real estate license as a front for his mob businesses, but he also posed "as a car salesman for a Brooklyn Buick dealership." Regarding the Italian Anti-defamation League Colombo had started, Fine wrote that it was nothing more than "Joe Colombo's sophisticated mob shakedown racket."

With Colombo incapacitated from his wounds from the failed assassination attempt, a new leader was needed. Joseph Brancato, who was part of a tough Colombo crew that operated in Suffolk County, received the crown. F.B.I. files, however, state that by February 22, 1973, Thomas Di Bella, an old-time hoodlum, was designated the new Colombo family boss with Brancato becoming a Capo. Although the Colombo family controlled Brooklyn, his territories also extended into other parts of New York and New Jersey.

According to Butch DeFeo, his grandfather's dealership was a front for the Mob, with reputed ties to Colombo and Gambino. Money laundering and evidence disposal were just some of the things the dealership was used for. This included melting weapons down in the dealership's melting pot and disposing of dead bodies for the Mafia. At his trial, Butch DeFeo also described how his father embezzled money from the dealership and ran a stolen-car ring.

Often, Butch would ride into work with his father, especially if he had spent the night in Amityville. This, however, forced Geraldine to come into Brooklyn to pick up Butch from work.

One summer day, while waiting for Butch to finish work, she noticed a truck delivering blocks of ice to the dealership's storeroom. Curious about the delivery, Geraldine approached Michael Brigante Sr., who was standing outside it. Geraldine said, "The closer I got to the storeroom, the worst the smell got. I asked Mike what was the ice for, and he told me to forget about it. Later, I found out from Butch that they had a couple of corpses in there, and the ice was for them."

Growing up in New Jersey, Geraldine was not unfamiliar with the ways of the Mob because her own friends and family were connected to the Genovese crime family.

"When they found out I had married Butch, they were not happy," Geraldine said. "They considered Big Ronnie a wannabe. And they viewed the dealership as the lowest form of Mob business because they disposed of corpses."

Despite her friends' and family's misgivings, Geraldine continued to grow closer to her in-laws. She would often notice that Big Ronnie brought home the dealership ledgers for an operation he called "Going South."

Out of all of Big Ronnie's responsibilities for the dealership, the most important involved balancing the legitimate books against the books that showed the actual cash flow from illegal sources. Not only was he a master in his ability to hide the dealership's true cash intake, but he was also successful in hiding his own embezzlement. Since the books practically named every crime figure involved with Colombo and the dealership, including cops on the take, whenever Big Ronnie brought the books home, he hid them in the cellar behind a loose panel.

FOOTING THE BILL

According to Geraldine DeFeo, Mike Brigante Sr. knew he had to accept Big Ronnie because his daughter loved him. He also made sure that she had everything she had wanted. It was Brigante who had to fork over the money for their Amityville house.

"If Louise was out of perfume," Geraldine said, "she would call her father at work. Later, that same afternoon, Mike would have a case of either Chanel or Shalimar delivered to her. If she was out of meat, her father would send over half a cow."

Commenting on this, Butch said, "How could my father be a man when her father was always there?"

Yet it was not only the Brigantes who spoiled Louise. "Each time Rocco DeFeo would come over," Geraldine said, "he would leave $50 underneath his coffee cup or saucer for Louise. I think it was his way of saying he was grateful to her for putting up with his son."

In the early 1970s, Big Ronnie decided that he wanted a series of portraits created to immortalize his family. So once more, Brigante picked up the tab, which was estimated to between $50,000 and $75,000.

Painstakingly detailed, the portraits took nearly a year to complete. Upon their completion, the life-size portraits hung in large golden frames on the staircase wall in between the first and second floors of the DeFeo home.

The first portrait showed Allison and Dawn DeFeo seated together on a couch. The two sisters, both wearing flower-patterned dresses, seemed to be reading from the same book.

The next portrait depicted Butch and his father, who was pouring a drink for his son. The detail was so remarkable that it appeared that Big Ronnie, who was staring straight ahead, would overflow his son's glass at any moment.

At the top of the first landing hung the portrait of Marc and John DeFeo. In a tender moment, Marc had his arm around his brother with his other hand on a toy dog, while John sat cross-legged, enjoying the park-like setting of the portrait.

At the end of the foyer sat the portrait of Louise DeFeo sitting on a chair, looking very regal in a red dress. With strands of pearls around her neck and expensive rings on her fingers, Louise's portrait was, by far, the most exquisite. From her picture, it was incomprehensible that Louise was the mother of five.

Michael Brigante Sr.'s portrait also hung in the house. Growing up, Louise and her father were very close. So when it came time to sit for the portraits, she insisted her father take part.

In his portrait, Brigante's formal attire, a black suit and tie, gave the unmistakable impression that he was the patriarch of the family and not Big Ronnie. After the portraits were hung, Big Ronnie could not escape the constant reminder that his family's prosperity was due to his father-in-law's generosity.

This was not the only aggravation the portraits added. Maybe it was the attention to beauty and detail that the artist had adhered to with Louise's, or maybe it was just Big Ronnie's paranoia, but he suspected his wife of having had an affair with the artist.

The Portraits.
In the early 1970s, Big Ronnie decided that he wanted a series of portraits created to immortalize his family. So once more, Michael Brigante picked up the tab, which was estimated to between $50,000 and $75,000.

To combat this fear, Big Ronnie installed a series of red phones throughout the house. Since he was the only one who knew their numbers, he could check up on Louise whenever he felt like it. Even though Louise was a lady and had never thought of cheating on her husband, there were suspicions that Big Ronnie had a girlfriend in the city.

BUTCH DEFEO AND HIS FAMILY

Womanizing may have been a bad habit that Butch picked up from his father. According to Geraldine, she often left Butch because she caught him with other women. "One time, I came into The Chatterbox Bar and found Butch having sex with a woman in the corner near the jukebox," Geraldine said. "When I confronted him later about the incident, he gave me a lame excuse, saying that it was not him but a Puerto Rican guy who looked like him."

Before Butch was allowed to sleep in the same bed with her, his wife forced him to do something that most men would refuse.

Geraldine explained, "He came home, and on the end table there were two jars. One was rubbing alcohol; the other peroxide. I told Butch that if he ever wanted to have sex with me again, then he would have to stick his penis in them because I did not want to catch a disease from one of his bimbos. He told me I was crazy, and he refused to do it. But he knew I was serious and would not back down, so after a few minutes of walking around the room, he unzipped his pants and dipped it in. Afterward, he was wailing in pain."

But even though Butch knew he would have to endure the wrath of his wife or risk losing her altogether, his extramarital affairs continued. He would later reason that it was due to an extraordinarily high sex drive.

Geraldine, nevertheless, made good on her promise and left Butch several times. Geraldine said, "Every time I threw Butch out, he would come back and beg me to take him back. My love for Butch was like a disease that I could not get rid of. When he did something really, really bad, he would place a red rose on the bed and then sing either 'A Sunday Kind of Love' or 'Maybe' to me. And Butch never hit me or the kids. This meant more to me than you can imagine, since my first husband was very abusive."

According to Butch and Geraldine, every time they reconciled, they would retake their vows as a sign of a new beginning. But according to Geraldine, Butch would stay "a good boy for only six months and then revert to his old ways."

And Geraldine's anger never lessened over time. She said, "Butch might have been the womanizer, but I was the abusive one in the marriage because I constantly slapped him and threw things at him. In fact, one time we were both in bed and I decided to get my revenge on him for his latest conquest. So I lit a cigarette and extinguished the match on the head of his penis.

"He leapt out of bed and started calling me every name imaginable as he proceeded to ice his penis down. I told him he deserved it because he could not keep it in his pants. I half expected him to kill me, but instead he picked up the phone and called his mother. Afterward, he went home to her. I didn't see him for days."

His father, on the other hand, could not understand why Butch put up with a wife like that. One time while the entire family was eating dinner at the pizzeria in Amityville, Big Ronnie yelled at his son that "he needed to be a man and show his wife who was boss before his penis rotted off because of his wife's maiming." The other customers just stared in amazement upon hearing the tumultuous man's conversation.

Despite Butch's marital problems, he was a good stepfather to Geraldine's two young daughters, Stacy and Jill.

"Butch would often read to my daughters a bedtime story," Geraldine said. "He would play with them, help them with their homework and do regular fatherly things with them. The one thing Butch wanted to have for his new family was normality, something his family didn't have. For him, this meant eating dinner at the table and not in front of the TV, having a strict routine, and trying to be a good example to the children."

When Butch and Geraldine finally decided to have a daughter of their own, Butch took great lengths to ensure his pregnant wife was comfortable.

Geraldine said, "When I was pregnant with my daughter, Shea Marie [pseudonym], Butch would carry me to and from everywhere. He was more concerned with the well-being of the baby than I was. Often when we would sit down together, he would put his head to my belly and just listen. He would speak softly to our unborn daughter, telling her he was her daddy and that he loved her. He was so excited about the pregnancy."

But according to Geraldine, it was while she was pregnant that she considered leaving Butch for good over an affair he was having with a barmaid by the name of Mindy Weiss. It was Butch's belief, as it was his father's, that a wife should be a lady in the street, but a whore in bed. Because Geraldine was pregnant, Butch refused to have intercourse with his wife, so once again he strayed. In August 1974, Butch's daughter was born, so he ended the affair and reconciled with his wife by once again reaffirming his vows.

Butch showed a similar type of love and care for his younger brothers and sisters. Although she was only an in-law, the DeFeo world was a strange and dysfunctional one to Geraldine. She did her best to spend time routinely at the DeFeo house and observed both the good times and the bad times.

According to Butch, he was extremely close to his sister Allison. Geraldine said, "Each time Allison would find out that Butch and I planned to go for a boat ride, she would run up to her big brother and jump into his arms. Ally always ran her hands through his hair, messing it up. She was the only person Butch allowed to do this. She was his favorite, and he called her his golden child."

Often, when Geraldine would accompany Butch to Amityville, she would bring along her daughters. It was at that time that Stacy befriended Allison. The two girls would sit in Allison's room looking at fashion magazines and catalogs, picking out the makeup and clothes they would buy once they were old enough.

Recalling her visits to 112 Ocean Avenue, Stacy said, "I remember hoping we would leave before Mr. DeFeo came home. The dock and the water near the house was what I really liked the best. I also liked sitting at the end of it with Allison."

The feeling in the DeFeo house would change from a happy, relaxed feeling to an oppressed, fearful one when Big Ronnie was due home from work. Often, to avoid any confrontations with her father, Allison went up to her room and closed the door.

Commenting on this, Stacy said, "The DeFeo family was so sad. They had so much, but they never enjoyed it. I don't think they knew how to be happy or live with each other without trying to control each other. Especially Mr. DeFeo, because he wanted to control everyone. Allison was not like that. Allison drew pictures, did puzzles, and colored in her room a lot so she could stay upstairs when her mom and dad were in bad moods or fighting. She just wanted to be full of laughter and jokes, and not hear all of the yelling. She hated the yelling."

Allison was nicknamed "Happy" because she was always so cheerful. And she would spend hours doing crafts, puzzles or coloring by herself. To avoid any embarrassing situations, Allison did not invite over too many friends to her house because she did not want them to see her father and mother fighting. It was a trait she shared with her mother, who was allowed by her husband to have just a few friends.

"Allison needed to be loved," Geraldine remembered. "She would often spend time over at my house in New Jersey, so she could play with my daughters, or be with her big brother. She would try to seek out attention in the smallest ways by making Butch tie her shoes. He teased her and called it 'cheap affection.' So every time Butch would tell Ally she knew how to tie her own shoes, or braid her own hair, she sarcastically replied back that she needed some 'cheap affection.'"

Butch also was very proud of both of his brothers and often boasted of Marc's gifted ability in sports. Although Butch did not care too much for sports himself, he always made it a point to try to come to his brother's games.

In September 1974, Marc injured his leg during a football game. At the hospital, Butch broke down in tears, and Big Ronnie, who did not understand this open display of affection, ordered Butch to leave.

Chapter Three

In addition to Allison, Butch also took his youngest brother John on many boating excursions. John loved to run and chase Shaggy, the family dog, around the backyard. Like most kids, during the summertime, John would spend most of his time in his pool.

Regarding his parents, Butch loved them just like any son loved his parents. Although his father was extremely abusive and violent, Butch considered him "his partner in everything" and considered himself "shit without him." Among the many bad habits Butch picked up from his father, thievery was one of them. Because Butch had stolen money from his father before, Big Ronnie kept most of his jewelry and money in a bank's safe deposit box rather than in the house.

Marc may have been the son Big Ronnie had always wanted because of his athletic ability, but Butch was the son he needed to carry out his schemes.

Butch was extremely close to his mother. According to Linnea Nonnewitz, Butch would spend hours gossiping with them at the kitchen table.

Linnea explained that on one occasion Louise was so despondent over living life with Big Ronnie, she told Butch she wanted to die. So Butch brought down a starter pistol from his room and pointed at his mother.

Louise told her son, "Go ahead and shoot me," knowing well the gun was broken. According to Linnea, at that point, they both entered into hysterics over the situation.

In spite of her constant complaints about her husband, Louise was a loyal wife. "She must have really loved Big Ronnie," Geraldine said. "Otherwise, she could have left him or had her father intervene. Instead, both would often act like little kids in love.

"She put up with Big Ronnie's obesity and weird sex habits like a mirrored wall in their bedroom. And because he was so obese, Big Ronnie would often break the bed during intercourse. They eventually stopped using a bed frame and just placed their mattresses and box springs on the floor."

Although her husband weighed 270 pounds, Louise was terrified to get fat. She even went as far as to warn Geraldine that a wife should never allow herself to get fat, out of respect for her husband.

Even if the entire house could hear Louise and Big Ronnie in their bedroom while they had sex, Butch and Geraldine were forbidden to have intimate moments in the house. "When we were dating, Butch and I snuck down to the basement because we wanted to fool around. All of a sudden, we heard Louise in the living room playing the piano and singing, 'This is not a house of ill repute.' It did not matter what time it was; she would always get out of bed and tell us to get a motel room."

However, Louise could not prevent her husband from turning violent. Thankfully, Big Ronnie usually spared the younger children from his abusive outbursts. This, however, meant that Louise, Butch and Dawn were the prime targets.

Like his other siblings, Butch genuinely cared about his sister. Frequently, Butch would hand over the keys to his car, so Dawn could disappear for a few hours while he stayed and took the beatings meant for both of them. Butch later explained at his 1999 parole hearing, "We were like dogs on leashes. We were always beat up and abused by our father."

But even Butch could not always save Dawn from the hand of their father. Geraldine recalled, "One afternoon, I came to Amityville to pick up Butch. As I pulled up the driveway, I could hear Big Ronnie screaming inside. I then noticed Butch sitting on the other side of the Amityville Creek. So I drove over and saw he was crying. When I asked him what was wrong, he told me he could not stop his father from beating up Dawn."

Although Butch loved Dawn, he also disliked her slovenliness. Apparently, the more grotesque episodes of Dawn's slovenliness included half-eaten chicken wings underneath her bed and used sanitary napkins hidden in her drawers. Of course, this attracted bugs, especially flies from outside.

According to Geraldine, Dawn was quite jealous of her little sister. "Dawn was a slob, boisterous and big. She was the complete opposite of Allison, who was neat, quiet and petite. Out of spite, Dawn sometimes would enter Allison's room just to mess it up,"

Geraldine said.

Dawn would often accompany her brother to a bar, a party, or to Butch and Geraldine's favorite restaurant, the Nautilus Diner in neighboring Massapequa.

Butch allegedly was a "Jack Daniels" man. He purportedly liked whiskey and was also a "chippy" user of heroin, meaning he did not use it on a regular basis. When he was in his late teens, Butch used a lot of speed to lose weight.

Dawn had followed in her brother's footsteps and used speed for her weight problem, but, in addition, also used LSD, mescaline and Quaaludes as a way to escape the problems at home.

In a way, Butch looked up to Dawn because she was going to secretarial school. He told Allison, Marc and John that they should follow Dawn's example and stay in school and "not to take after his example."

Despite the turmoil, there were good times at the DeFeo household. During the summer months, Big Ronnie would plan an excursion to Coney Island for the family. "He was like this big kid," Geraldine said, "because he woke everyone up bright and early because he was so excited to go ride the rides at the amusement park."

During Christmas, Big Ronnie would go all out. From the intimate conversations she had with her mother-in-law, Geraldine learned that as a child Big Ronnie did not always have a Christmas. So when the holidays arrived, Big Ronnie bought gifts, hosted parties, and repeatedly had the family gather around so he could read a story. Most often, it was the short story he had written about the donkey that carried the Virgin Mary.

On November 16, 1974, Big Ronnie would have turned 44 and had planned to celebrate the occasion with a party. But three days before, his life came to an abrupt end.

BUTCH AND HIS FRIENDS

Soon after Butch moved to Amityville with his family, he met Barry Springer, Chuck Tewksbury and Frank Davidge, whom Butch nicknamed "Remus." The group did practically everything together.

Butch and Barry even started a clamming business together. "Butch loved clamming," Geraldine said. "Many times we would be walking on the beach, and Butch would see the conditions were right to go clamming. So we would get Barry and some of the other guys and go out on the boat. It was a tremendous amount of hard work, but Butch enjoyed it. And it was not about the money because Butch gave his earnings to his mother."

Butch also liked to go hunting with his friends, even though he had bad eyesight and did not particularly care to kill animals.

In November 1972, Butch and Frank Davidge were hunting deer in the woods. Although Davidge was to the left of Butch, he accidentally shot in Davidge's direction. Geraldine said, "Butch had such terrible eyesight that he truly did not see Frank there. Frank knew it was an accident and remained friends with Butch. If Frank had thought Butch was trying to kill him, then he would have shot back and definitely would have had no more to do with Butch. Frank later told me that Butch was very apologetic over the incident because the last thing he wanted to do was shoot a friend."

Both Frank Davidge and his brother, Billy, spent much of their time at the DeFeo house hanging out with Butch. In addition, Dawn and Billy Davidge began a courtship. According to friends and family, Dawn fell head over heels in love with Billy.

By 1974, Big Ronnie's abusive tendencies were worsening. On several occasions, Frank Davidge witnessed this cruelty firsthand. According to Geraldine, after one too many incidents, Frank refused to come back into the DeFeo house. Nevertheless, Dawn and Billy still saw each other. And for her senior prom, Billy explained, "Butch even gave me money to take Dawn to her high school prom."

In the late 1960s, Butch met Robert "Bobby" Kelske, who quickly became his best friend and confidant. A gifted athlete, Kelske was named to the Suffolk County league team during his senior year at Amityville High School. In fact, in one game, Kelske, #31, was credited with scoring 19 points. Butch was extremely proud of Kelske and often boasted about his friend's athletic ability.

Not only did Bobby do regular things with Butch, such as hanging out at bars, but also was intimately involved with the Brigante operation and the DeFeo family. According to Butch, they hung out together, scammed together, and even worked for the Mob as bag men responsible for money drops.

Another friend who had ties to the Mob was Augusta "Augie" Degenaro. According to Butch and Geraldine, Augie hung out with "made men" connected to the Gallos and then later the Colombos. Butch summed Augie up by saying he was a "wannabe who talked the talk, but did not walk the walk."

According to Geraldine, when her husband drank, "he got guts." On one occasion, he had a confrontation with Bobby outside Henry's Bar. Because Butch had made a pass at Bobby's wife, Bobby hit him. So Butch got a gun from his car and pointed it at his friend, pretending he was going to shoot him.

"Bobby just stared Butch down," Geraldine said. "Bobby's nickname was 'the brick' because he was so big and tough and could not be physically intimidated and because he was a bricklayer. Bobby knew Butch was a braggart and did not have the guts to make good on his threats. Afterward, when Butch was laughing about the incident, Bobby just threw his gun on the roof of Henry's Bar forcing Butch to get it the next day."

Henry's Bar was known to Butch, his wife and their friends as "Highs" because they often got either drunk or high at the bar. Bobby even sold his drugs there to make some extra cash. Out of all the bars in the area, Henry's was the one that Butch and his friends frequented most often because it was right up the street from the DeFeo home, their after-hours hangout.

Irene Reichelt, a former acquaintance of Butch's and who had also been a patron of Henry's Bar, said in a 1999 interview, "He [Butch] was always buying people drinks. He used to say his father would give him five thousand dollars if he asked. Always fancy clothes, fancy cars. He had a car with one of those cucaracha horns."

A barmaid from The Chatterbox Bar, another popular bar for the group, recalled how Butch was part of a crowd that "would drink and then get into fights, but the next day they'd apologize."

Regardless of the day, time or the occasion, 112 Ocean Avenue served as the main hangout for Butch and his friends after the local bars had closed. Moreover, the finished basement provided a refuge to smoke dope, drink and play pool. However, nobody could overlook the growing hostility within the DeFeo house. The atmosphere was changing, and everybody knew things were worsening.

Dawn with high school friends (above).
Mike's Pizzeria in Amityville (below).
Here, the DeFeo family would sometimes dine or come for takeout. Two doors down, at the village's shoe store, Brigante Sr. would treat his grandchildren to a new pair of shoes each week.

CHAPTER FOUR
On the Road to Disaster

OUT OF ALL the tumultuous events in their household during the DeFeo family's final months, the prime factor leading to the impending tragedy was Big Ronnie's cruelty. Describing the abuse, Butch said, "It just went on and on. My mother, everybody [were targets]; nobody could control my father."

On one occasion, Frank Davidge was over at the house eating dinner with Butch and his father. At Butch's trial, Davidge, under oath, testified, "The kids were running around the house; the mother was yelling at the kids. She was doing the laundry, and doors were slamming. And the father had asked the mother to please be quiet so that he could eat in peace a number of times.

"The noise still continued to go on, at which time Mr. DeFeo got up from the table. Mrs. DeFeo was coming upstairs from the basement, which was where the laundry room was, and she had an armful of laundry or a bundle of laundry in a basket. Mr. DeFeo walked over to her and punched her . . . and I didn't see her fall down the stairs, but I heard the noise of something falling down the stairs."

Although Butch constantly protested when he saw his father hit his mother, there was little else he could do to stop it. On one occasion, Butch pulled off his father, knowing he would suffer the consequences. But before Big Ronnie could react, Louise grabbed an empty champagne bottle and broke it over Butch's head because he had interfered.

Yet Butch would never hit his father or defend himself even if he had done nothing to deserve the beating. Geraldine recalled, "Big Ronnie must have been insane. I mean, he would fly off the handle for no reason at all. One time, all of us were sitting at the dining room table eating a nice dinner. Butch dropped his napkin, so naturally he bent down to pick it up. When he raised up, Big Ronnie asked him calmly, 'Why did you leave the table without excusing yourself?'

"Butch said that he just bent down to pick up his napkin. Well, this was not good enough for Big Ronnie. He got up from his chair, picked up Butch by the throat and pushed him against the wall. Despite our shouts and cries for him to stop, Big Ronnie proceeded to punch his son in the gut and the face until he was a bloody mess. After Big Ronnie got tired, he returned to his seat and proceeded to eat dinner like nothing had happened. That was how unstable Big Ronnie was."

Ever since Butch was a child, his father would strike him with one hand while he used the other to show he loved his son. In 1973, Butch got arrested on a grand larceny charge because he was in possession of a stolen outboard motor. In spite of the fact that his father beat him up for getting caught, Big Ronnie did everything in his power to protect his son, including boasting to police that he had ties to organized crime.

Moreover, Big Ronnie did not limit his aggression to just his family. As a scare tactic, he would often threaten to flex his "Mob" connections. In fact, many of these quarrels ensued between Big Ronnie and his neighbors, some of whom realized that Big Ronnie carried a revolver and should be taken seriously. Besides, Ocean

Avenue had seen its share of incidents at the DeFeo house to know that Big Ronnie was not someone to fool with.

In the early 1970s, Big Ronnie promised his wife that he was a changed man. To symbolize this "new Ronnie," he constructed a rock garden in the backyard that he dedicated to his wife. As promised, Ronald DeFeo Sr. was a changed man, a gentler father, a kinder husband, and a better neighbor. But it would not last.

At the end of two weeks, Big Ronnie destroyed the rock garden to indicate he was reverting to his old self. It was clear that Big Ronnie felt a need to demonstrate that his home and family were his to do with what he pleased.

This became evident to Geraldine late one night after the family had returned home from dinner in New York City. She explained, "After getting out of the car, Big Ronnie went to the corner of the house, next to the driveway, unzipped his pants, and began peeing on the side of the house in plain sight for everyone to see. It was explained to me that Big Ronnie felt a need to mark what was his."

But a person who challenged or questioned Big Ronnie's authority ran the risk of a physical confrontation. Geraldine said, "One evening, Big Ronnie and I were having a disagreement in the kitchen. Although I could tell Butch and Louise were eyeing me to shut up, I persisted to argue with Big Ronnie. All of a sudden, Big Ronnie placed his hands around my throat and began choking me. It was not a playful choke, but his huge hands were actually cutting off my air supply. My punches did little good to fend off the attack.

"I expected Butch to come to my rescue by hitting, kicking, biting, anything to free me. Instead, in a meek voice, he pleaded for his father to stop. He said, 'Dad, please don't choke her. That's my wife, dad. Please stop.'

"I was about to pass out when Butch finally said, 'Dad, if you keep doing that, I will leave this house and never come back.' With that, Big Ronnie released his grip on me."

In spite of the fact that Geraldine was nearly unconscious, she managed to drive home. Although angry at Butch, he convinced her not to call the police because his father had too many connections with cops and because his mother would face the consequences. It was weeks before Geraldine would recover fully, or return to Amityville. But it was not the last time Geraldine and Big Ronnie would engage in a physical altercation.

Butch and Geraldine often would accompany Big Ronnie and Louise to dinner in the city. On one occasion, they arrived at 112 Ocean Avenue and witnessed Big Ronnie dragging Allison, by her hair, up and down the stairs.

"Her head was striking every step," Geraldine said, "as Big Ronnie went back and forth dragging his daughter up the stairs and then back again. Everyone was shouting for him to stop, but nobody was doing anything about it. So I picked up a crystal candy dish and smashed it over his head. If there had been a gun there, I would have gladly used it."

The candy dish was fine crystal, so it was a heavy weapon. Bleeding from his wound and shocked that someone had actually intervened, Big Ronnie released his grip on Allison. But before his father could retaliate, Butch grabbed his wife by her shirt, tearing it in the process, and led her outside. A few seconds later, he returned, carrying his semiconscious sister.

Geraldine said, "We both were panicking because we didn't know how badly hurt Allison was. Butch kept yelling to me not to let her go to sleep as he raced to a hospital. Later, when Allison was coming around, Butch called his parents to tell them she was fine. I guess he told them where we were because they showed up shortly thereafter. Instead of worrying about Ally, Big Ronnie cursed his son, saying he was a 'no good son-of-a-bitch' because that was his daughter and he could do with her what he wanted to."

As had happened other times, the doctors were given an excuse. This time they were told that Allison had fallen down the stairs by accident. Friends and relatives alike felt they were powerless to stop Big Ronnie. However, the one person Big Ronnie may have been frightened of was his own mother.

At about age five or six, Butch recalled seeing his father anger his grandmother, Antoinette DeFeo. In retaliation, Butch described a horrifying scene of his father cowering as his mother beat him, one hand with a razor strap, the other with the buckle end of a belt.

Incidents such as these would carry over to Big Ronnie's own family. He would often tell his son, "He ain't shit with out him." On other occasions, Butch, according to Big Ronnie, was not even his. Apparently, he enjoyed this form of cruelty, even lowering himself to remind Louise about her father's extramarital affair that resulted in an alleged stepsister.

During the last months, Butch began detesting his mother's weakness more and more because he felt she could have ended the abuse with one phone call to her father. Yet instead, she always protected her husband, seemingly choosing to be a loyal wife rather than a devoted mother.

THE FAMILY BUSINESS

Even though Big Ronnie had contempt for his father-in-law, he knew that he needed the generous income the man paid him. Instead of sitting down in an intelligent manner to discuss his problems, Big Ronnie would revert to methods like filling up an entire notepad with the words "fuck you" and then handing it to Michael Brigante Sr.

Rather than being grateful for his position at the dealership, Big Ronnie chose to embezzle money. Linnea Nonnewitz recalled Louise's fears about what her family would do for an income if her father ever fired Big Ronnie. This being the case, it is understandable that Louise did everything in her effort to pacify her father.

Witness to this, Geraldine said, "I came in one day unannounced and heard Louise on the phone. So I stood by the dining room because I did not want to disturb her. I could not help overhearing her say, like a little girl, 'Daddy, he is getting better.' She did everything she could to placate her father."

Despite his daughter's insistence, Big Ronnie was not improving. One day, Brigante walked into Big Ronnie's office to discuss business, when a black bag suddenly fell out of the loose ceiling panels. Although the bag contained money, Big Ronnie denied any knowledge, even in light of this evidence, of the bag or the money.

Blue T (above) is loacted down the street from the DeFeo house and next door to Henry's Bar (now Cloud Nine). It was here that Dawn began revealing a twisted plan to Butch and Geraldine. The DeFeo children (below) pose for a picture five years before the tragedy.

There were two reasons why Big Ronnie needed to embezzle money. First, Michael Brigante Sr. had toyed with the idea to close down the dealership rather than just fire his son-in-law. His daughter's constant pleading had repeatedly postponed this. A new problem, however, arose that Brigante could not ignore.

In 1974, Brigante faced insurmountable difficulties. Not only was another Mob war imminent, but Brooklyn authorities were beginning to focus their attention on the dealership since key crime figures like Joseph Colombo Sr. were involved with it.

The Colombo organization had taken a significant hit ever since their patriarch was incapacitated. Colombo's Italian Antidefamation League, a thorn in the F.B.I.'s side, was no longer a threat since its publicity-seeking leader had been gunned down. And despite Colombo's injuries, prosecutors wanted him to stand trial for his part in a 1968 robbery of $750,000 from the Long Island Diamond and Jewelry Exchange. But officials did not stop there. Wanting further indictments, they kept every Colombo member under surveillance, from the lowly soldier to the new head of the family.

Rather than face an investigation, and possible indictment, Brigante knew he had to close down his lucrative business. Knowing his ride on easy street was near an end, Big Ronnie began preparing for tougher times by embezzling more than $250,000 from the dealership.

Sometime before November 13, 1974, Big Ronnie decided that it was too risky to keep the money at his house. So he enlisted his son to bury the money at a nearby dock and beach in Amityville. It has been alleged by Butch that after the murders, the money was finally recovered by some Suffolk County police officers who kept it for themselves.

Big Ronnie's plan was to live off the money and move the entire family to Canada close to Saint Joseph's Oratory in Montreal. After visiting the holy place a few years earlier, Big Ronnie had been convinced that he had the ability to predict the future and had been given other E.S.P. abilities.

"Big Ronnie," Geraldine said, "was convinced by a charlatan

priest that there was this underground movement that was preparing for the second coming of Christ. In order to help, Big Ronnie sent thousands of dollars to him. It just fueled his insanity because the priest would write letters back stating how Big Ronnie had psychic powers. It was sickening."

Big Ronnie truly believed he had psychic powers. In fact, he would constantly tell people close to him that his premonitions led him to believe that they were in danger. If they lived near the water, Big Ronnie would wake them up in the middle of the night to inform them they were in imminent danger of a tsunami. He even ordered, and convinced, his wife to cease driving her car because he feared she was going to be in a traffic accident and be decapitated.

Thinking he could pray his way into heaven, Big Ronnie ordered Butch and Bobby Kelske to construct religious shrines in the front and back of the DeFeo house.

When they were completed, the front of the house had a large statue of Saint Joseph holding the baby Jesus, surrounded by flowers and three small statutes of praying children.

The back yard, on the other hand, had a brick and rock grotto constructed by Bobby Kelske. After its completion, the grotto contained a magnificent statue of Jesus Christ.

Friends, family, and neighbors would see Big Ronnie out there praying to the statues at all hours of the day and night. Geraldine explained, "Usually after he finished one of his rampages, Big Ronnie would go outside, dressed only in his underwear, and pray in the front yard for forgiveness. Louise, bloody and bruised, would come outside and would yell at him to stop making a scene. By this time, the neighbor would stick her head out and yell that Louise was acting like a fishmonger's wife. Louise would yell back to mind her own business and then yell at Big Ronnie again to come inside. Big Ronnie then would threaten Louise to shut up or he'd give her another beating. He then would go on praying. It was a circus."

Ever since he had started working for his father-in-law, Big Ronnie had wanted to become a "made man" in the Mob. But his big mouth was his undoing because he was subsequently turned down. For that reason, Big Ronnie decided to start his own "family." Next to his son, Big Ronnie's first choice for enrollment was Bobby Kelske.

Kelske not only spent most of his free time hanging out at the DeFeo house, but also was paid handsomely for the odd jobs he performed for Big Ronnie. So when Big Ronnie wanted to indoctrinate Kelske into his family, Kelske obliged and followed him downstairs. There, Big Ronnie performed an impromptu ceremony, in which he prayed over Kelske. Afterward, he told Kelske he had been blessed and now was a member of *his* family.

In reality, Butch DeFeo and Bobby Kelske already were associated with the real Mafia by way of Michael Brigante Sr.'s dealership. According to Butch, not only did Kelske and he act as bag men, but they disposed of corpses, and even burned down a house under orders from Carlo Gambino.

Butch explained, "Tony Mazzeo [a purported mobster] did something to offend Carlo Gambino. Gambino asked my grandfather to burn down his house, I think because they feared Mazzeo was going to turn into a rat. Afterwards, my grandfather told my father that he had to take in Mazzeo, so that Mazzeo would not become suspicious. But it did not end there. Kelske always held the fire over my grandfather's head because the rags we used to burn down Mazzeo's house had laundry marks on them that could be traced back to the dealership."

This would not be the last time the two friends practiced arson. Wanting to collect the insurance money on his boat, Big Ronnie ordered his son and Kelske to take his boat out into the Great South Bay and burn it. Ironically, a claim of $2,200.99 was paid on November 14, 1974, one day after Big Ronnie's death.

But all of Big Ronnie's scamming was coming back to haunt him. In early autumn 1974, two unidentified men visited 112 Ocean Avenue with a message for Louise to give to her husband, who was not home at the time. Geraldine, there visiting with Shea Marie, recalled, "These two guys told Louise that Big Ronnie better change his ways or we'd find him in the gutter."

Fearing for his life, and possibly feeling that his father-in-law instigated the threat, Big Ronnie ordered Butch to kill Michael

Brigante Sr. Since Butch loved his grandfather more than his own father, he refused. It was one of the only times Butch disobeyed his father.

A few weeks later, Butch's brake lines to his Buick were cut. Although he avoided an accident and made it into the dealership without injury, he was visibly shaken. He felt, without a doubt, that his father was responsible. Thus, fearing for his grandfather's life, and now his own, Butch enlisted the aid of Bobby Kelske and Augie Degenaro to help kill Big Ronnie around Christmas time 1974.

Big Ronnie would be killed in Brooklyn because Brigante had more influence with the cops there than in Suffolk County. In the end, the murder would be attributed to a robbery gone wrong. Besides, there was indication that Brigante and the heads of La Cosa Nostra approved of the hit and had even planned to take out Big Ronnie themselves.

Although Bobby Kelske was not overly enthusiastic about killing Big Ronnie since the man paid him well, he knew he owed Butch. In 1973, Bobby had gotten himself into a scrape and had asked Butch to help him out. Geraldine recalled, "Butch and I were in Henry's Bar drinking up a storm late one night. Bobby came rushing in, out of breath, and told us that he thought he had just killed someone. Bobby told us that he followed this drunk black guy because he wanted to rob him. Bobby said he hit him, and the guy fell backwards into the canal, disappearing from sight. We learned later that the man drowned."

The body was found later by police at the foot of Ocean Avenue. The day before his death, the victim had just borrowed $211 from a finance company in Amityville. To celebrate, he had gone out drinking and even bought a few rounds of drinks for other patrons. His autopsy showed he had an alcohol level of 0.15 at the time of his death. No charges were ever brought against Kelske.

In all of his life, Butch never raised a hand to defend himself against his father's attacks. So there is considerable doubt whether Butch's planned hit would have been carried out. Regardless, by that time, Big Ronnie's rampages were worsening, and something drastic had to be done.

Learning that his son was having problems, Rocco DeFeo approached Big Ronnie. It may have gotten back to Rocco's brother, Pete DeFeo, a one-time hit man for the Genovese crime family, that Big Ronnie was in serious trouble.

Recalling seeing Rocco confront his son, Geraldine recalled, "During a family gathering at Amityville, Rocco told Big Ronnie he wanted to talk to his son. The two went outside and began having a heated argument. All of a sudden, Big Ronnie started beating up his own father, pushing him to the pavement and pounding Rocco's head into it. He finally stopped after a neighbor said she was going to call the police."

Big Ronnie, however, was not the only one to steal from the dealership. On November 1, 1974, Butch orchestrated a phony robbery where over $19,000—mostly checks—were stolen. Big Ronnie knew his son too well and wanted his cut of the action.

According to Butch, his father had gone through his room looking for the money. After he could not find it, Big Ronnie had began asking around. A vagrant, who was a Vietnam veteran and who had been doing odd jobs for Big Ronnie around the house, overheard Big Ronnie offer Kelske $500 if he told him where Butch had stashed the money. Kelske played dumb, but the veteran said he knew where the money was.

Later, the subject of the veteran came up at the dinner table. Geraldine said, "Right in front of the children, Big Ronnie asked Butch if he'd taken care of the man's body."

After Big Ronnie had learned where Butch had stashed the money, he took the veteran into the boathouse. With machinery running to mask the sound, Big Ronnie pulled out his pistol and shot the guy in the head. His reasoning was that if the guy would rat out somebody for $500, then who knew what he would do for $5,000?

Purportedly, Butch and Bobby were assigned the task of chopping up the guy's corpse and dumping it into the Jersey swamps. Offering credence to this, Geraldine said, "I saw the bloodstain in Butch's car trunk afterwards. It was where the body had been stashed."

The Boathouse.
Prior to the murders in November 1974, the boathouse was the scene of a shooting, where Big Ronnie "offed" a vagrant who he felt was a liability.

The incident was a further indication of the danger Big Ronnie had become. By cutting Butch's brakes, trying to orchestrate a hit on his father-in-law and killing a man in his own boathouse, it became clear: Big Ronnie was prepared to kill anyone and everyone who posed a threat to him.

WANTING OUT

By the end of summer, Dawn DeFeo had begun rebelling against her parents' wishes. She did not want to attend Katherine Gibbs Secretarial School in nearby Melville. Rather, Dawn wanted to join Billy Davidge, who had relocated to Florida with his family. Big Ronnie, however, refused to allow Dawn to leave his home.

Big Ronnie repeatedly threatened Dawn that if she did not go to secretarial school, then she would not get Butch's old car, a turquoise Buick Wildcat. Since she had hated the color, it was currently at her grandfather's dealership awaiting a paint job.

Regardless, Dawn wanted out of her house because she wanted to be reunited with her boyfriend. According to Linnea Nonnewitz, her own daughter had plans to go to Florida, and Dawn wanted to come along. But because Linnea was best friends with Louise DeFeo and was her housekeeper, she refused Dawn's request. Dawn, who was driving with Linnea at the time, was so incensed that she purposely crashed her mother's car.

"Dawn DeFeo, as she was in love with me," explained Billy Davidge in an affidavit, "wanted to come to Florida to live with me, but her mother and father forbid her from doing so, which led up to hostile incidents between Dawn and her mother and father over all of this. And Dawn was determined to come to Florida, no matter what."

In August 1974, the band Paper Lace had a hit song titled "The Night Chicago Died," about gangster Al Capone's war with law enforcement. The song embodied everything Dawn was feeling about her own family.

The following month, Dawn asked her sister-in-law to help her change some of the words to the song. Geraldine recalled, "Butch and I were at Henry's Bar drinking when Dawn showed up. She figured since I wrote music I could help her because she was having problems with replacing the words to complete her version. Since I was drunk, and Dawn was high, I figured what the hell."

Upon completion, Dawn called her version of the song "The Night the DeFeos Died." The lyrics would later prove to be prophetic. An excerpt read:

> *In the sweat of an autumn night*
> *In the land of the dollar bill*
> *In the town of Amityville*
> *And they talk about it still*
>
> *When a man named Butch Capone*
> *Tried to make that town his own*
> *And we called our punks to war*
> *Against our parents and their law*
> *I heard my mama cry*
> *I heard her scream, Big Ronnie we're going to die*
>
> *I heard her pray the night my family died*
> *Brother, what a night the people saw*
> *Brother, what a plight the people saw*
> *Yes, indeed!...*
>
> *And the sound of our shots sang*
> *Through the front and back and side*
> *'Til the last of the DeFeos cried*
> *And had given up and died...*
>
> *There were crowds in the street*
> *And policemen off their beat*
> *And I heard what someone said*
> *That all the DeFeos are dead!...*

Aerial view of 112 Ocean Avenue (above).

Despite their perfect life, the DeFeos were on the road to disaster.

The back of 112 Ocean Avenue (below).

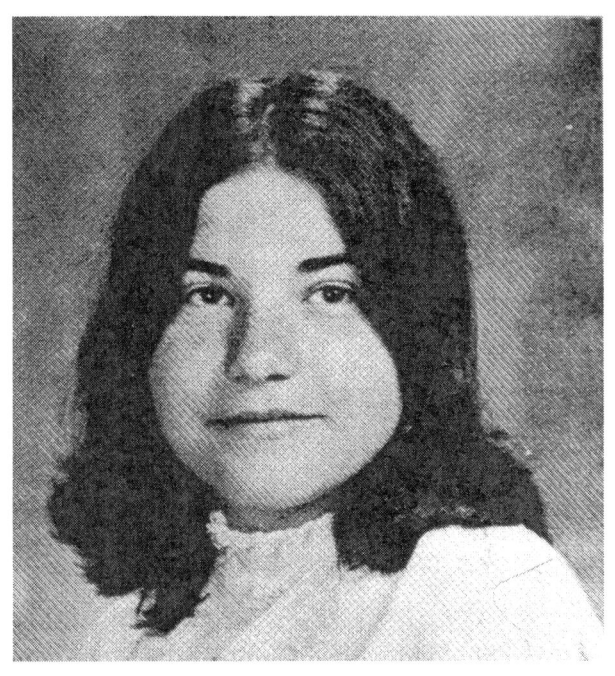

Dawn DeFeo's senior picture for her high school (above).
Allison's room (below).
Here, Allison informed her brother that things were not going to be "alright."

Nobody in the family took Dawn's song or her antics seriously. The song wound up being another neglected warning sign of an impending tragedy.

In an affidavit to Butch's attorney, Jacob Siegfried, Augie Degenaro allegedly stated, "Dawn DeFeo had begun talking with him about wanting a gun that was clean [no markings] and to have him assist her in the crime of killing her father. She knew he had money hidden, and if he helped her, she would find it and give him half. She [Dawn DeFeo] also wanted him to get her heavy-duty sleeping pills." Although Siegfried is now dead, his son authenticated his father's signature on the affidavit. As for Augie, he has effectively disappeared.

Augie Degenaro was not the only one Dawn had approached about wanting to kill her father. She told other people that she was prepared to kill her entire family if that was what it took to get out of the house.

Eventually, Dawn learned about Butch's planned hit on their father in Brooklyn. But for Dawn, Christmas time was too far away; she wanted out sooner.

At the Blue T Pizzeria, next door to Henry's Bar, Dawn confronted Butch and Geraldine. Dawn could not wait any longer and demanded that Butch and she kill their father that night. The confrontation led to an argument with Butch telling his sister "to shut the hell up."

Even Billy Davidge knew that Dawn had a bad temper. According to an affidavit made by Davidge, he had direct knowledge of Dawn's hatred toward her mother and father. Years later in court, Davidge also admitted that Dawn's only use for Butch was for money and as a resource to get out from their home.

Although Dawn was the most volatile member of the family, she was not the only one who wanted out. Butch said, "I was tired of being constantly called back from my home in New Jersey to intercede in my family's battles."

Geraldine added, "Butch had thought about going legitimate and had plans to apply for a job as a postman. We had a nice house, three beautiful daughters, and we loved each other, so what else could we want? I have doubts whether Butch could have really carried out the assassination of his father in Brooklyn. But I do know he would constantly say to me that he wanted his family to just move to Canada already and get out of his life."

Big Ronnie knew he was losing his son both as a partner and as a member of his household. This may have been another reason why he attempted to kill Butch by cutting his brake lines.

Louise faced a similar dilemma. Her relationship with Butch had begun to sour. To his wife, Butch even had begun referring to Louise as "that woman" instead of his mother. He was beginning to blame his mother for allowing his father to get that much out of control. On the flip side, Louise was beginning to blame Butch for causing more turmoil in the house because he was beginning to rebel against his father's wishes. After all, when Big Ronnie was upset, Louise physically suffered.

According to Linnea Nonnewitz, Louise had told her friend, intuitively, "Lin, I am going to warn you that something so tragic is going to happen, no one will think of it as a miracle." Although she did not understand what her friend was referring to at the time, today, Linnea feels that Louise knew that, one way or another, her family was going to die. According to Linnea, the miracle Louise mentioned was the fact that nobody would have to live with Big Ronnie anymore.

On several occasions, Louise even put her head into the kitchen stove, wanting to turn on the gas to kill herself. It was just another indication how bad things had become in the DeFeo household.

But the worst, Geraldine explained, was when Louise revealed to her that she wanted to poison her entire family. Geraldine said, "Louise warned me not to come to Thanksgiving Dinner because she wanted to poison everyone, including Butch. She was tired of all the fighting, chaos, and abuse. I doubt she was serious, but she was so tired of the constant war."

By August 1974, things in the DeFeo family began falling apart dramatically. By that time, Big Ronnie had begun abusing even the younger children. Almost in a show of defiance, Marc and John had a food fight when their father was not present. Meatballs and sauce flew across their expensive portrait.

More and more, Marc was becoming enraged. Big Ronnie was pushing his son so hard to make a career out of sports that Marc was beginning to hate sports altogether and was turning violent.

"One day when Butch and I were leaving," Geraldine said, "Marc asked me to tell him, again, about the time a horse had kicked me. Before I could even rehash the story for him, he asked, 'Did the horse kick you like this?' He then kicked me as hard as he could in the shin before running away. Butch wanted to go after him to punish him, but I told him not to, even though my shin was bruised. I knew that was not the same sweet boy I was used to."

Geraldine was always reluctant to bring Shea Marie to the house when Big Ronnie was around. Because Big Ronnie had always told Butch that he doubted if he was truly his son, she did not want him to say a similar thing about Shea Marie being Butch's. Toward the end, even Linnea refused to come over to socialize or work if Big Ronnie was around.

By November 1974, Geraldine was seeing very little of her in-laws. Therefore, on November 12, 1974, Geraldine was surprised to get a phone call from her mother-in-law. Louise needed Butch to come back to Amityville right away. Since Butch had not returned home from work, Geraldine told Louise that she would let him know that she had called.

"Today, I wish I had never answered that phone," Geraldine said. "A short while after Butch got home from work, he called his mother and found out that Dawn had tried to stab her father with a butcher knife because they had another argument. Louise told Butch that the family needed him."

THE LAST NIGHT

Obediently, Butch got dressed, grabbed one of the chicken cutlets Geraldine had made for dinner and drove 90 miles to Amityville. Geraldine was furious, but knew that Butch was the only person who could resolve the conflict in the DeFeo household.

On the phone, Louise had informed him that Dawn was at her

worst that night. "Her eyes were ablaze," Butch said, repeating what his mother told him, "and she threatened to kill everyone in the household."

After returning home, Butch raced in the doorway and was greeted with the ghastly sight of his little brother, John DeFeo, sprawled out on the marble tile of the foyer. Butch said, "John Matt had a bloody nose and lip. There was blood all over his face because he must have smeared it."

Crying hysterically, John informed his brother, "Daddy is going to kill mommy!"

Bypassing his injured brother, Butch took the stairs two at a time to reach his parents, who were arguing upstairs.

Butch reached his parents' doorway and saw that his mother's blouse had been torn, partially exposing her breasts. Before Butch could say anything, Big Ronnie slapped Louise and then punched her breast.

Seeing his son standing there, Big Ronnie turned toward Butch and charged. Although Butch was knocked over, he quickly got to his feet.

From the third floor, Dawn yelled down, "You motherfuckers! You are all no Goddamn good, motherfuckers! I hate you all!"

Marc, still having a difficult time getting around because of his football injury, yelled out from his room, "What's going on? Should I come out? Can I come out?"

Marc's questions went unanswered as Butch raced down the stairs toward the cellar, hoping to outrun his father, who had every intention of hurting him. According to Butch, the only person he did not hear during this time was Allison, who he figured was hiding in her bedroom.

As Big Ronnie began to give chase, he tripped over a pile of clothing left in the hallway. Butch said, "As I ran down the stairs, I thought to myself, 'God got you, you fat prick. You ain't going to get me.'"

Butch, now on the landing between the first and second floors, stopped to see his father wailing over his injured foot. Butch shouted up to his father that he was "a big fat whale."

Hearing the loud "thump" of Big Ronnie falling, Louise came out of her room to investigate. Butch said, "My mother, whose eye was bleeding, asked my prick father if she should get him a cold rag or something. It was like she had forgotten he just beat her up."

Looking on from above, Dawn sarcastically asked, "Hey, pop, you want a toot off my pot pipe?"

Taking a moment to let the scene sink in, Butch placed his hand to his head and thought, "I am in a crackerbox palace."

Dawn continued to laugh hysterically at her father's clumsiness while Louise shouted to her to shut up because her father was hurt. She then went to Big Ronnie's side to help him up.

Big Ronnie yelled, "You fucking phonies. You are worthless, all of you. None of you are shit without me."

He then turned toward Dawn and said, "I'll kill your punk boyfriend and you."

To Butch, Big Ronnie said, "What are you looking at, you *stronzo*?" Because I will kill you, your goddamn wife, and all your fucking kids."

Despite the threat, Butch just kept on laughing while his father continued to call him "a no good piece of shit."

Incensed at the situation, Big Ronnie ordered Butch and Dawn to stop laughing, reasoning the commotion would give him a heart attack. Butch explained the laugher, saying, "My father could not get up because all of his blubber was on his leg."

It was a madhouse. Butch and Dawn continued to laugh, John was still downstairs, crying hysterically, and Marc kept yelling out from his room, "What should I do? Should I come out?"

Not wanting his brother to walk out into a war zone, Butch shouted back, "Shut the fuck up, and stay in there!"

Suddenly, Dawn broke into the Bristol Stomp dance, saying, "Butch, this will take off some of my weight."

Butch insisted, "I swear on my mother's soul, may she turn in her grave, with all that was happening, Dawn started dancing the Bristol Stomp. I realized then we were a house of maniacs."

A few minutes later, Dawn shouted out that she was going to get some cookies and milk, and she disappeared into her room.

Chapter Four

The performance was over. Butch proceeded down to the cellar to answer the ringing phone. His father, down but not out, yelled at his son, reminding him it was his phone, and he was going to chop the lines because he paid for it.

Ignoring his father's warning, Butch said, "On the phone was Bobby Kelske. He presumed I was high on some good shit because I was laughing so hard. So he said he'd be right over to join in. Kelske got there in greased-lightning time because he thought he was going to get some good dope. He didn't even comb his hair."

Kelske, finally realizing his friend was not in the cellar getting high, asked Butch, "What the fuck went on here? John Matt is rolling around the hallway, screaming."

Realizing he had forgotten all about his injured little brother, Butch, who was squeamish at the sight of blood, asked Bobby, who had sons of his own and who was good with kids, to clean John up and get him to bed. Meanwhile, Butch would look in on Allison to make sure she was all right.

Softly knocking on Allison's door, Butch asked for permission to enter, even though he had already opened the door. Next to Butch's, Allison's bedroom was the neatest in the household. But not only was it organized, it was bright and cheery. Pink, green, and yellow flowered wallpaper decorated the walls. Drugs may have been Dawn's release, but jigsaw puzzles were Allison's. Therefore, it was not unusual to find Allison working on one or two puzzles at the same time. Parallel to the doorway sat two twin beds with Allison's being the closest to the door.

Seeing his sister with a red mark on her face, Butch asked, "Did daddy hit you?"

Since Allison did not answer him, Butch tried to change strategies, asking her if she had been doing her jigsaw puzzles.

Allison finally replied, "How can I do my puzzles if it is so loud? Everything is just so loud."

Feeling she needed consoling, Butch sat down on the spare twin bed across from his sister's. Allison asked him to be careful because he was sitting on her school clothes, which, as usual, she had laid out on the extra bed for the next day.

Allison asked her brother if he thought the weather was going to be good enough for the coming weekend. She had wanted one last ride in her brother's boat before winter set in. In reply, Butch said, "I have to talk to ma about it."

When asked if she wanted to come spend the weekend in New Jersey, Allison informed her brother, "I have too much homework. But if I can come up for a little while, I'd like to go on the boat."

As Butch got up to leave, he placed his hand on Allison's hair to mess it up, an affectionate act he normally did to his kid sister. Although she knocked her brother's hand away, she finally cracked a smile.

Butch told his sister not to worry because everything was going to be all right. "Allison's reply almost floored me," Butch said. "She rolled her eyes at me and said, 'Yeah, sure.'"

Outside Allison's room, Butch heard Bobby Kelske and Dawn upstairs fighting. Bobby wanted Dawn to hand over some blue Valium that her black friend had brought back from Mexico. Butch ignored them and went down to the cellar. He turned on TV and chalked up his pool stick, figuring Bobby would be down soon enough.

After Bobby Kelske came downstairs, he told Butch that after he doctored up John, he put on his pajamas and placed the little boy into bed. Before they started to play pool, Kelske took some of the blue Valium and cocaine he had scored from Dawn. Butch passed, explaining he was not yet in the mood.

A few moments later, Dawn came downstairs and began telling Butch that their father was going to make good on his threats. Ignoring Dawn, Butch took aim, preparing to make his shot. But Dawn was insistent, stepping in front of Butch so he could not shoot. Whispering so only Butch and Kelske would hear, Dawn appealed to them to do something because she felt the threat was serious.

"You know my father's mind snapped about a year ago. Just look what he did to you," Dawn told Kelske, referring to her father's impromptu ordination into his family.

Dawn continued, reminding them that Big Ronnie was living

in a fantasy world. Not only did he think he was a big Mafioso, but he also believed that God came down, sat on the couch next to him and spoke to him.

Dawn reasoned, "The only way is to kill him. And we have to kill ma, too, because she is just as sick as him."

Since his sister would not give up, Butch tossed her his car keys and told her, "Get lost for awhile. Blow off some steam, but just make sure you don't get killed."

After Dawn had left, Kelske told Butch, "Do you really think your father is wigging out? If he is, then maybe we should call Big Mike [Brigante Sr.]."

Butch replied, "Wait a minute, Bobby. What do you hear?"

Kelske answered, "Nothing."

"Just like every other time," Butch said, reminding his friend that after every one of his father's outbursts, there was always a peaceful resolution.

Still not convinced, Bobby again asked Butch if he was sure they should not notify his grandfather. After all, Bobby argued, he even beat little John up, which, for Big Ronnie, was a line that he rarely crossed.

"Nah. I'll just kill the motherfucker," Butch boasted.

While Dawn was away, Butch accompanied Bobby on an errand. After they returned to 112 Ocean Avenue, Butch was ready to join Kelske in his binge. For the next hour, the two friends continued to get high and play pool.

Their concentration finally was broken when they heard the blender in the kitchen upstairs. Upon investigating, they found Augie Degenaro making a tonic for Dawn, which would help the girl sober up.

Butch explained, "During this time, Dawn was in between the crapper and her bedroom. When she came downstairs, she showed us bullets that she had marked, including one for me. She then put her .25-caliber gun to my head and pulled the trigger. I knew the gun was empty, so I just stood there while she laughed hysterically. Bobby, however, turned several shades of green."

After the group returned to the cellar, Louise came downstairs.

As if nothing had happened, she asked, "If you boys want to make some snacks and sandwiches, feel free. Help yourselves, and have a good time."

Dawn turned to her brother and whispered, "Now tell me she ain't crazy, too. Just look at her face. It's all fucked up from our pig father, and she wants us to make sandwich treats. She needs to die, too, Butch."

After his mother returned upstairs, Butch grilled Dawn on the cause of the fiasco, saying, "Who the fuck started this? You?"

"No!" Dawn insisted. "Dad was supposed to go pick up grandma tonight, but he didn't want to because he said he was sick of the old bag and tired of the Brigantes throwing their money in his face."

Dawn continued to relay the evening's earlier events from the time the argument started until Butch arrived.

It purportedly all started when their mother, who was defending her parents, accused Big Ronnie of having hallucinations. She was reprimanded with a slap to the face. Next, Dawn, who had mistakenly walked into the middle of the argument, was scolded by her father. Big Ronnie said, "And you, Ms. Bitch, are not going anywhere. You will live underneath my roof until I tell you to get out."

In an attempt to calm her husband down, Louise placed her hand on Big Ronnie's shoulder. Big Ronnie returned the loving gesture with a punch to the face. After that, the couple began beating each other up.

Wondering what the commotion was, little John DeFeo came out of his bedroom to investigate. Showing no mercy, Big Ronnie punched the little boy and told him, "You're a wimp and a little bastard." John, on his knees and holding his bruised face, was then kicked by his father into the staircase railing.

By this time, Allison also had come out of her room to investigate the commotion. Dawn informed Butch that it was an amazing sight because their father briefly lost it.

For a split second, Big Ronnie told Allison to get back into her room and take care of her baby in the crib. Everyone was dumbfounded to hear Big Ronnie talk like that because he had forgotten completely where he was.

Chapter Four

After snapping out of it, he ordered Allison back into her room, saying it was family business and it was not her matter. Defiantly, Allison told her father, "It is my matter when you beat up everybody in the house like an animal. This is my family."

Allison's reply not only infuriated her father, but brought out his paranoia. He accused his daughter, saying, "You've been talking in school, haven't you? You've been telling everyone our business, haven't you?"

Allison replied, "No, daddy. I am ashamed to. Daddy, nobody comes here because you and mommy are like animals. We don't have any friends."

Dawn told Butch, "Because she had said something nasty about ma, Dad proceeded to slap, push and kick Allison all the way back to her room."

In an act of insanity, knowing full well that Allison was very neat, Big Ronnie jumped up and down on her beds, shouting, "This is my house, and I can do whatever I want."

Dawn then came into Allison's room and told her father that he was going to break the damn bed. By this time, Marc began yelling for someone to inform him what was going on. And little John, who had recovered from the first attack, spied on his father in his sister's room. His inquisitiveness cost him.

Big Ronnie bypassed Dawn and chased the little boy all the way to the foyer. There, Big Ronnie again hit his youngest son, this time giving him a bloody lip. Crying hysterically, John DeFeo would remain there until his brother arrived later in the evening.

Big Ronnie continued his rampage by heading back upstairs to deal with Marc, who was still hollering for someone to tell him what was going on.

Although Dawn was outside the boys' room, she told Butch that she heard their father throw around Marc's wheelchair and bang his crutches on the wall. He then proceeded to belittle the boy, telling him he was a "fucking slob and worthless." He informed Marc that he was going to starve him because he had fallen off the diet he had established for him for football.

Angered by her father's rampage, Dawn ran downstairs to grab a knife. When asked later by Butch why she had not grabbed a gun, she replied she had not been thinking because everything happened too fast.

Ready to stab her father, Dawn ran back upstairs. Louise, however, cut her daughter off, and screamed that "she was no goddamn good" to want to kill her own father.

Dawn screamed back at her mother, "You're just like him!"

By that time, Big Ronnie had come out into the second-floor hallway. He slapped Dawn and wrestled the knife away, telling her he was going to kill her in her sleep, repeating what Louise had said that "she was no goddamn good."

Realizing the family was out of control, even by their standards, Louise called Butch in New Jersey. But until Butch arrived, things got progressively worse.

After Dawn had finished relaying the evening's events, Louise returned downstairs. She informed them that Big Ronnie, she and the younger kids were going to have a bowl of ice cream and invited the rest of them to join them.

Butch explained, "After my mother said this, Dawn started laughing uncontrollably. She was laughing so hard that she was crying and holding her stomach."

Butch told his mother, "Geez, ma. We just had the Battle of the Bulge here, and you're having ice cream?"

Louise informed her son, "Daddy, Allison, John Matt and I are going to have a bowl of ice cream because it soothes you."

By this time, Butch and Bobby joined Dawn in laughing uncontrollably. Louise paid no attention to them and returned upstairs.

After her mother had left, Dawn told Butch, who was still laughing, that they had to kill them, including the kids, to put them out of their misery. Dawn rationalized the thought, saying, "Butch, we're grown up. The kids aren't so they'll need a mother and father." Besides, Dawn felt it was too risky to let the kids live. She theorized that either they would grow up and seek their revenge or turn them into the police.

While Dawn was trying to convince her brother about the need

Chapter Four

to kill everyone, Augie began playing the piano in the living room. Fearing his mother would return downstairs to complain about the noise, Butch raced to the living room and asked Augie, "What are you, a nut job?" Just then, Butch realized Augie's reason for playing the piano.

While the others were laughing downstairs, Augie heard Big Ronnie and Louise conferring in their bedroom. Big Ronnie was shouting how he had to take care of Butch and Dawn once and for all. Augie did not want the others to hear Big Ronnie's twisted plot, but instead of drowning out the noise, his piano playing attracted Butch's attention.

Now Butch heard his parents conspire against him and Dawn. Big Ronnie was badgering Louise that they had to institutionalize Dawn and kill Butch. Louise said she could never do that to her son. Big Ronnie reminded her, "I gave him life, so I can take it away." According to Big Ronnie, it was his God-given right.

Just then, Butch heard his mother start crying. At that point, Butch knew his mother had caved in and that she would agree with anything his father wanted to do to them. Dawn, who by that time had come upstairs with Bobby Kelske, reiterated to Butch that there was no defense from their father's plan to kill them or pay a quack doctor to commit them to a mental institution.

It was a tough decision because Butch, at one time, had been extremely close to his mother. Now he had to choose either take his chances and hope his father's threats were idle or follow through with Dawn's plan to kill their parents.

Commenting on his father's plot to Geraldine, Butch said, "A sane man could not be able to do that to his own flesh and blood. But an insane man, who did not feel connected to his own flesh and blood, could easily do that. My father was not a sane man. His illusions, paranoia, and delusions of grandeur made him a very sick man."

When asked why he had to kill his mother, Butch answered, "First, she would have hated me because she would have known or figured out that I killed my father. I would have hated that. But everybody seemed to forget that my mother was deeply in love with my father. The man wrote a song for her."

There was another danger that could not be overlooked. According to Geraldine, Butch even believed it was possible that Louise could convince her own father to betray Butch and Dawn as she convinced him to overlook the years of abuse Big Ronnie had inflicted on her. But it is doubtful that this would have occurred. In fact, this perhaps is just one of Butch's many excuses as to why he felt justification for plotting to kill the woman that gave him life.

The group, who quickly sobered up upon hearing Big Ronnie's heinous plan to get rid of his oldest children, sauntered downstairs, where they sat quietly chain-smoking.

After several minutes, Dawn was the first to speak, saying, "See. He made her crazy just like himself."

Butch agreed with Dawn that their mother had been exposed too long to their father's illness and had become just as crazy as he was. Stuttering, Butch said, "I . . . I agree with you. She belongs in the ground, too."

Crime-scene photo.
Two ice cream bowls and a wine glass are pictured here.
Unknowingly, this proved to be the last meal for some of the DeFeos.

CHAPTER FIVE
In the Sweat of an Autumn Night

IN AMITYVILLE, THE weather report had called for wind and light rain with low temperatures in the mid-40s. Except for the patrons at the local bars, the residents of the sleepy South Shore community had nestled in for the night. On Ocean Avenue, a tide of multicolored leaves blew up and down the street and across the manicured yards.

Butch and Dawn had finally agreed to kill their mother along with their father. Butch said, "Over the last year, my father was pounding on my mother day in and day out. He even had her starving her own son [referring to Marc's football diet]. He even convinced her that she would drop dead if she ever left him."

Butch felt in his heart that his mother had, at last, completely lost all her own free will. She now would agree to anything that Big Ronnie had wanted to do to them. So Butch and Dawn figured it was either them or their parents. Butch also figured his grandfather was no help because he would do anything his daughter wanted. Besides, if they killed only Big Ronnie, Butch figured that his mother would eventually figure out they did it and then seek out her own revenge. Although they agreed to kill both their parents, they could not agree how to do it.

* * *

"Maybe we can talk the old man into going to Brooklyn," Bobby Kelske said, suggesting they hit Big Ronnie as planned, but only sooner.

Butch replied, "Yeah, but what do I do about my mother? Run her over in the streets?"

Augie chimed in, saying, "Yeah, it would look good, like Louise had suffered a hit and run."

Dawn jumped up and said, "This is stupid. This is not the way."

Turning to Butch, she said, "You're all talk. You never do shit. When you want something done, you got to do it yourself." Dawn then began laughing loudly, causing Butch to think she was suffering from hysteria.

Butch walked upstairs to his parents' bedroom door to eavesdrop. His father was apologizing to Allison and little John, blaming his actions on Louise, Butch and Dawn's lack of respect for him. He continued, telling the children the Brigantes were no good and "deserved to be dead and sent to hell."

Although Louise was in the room, she refused to speak out in support of her own family. Butch, describing what he overheard, said, "My father kept on saying how my mother should go to court and declare all of her family incompetent. That way, she would get all of their money. My father said he knew a doctor who could fix them all up."

It was only natural for John DeFeo to ask his father if his grandmother was sick. Big Ronnie replied, "You know she is sick."

Because Butch did not hear anything from his mother, he again rationalized that she was too far gone to be saved. At that point, the room grew silent. Butch could only make out the sound of spoons scraping the bottom of bowls. As he turned around to go back to the basement, he saw Dawn standing there.

Dawn said, "See? What can we do?"

Butch and his sister returned to the basement. There, Augie and Bobby were getting high and playing pool. By this time, however, the basement was a mess.

Not thinking, Bobby threw an old cigarette butt on the pool table next to the loaf of bread he had brought down to munch on. The basement's vibrantly colored couch was also a wreck. A pink blanket had been thrown across it, and one of the cushions was askew. According to Butch, he told everyone they had to clean up the basement before they left; otherwise the filth would set off his father.

It was shortly after midnight on November 13, 1974. On the basement TV, "Castle Keep" was playing on Channel 5. Burt Lancaster starred in this World War Two thriller about a bunch of American GIs ordered to defend an 11th-century castle from an advancing column of Germans.

Butch sat on the couch with his head between his legs. While he rubbed his beard, pondering his dilemma over his father's threats, Dawn left and went upstairs. Butch assumed she had had her fill and had gone to bed.

Butch said, "Dawn came back downstairs saying we were never going to be free. I knew she had something in her hand, but my head was still between my legs. Everyone was talking all at once, so I could not make out what she was saying. I saw she had black gloves on and thought it was weird for her to wear them since it was not that cold outside. All of a sudden, she went stomping out of the room."

A few moments later, Dawn returned to the basement. She told her brother that he was a coward and complained how they were going to be trapped for the rest of their lives. She insisted they had to do something.

Finally raising his head, Butch asked, "What?"

Dawn calmly replied, "Kill them."

With that, she leaned over and kissed her brother on his cheek in a similar way that Judas kissed Jesus right before he betrayed him. She repeated herself, saying, "Come on; let's kill them now."

After seeing Dawn's antics, Bobby and Augie laughed, thinking it was all a joke. It was then that Butch realized that his sister was holding his deer-hunting rifle, a .35-caliber Marlin.

Butch explained, "All of my emotions had erupted. Dawn and I looked at each other and knew there was no going back."

"What the hell are we going to do about the kids?" Butch asked.

Dawn suggested, "The noise could be covered up by saying the shots were a backfire."

Dawn went on to say that she would take the kids to their grandparents' house in Brooklyn after they were finished. In reply to Butch's wanting to take the kids before they acted, Dawn said, "If we don't do it now, we are both going to piss out."

Since they could not begin until the younger children left their parents' bedroom, Dawn volunteered to go up and make sure they had left. When she returned, Bobby grabbed a flashlight from one of the utility shelves in the basement and followed the others upstairs.

"At that point, we went upstairs, and I told Augie to wait outside in his car," Butch explained. "The plan was for him to act as lookout."

The others proceeded to the second floor. Butch carried his Marlin rifle and Bobby a military-type flashlight. Except for the bathroom light next to Allison's room, the second floor was dark. While Dawn went into Marc and John's bedroom to instruct them to stay there, Butch went into his younger sister's room. "I told Allison to stay in her bedroom, no matter what she heard. She asked 'why?' so I told her a burglar was in the house," Butch admitted.

Afterward, Butch rejoined Dawn and Bobby in the hallway. The children's rooms were only 10 or 11 feet across the hall from the master bedroom. Dawn's job was to stand by their doors and make sure none of the kids left their rooms when the shooting began.

According to Butch, the plan was simple. They would kill Big Ronnie and Louise; then Augie and Dawn would take the children to the Brigantes' house in Brooklyn. Butch and Bobby, on the other hand, would stick around to make sure the crime look like a botched robbery.

In the master bedroom, shadows on the wall danced from the flicker of a small votive candle located on the top of Big Ronnie's dresser, which had been turned into a religious shrine.

Standing at his parents' doorway, Butch could barely make out their forms in bed. Bobby stood next to him and turned on the military-type, angled flashlight he was holding. After the flashlight's beam found its mark, Butch raised the rifle and took aim. Because he had never killed before, he hesitated and was unable to pull the trigger. Infuriated, Dawn grabbed the gun from him. Without a second thought, she raised the rifle and took aim at her father's illuminated form.

The shot was incredibly loud. Shaggy, who was sleeping near the backdoor in the kitchen, sprang to life, barking wildly. One of the boys yelled from his room, "What's going on?"

Big Ronnie had been sleeping on his stomach when the bullet penetrated his bare back. The large man grunted in pain as his whole upper body involuntarily reared up and sent him lunging forward. Now that the first shot had been taken and they were past the point of no return, Butch grabbed the gun from his sister. But before he could fire a second time at his father, his mother raised up on her side, instinctively clutched the large chain around her neck, and yelled to her husband, "Oh, my God, Ronnie!"

That very instant, all of the pain and anger Butch was feeling overwhelmed him. He blamed his mother equally for his father's years of abuse because, according to Butch, "she could have stopped it." Butch squinted as he took aim at his own mother, the woman who had given him life and whom he had once been so close to. Besides, Butch felt that his mother's love for his father would have prompted her to turn him into the police or seek revenge. He knew what he had to do.

Still clutching the chain around her neck, Louise looked on in horror. Her husband had just been shot. She looked toward the doorway as her son fired. The impact of the bullet threw her backward into the mattress.

Bobby, believing it was over, backed up and discarded the flashlight on the brown recliner in the hallway. The children were calling out from their bedrooms. Dawn walked to the their closed doors and yelled, "If you get up, you're going to get the beating of a lifetime, and I'm going to be the one to give it to you!"

But the nightmare was far from over. Needing leverage, Big Ronnie placed his hands behind his back to help push himself out of bed. Even though he was coughing and choking, Big Ronnie swung his leg out of bed. Since his wound prevented him from straightening up, Big Ronnie turned toward his attackers hunched like a bull and charged. Grunting from the pain and growling in anger, he picked up speed as he headed for the hallway.

"I was scared to death because I thought my father was going to kill me. I forgot I still had the rifle in my hands," Butch explained. According to Butch, Bobby Kelske was also frightened by the sight and continued to say, "Oh, my fucking God! Jesus Christ!"

Butch stepped deeper into the hallway and finally realized what he was holding. As his father entered the hallway, Butch fired, barely having time to aim. "The look on my father's face was unbelievable as he stopped dead in his tracks." Butch recalled, "He finally just fell over."

Apparent from her cries of pain, Louise also had survived. Wanting to silence the woman and put her out of her misery, Bobby took out his Colt Python and fired once. In a twisted sense of loyalty, Butch turned to reprimand Bobby for shooting his mother. As he turned, however, Butch struck Bobby's elbow by accident with the butt of the Marlin. Bobby then lost his grip on his pistol, causing it to fall to the floor into a pool of Big Ronnie's blood.

It was over. Both Big Ronnie and Louise lay dead. Like a schoolgirl who had just been kissed for the first time, Dawn ran happily up to her room. Butch called after his sister to remind her to take the kids with Augie to his grandparents' house in Brooklyn. "All of sudden, Bobby lost it. He took off running downstairs and out the front door," Butch explained. "He stopped in the front yard and started puking his guts out. I told him to get back inside because we had to clean up the mess."

Standing at the front door, waiting for Bobby, Butch heard

Marc call out from his bedroom, "What's going on?" Not wanting his brother to see his father lying in the hallway, he told Marc to stay in his room because there was a burglar in the house. Butch turned and went back to get Bobby inside. As he approached the front door, Butch saw from the foyer clock that the time was 1:05 a.m.

Wearing only his white socks, Butch went outside to find Bobby, who was nowhere in sight. Seeing Augie sitting in his car in the driveway, Butch asked him, "Where's Bobby?"

"Somewhere down that way," Augie replied, pointing down Ocean Avenue.

Knowing Bobby was not going to return on his own accord, Butch ran upstairs to put his boots on. Before leaving the third floor, however, Butch shouted to Dawn, "I'll be right back. Get the kids ready!"

A few minutes had passed, and Butch was getting nowhere with his search for Bobby. Suddenly, the silence of the night was broken by Augie's car racing down Ocean Avenue toward him. The car finally screeched to a halt, almost hitting Butch. "I asked Augie what the hell was the wrong," Butch said.

Agitated and angry, Augie told him that Dawn was stoned and acting like an idiot. She purportedly had placed a gun to his head, but instead of killing him, fired it into the car. Although Butch tried to convince Augie to return to the house with him, the bullet hole in his car's floor was reason enough for him not to.

With Augie gone, Butch's problems were multiplying. Dawn's state of mind, however, was not Butch's first priority. "Rather," Butch explained, "I had to find Bobby because, knowing him, he'd shoot his mouth off." So Butch ran back home, jumped in his car and drove around the neighborhood looking for his friend.

After an unsuccessful search, Butch returned to 112 Ocean Avenue. Knowing he needed to start formulating an alibi, Butch called Geraldine at their New Jersey home. Geraldine recalled, "I was awakened by Butch's phone call at around 1:25 a.m. He wanted me to come down to the Lincoln Tunnel because he said he had no money for the toll and had no cigarettes on him. Since it was a school night, I wasn't about to wake up the children, so I told him to go back to Amityville to get money."

In order for it to look as if his parents had died in a botched robbery, Butch had to get his father back in bed. Try as he might, he was unable to move the 270-pound body, even though rigor mortis had not set in yet. His failed attempt confirmed what he already knew: He had to bring Bobby back.

Worried about Allison, Butch, who was now covered in his father's blood, entered her room. "I told her that mom and dad got hurt and that we were waiting for an ambulance. I asked her not to get out of bed," Butch said. Allison did not argue with her brother, but simply pulled the covers over her face.

When Butch went into Marc and John's bedroom to tell his brothers the same thing, he was confronted with a new situation. Butch said, "Marc wanted to go to the bathroom. I told him he couldn't leave the bedroom, so he had a choice either peeing in the bed, or I'd bring him a can. All of sudden, he starts hitting me with his crutch, saying he wasn't about to pee in his bed."

Posed with this new dilemma, Butch went into the kitchen to find a coffee can for his brother. After failing to find an empty one, Butch had little choice but to open the brand new can of Maxwell House Coffee. After washing out the can and dumping its entire contents down the sink, Butch ran back upstairs.

While Butch was busy in the kitchen, Dawn was up in her room and had turned on her stereo. As Butch came back upstairs with the coffee can for Marc, he heard Dawn singing. Butch recalled, "Now picture this. The old man is lying dead in the hallway; my mother is dead in her bed. Marc is trying to beat me with his crutch because I'm trying to get the kid to piss in the can, John is whimpering and crying, and Dawn is up there screeching at the top of her lungs with her music."

After Marc had finished with the can, Butch dumped the contents out in the bathroom and returned with it to the kitchen. As Butch entered Shaggy's sleeping area, the sheep dog sprang to life and nipped him. Even though Shaggy was excited from the loud gunfire, it was not unusual for the dog to bite Butch. Ignoring the dog, Butch tossed the can into the kitchen's trash bag and then returned to the third floor.

He entered Dawn's room and found her laughing, singing, and dancing. "I didn't know what to do," Butch said. "She was like a mad woman, carrying on. She then told me she wanted to make a phone call to Billy Davidge to tell him what just happened."

As Dawn picked up the phone to call her boyfriend in Florida, Butch knocked it out of her hand and asked her, "What are you, stupid? What the hell did you take?"

"I then told her she better sober up and take one of the cars and get the kids to Brooklyn. I told her to tell grandma and grandpa that there was a burglary and that there were people hurt," Butch added.

Butch left his sister in her room and went to the second-floor bathroom to take a shower. In the hamper, Butch found a dirty pillowcase and put his bloodied clothing in it. Following his shower, he left the pillowcase there and went back upstairs to check on Dawn.

Butch entered Dawn's room and found her dialing a phone number, presumably Billy's. After he wrestled the phone away from her, he scolded Dawn, telling her, "Snap out of it! Take care of the kids!"

Dawn replied, "Yeah, yeah, yeah. I will."

Butch left Dawn sitting on her bed staring blankly into space, and returned to the second-floor bathroom where he had left the pillowcase filled with his soiled clothing. In the basement, opposite from the finished section, sat two washers and two dryers. The laundry area was filled with the usual materials: two super-sized bottles of Clorox bleach and a large box of Tide laundry detergent. In addition, the day's laundry sat on the concrete floor, waiting to be attended to.

Butch opened up one of the washers and placed both the pillowcase and its contents inside, followed by a large amount of soap and degreaser that his mother had kept around for washing his mechanic's shirts. While doing this, he noticed that he had blood on his bell-bottoms as well. He added them to the wash.

Now dressed only in his boxer shorts, Butch returned to the children's rooms to check on his brothers and Allison. "I looked in

The basement (above).
Butch, Dawn, Bobby and Augie sauntered into the basement, where they sat quietly chain-smoking, pondering their fate.

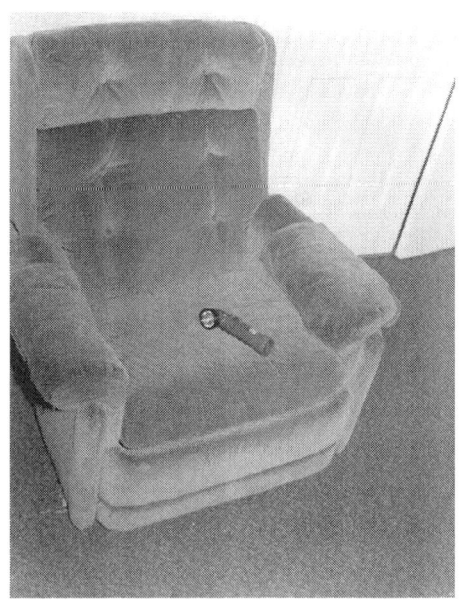

Outside the master bedroom (left).

This crime-scene photograph shows a military-type, angled flashlight located on a brown recliner in the second-floor hallway. Here is where Bobby Kelske dropped the flashlight after playing his part in the murders.

The master bedroom (above). This crime-scene photo shows the killing angle from the door, where the killers stood, to the bed, where the victims slept.

Front door (left). This photo shows the front door and clock Butch ran passed when he chased after Bobby Kelske.

on the boys first and saw John snoring, and I told Marc to stay in bed because the ambulance was coming. I then went into Allison's room and told her not to worry that everything was going to be okay," Butch said.

Unaware of the time, Butch got dressed and again reminded Dawn to take the children to Brooklyn because he was going out to look for Bobby.

Butch drove throughout all of Amityville, visiting Bobby's favorite hangouts. Still unable to find his friend, Butch headed home. Seconds after he turned onto Ocean Avenue from Merrick Road, however, Butch saw Bobby speeding toward him, away from the DeFeo home. Although Butch felt it was peculiar that Bobby was coming from the direction of the house, he swerved in front of him to block his hasty exit.

"I got out of my car and went over to Bobby's to pull him out," Butch said. "When I opened his door, his dome light went on, and I was surprised to see Bobby wearing my blue-striped shirt that I had been wearing when I left my home in New Jersey."

After arriving back at his parents' house earlier in the evening, Butch had taken off the shirt and placed it on the third-floor bathroom doorknob. Explaining the heating situation, Geraldine said, "Louise had such poor circulation that the temperature of the house was usually kept between 76 and 80 degrees. Because of this, it was not unusual for Butch to walk around in his white T-shirt."

Butch continued, "I noticed that the shirt Bobby was wearing, my shirt, was stained with blood from the left elbow to the cuff. My first thought was that he went back to the house and had also tried to put my father back in bed. Then, I panicked and was scared that the old man was still alive.

"Bobby was all shook up, but I told him he had to come back to the house. He said 'No way!' So I told him I would slap him up if he didn't and spent the next few minutes arguing on the side of the road."

According to Butch, before Bobby had worn his shirt, he had been wearing a brown corduroy shirt and a blue denim vest. It was not until later, however, that Butch would find out what happened to Bobby's clothes.

It was close to 4:00 a.m. when Butch finally convinced Bobby to return to the house. By this time, the house reeked of coffee grounds and the stench of death, and was lit up like a candle. Hearing them come in, Dawn yelled down from the third floor, "Butch, is that you?"

"Yeah, it's me. What are you still doing here?" Butch called back as Bobby and he went upstairs.

"As I approached Allison's room to check on her, Bobby suddenly got all nervous," Butch recalled. "Before I knew it, he took off running and was out the front door."

Butch, nevertheless, proceeded into his younger sister's room. "I immediately was sickened by the sight. It felt like my stomach flipped-flopped a couple of times, and I just about died," Butch said.

Allison, who had been Butch's golden girl, lay dead in her bed. She had been shot in the head, and her blood was dripping down onto the white shag rug, staining it red.

"It was never supposed to have happened like that," Butch insisted.

There had always been a sort of sibling rivalry between Dawn and Allison. From the disfiguring wound, it was clear that Dawn had committed the atrocity.

Believing his brothers had met a similar fate, Butch bypassed their door and headed for Dawn's room. Butch would learn later his assumptions had been correct.

Earlier, Dawn had entered her brothers' room and ordered both boys to lie face down in bed. She fired twice, hitting each boy once in the back. It happened so quickly that neither of them had a chance to escape. Death occurred in seconds.

Furious, Butch ascended the steps two at a time and called out to Dawn, "You fat bitch!"

According to Butch's recollection, Dawn shouted back, "Don't start. I'm slopped up because I just drank a gallon's worth of vinegar to sober up."

As Butch approached Dawn's bedroom, he could see her sitting on her bed. As he entered the room, his feet struck an object. The Marlin rifle, which Butch had previously left by his father's body on the second floor, lay at his feet.

"As I bent down to pick up the rifle, Dawn popped off her bed and charged at me," Butch explained. "We were both screaming. I was so angry I wanted to throw her out the window, but thought maybe her butt was too big to fit through it."

Enraged at the murder of his younger siblings, Butch wrestled Dawn for control of the gun. Finally able to get enough leverage to raise it up, Butch shoved with all of his might, sending Dawn flying across the room.

"I lambasted Dawn, and she flopped across the room. Her head struck her bed post, and she was knocked unconscious. As she lay there, catty-corner from her headboard, I watched her eye grow bloody, and her nose begin to puff up. I remember thinking that she was going to wake up and kill me. So I picked up the rifle and fired it. I don't know where the bullet hit. It could have hit in the front or the back of her neck, but blood splattered everywhere," Butch said.

Needing another shower, Butch returned to the bathroom and then proceeded to the laundry area to wash his clothes that were covered with Dawn's blood. Butch took out the clothes he had washed, put them in the dryer and then put the newly stained clothing into the washer.

Butch quickly dressed for work and left home wearing his Brigante work shirt, a quilted vest, boots, black socks and blue dungarees. But, according to Butch, he had forgotten something. "I fucked up. I left that goddamn piece of shit gun upstairs in Dawn's room. I didn't clean up, but just wanted to get the hell out of there. My whole family was dead."

At around 5:00 a.m., Butch arrived at Saul's Luncheonette, located near his grandfather's Buick dealership. There, Butch had a conversation with one of the patrons.

Already at work on his alibi, Butch claimed that he was early for work because Bobby Kelske and he were up most of the night playing pool and watching a war movie. Adding fuel to the fire, Butch

The tragedy unfolds. Pictured to the left and below are the lifeless bodies of Allison DeFeo (left) and John Matthew DeFeo (below). Death for the DeFeo children was almost instantaneous.

stated that Dawn had an argument with him over going to Florida to be with Billy Davidge. Butch continued, saying that Dawn had threatened to kill everybody in the house if she was not allowed to leave soon. Police would later learn from the patron that Butch mentioned needing to call home after his family was awake, so his mother could leave out his pay stubs because he had to meet his probation officer later that evening.

At around 6:45 a.m., Vito D'Iorio arrived to open up the dealership. Five minutes later, according to D'Iorio's statement to the police, Butch came in. Butch then informed D'Iorio that he could not bring in his father's car, which needed some repairs, because he had left home without the keys and did not want to wake up his father.

An hour later, Frank Boyd found Butch to tell him that Bobby had already left. "I asked Frank what he meant. And he told me that Bobby had woken him up and made him come down to the shop to burn something in the melting pot," Butch said.

Boyd went on to explain that Bobby wanted him to burn a knapsack full of clothing, his Colt Python, and a bloody handkerchief with the initials "RJD." At this point, it became clear to Butch that Bobby must have returned to the house to get his pistol and used one of his father's handkerchiefs to pick it up.

"Frank assured me he took care of it, but that the shop still stunk of the burnt clothes. He asked me what happened, and I just told him not to worry," Butch said.

Butch needed to leave work as soon as possible. He had to clean up the house and work on his alibi. However, since his grandfather was not around, Butch could not leave early.

Sometime after 2:30 p.m., Butch finally left work. According to Butch, as he walked out to his car, he met up with Allen Espasita. During their chat, Butch mentioned that he had to call his house so his mother would leave out his pay stubs to take to his parole officer. Seeing the large diamond ring on Butch's pinky, Espasita commented on it. Butch proudly boasted, "My father gave it to me, and hadn't given the other children a gift like that because I was his partner in everything."

Chapter Five

Five minutes later, Butch started the drive back to Amityville.

On County Line Road in Amityville, Butch saw Bobby Kelske driving toward him. After he finally got Bobby to pull over, Butch told him, "Look, man, my father must be stiff as a board by now. I got business in the house, and you got to help me take care of it."

Not wanting anyone to notice them, both Butch and Bobby parked down the street from the DeFeo house. With his house in plain view, Butch sat in the car for a few extra moments. The gravity of the situation was hitting him hard, and he knew he had to keep himself together for the time being.

"We entered the house and were immediately hit by the smell. The very first thing we did was go into the cellar where my father had hidden the books," Butch said, referring to the Mob books his father had stored behind of the basement's loose panels. The books had to be destroyed before the police found them because they detailed the entire Colombo/Brigante operation, from racketeering to money laundering and body disposal.

"After placing them in a bunch of garbage bags, Bobby and I took them to a nearby patch of woods. We first burned them and then scattered the ashes and the tiny pieces into the water," Butch said.

Returning to the house, Butch and Bobby had to move Big Ronnie into bed and clean up the best they could. Butch said, "I wasn't going to leave it messy. But the most difficult problem we faced was putting my father back into bed. He was stiff, and his leg was bent at the knee."

After his father was finally placed back into bed, Butch went over to his mother and straightened her up, too. Despite shooting her, Butch still loved his mother and wanted to make her look peaceful. Next, Butch and Bobby grabbed a bunch of rags brought home from the dealership and one of the Clorox bottles from the laundry area to scrub everything they could.

While they were on the first floor, Bobby saw Butch bend over to pick up a hairbrush in the middle of the foyer. He told his friend not to pick it up. Naturally, Butch asked the reason, so Bobby told him that it had Dawn's fingerprints on it, and it would implicate her in a fight with him. Butch followed his friend's wishes and left the hairbrush lying on the foyer tile. For the time being, he let the incident pass.

Because Butch could not look at Allison again, Bobby went into the teenage girl's room and cleaned up, or so Butch thought. Bobby had overlooked the dried pool of blood on the floor.

Careful not to get any blood on themselves, Butch and Bobby went into Dawn's room, wiped the blood off her headboard and positioned the girl into bed to make it appear she had died like the rest of her family. Because Dawn had been there all day, her hair was stuck to the mattress, causing it to look matted when they placed her correctly in bed.

Upon finishing, Butch and Bobby went outside. Butch wanted to walk by the boathouse one last time because he had a foreboding feeling that he would never see it again.

Over the course of a few minutes, Butch and Bobby did not speak. The trauma of the past evening's events was finally setting in. Butch, nonetheless, wanted Bobby to elaborate on the hairbrush.

Bobby supposedly, and reluctantly, told him that when he had returned to grab his gun, he noticed that Dawn had gone off the deep end.

Dawn told Bobby that the kids would have no life because their parents were dead. She wanted him to help her kill the kids. Bobby refused and left with his Colt Python wrapped in a handkerchief that belonged to Big Ronnie.

Butch said, "Bobby told me that Dawn then threw her hairbrush at him and yelled, 'They know! They know what we did!'"

During this time, Bobby also admitted to Butch he tried to get Big Ronnie in bed, reasoning that the man's open eyes made him nervous. It was how Bobby got all bloodied.

Butch said, "Bobby could not even look me in the motherfucking eye after he told me the story about Dawn. I asked him, 'What's wrong with you, man? Why didn't you fucking kill her ass? You let those kids die!' I then told him that I ought to go and kill his kids. Bobby started walking away, so I grabbed him and said, 'Nope. Nope. Nope. We got to make a plan.'"

Chapter Five

In response, Bobby suggested to Butch that he "go get fucked up," meaning get high because he thought that he could not be held accountable for his actions if he was caught. Butch agreed with the idea.

If Butch's story is correct, Bobby offered to get rid of the rifle and the dirty rags as he made his way home for his own shower. They would meet later at Henry's Bar for their big performance.

After Bobby left, Butch took another quick shower, put back on his work clothes, and then proceeded to gather up anything that he felt would "jam him up." This included his rifle case, a brown holster, the spent casings, one full and one empty box of ammunition, two live rounds and even the yellow towel he had used to dry himself after his showers. He placed all of the items into a blue-and-white pillowcase taken from the second-floor hamper in the bathroom. He forgot, however, the box in his closet that his .35-caliber Marlin had come in.

Figuring it would be a cool night, Butch grabbed his denim jacket. He double-locked the front door from the inside and instead went out through the veranda's double doors, locking them behind him.

Driving like a maniac, Butch made his way back to Brooklyn. "I wanted to get the stuff as far as way from me as possible," Butch explained. "So I dumped it near the place that Bobby, Augie and I had originally intended to kill my father."

Sometime between 5:00 and 5:30 p.m., Butch finally arrived back into Amityville. "I immediately drove over to Patty Geiger's house to get a hit of heroin. I had read in an article once that if you got arrested for something, they couldn't hold you responsible if you were on drugs at the time of the crime," Butch said.

During the remainder of the time, Butch went into Henry's Bar and had a Coke to drink. Shortly before 6:30 p.m., Butch left, making sure everyone in the bar, including Bobby, knew he was going to have to break a window to get into his house because nobody was answering the door and he did not have a house key. Although it was all a lie, the final scene was set.

Butch, in fact, did return home. Once there, he went into the

Coles Avenue Dock.
The picture above was taken on November 14, 1974. Inside the trashcan located at the Coles Avenue Dock was a rag that was tied to the DeFeo crime scene. Below, the image shows the dock in 2002. Obviously, little has changed, including the wire-mesh trashcan.

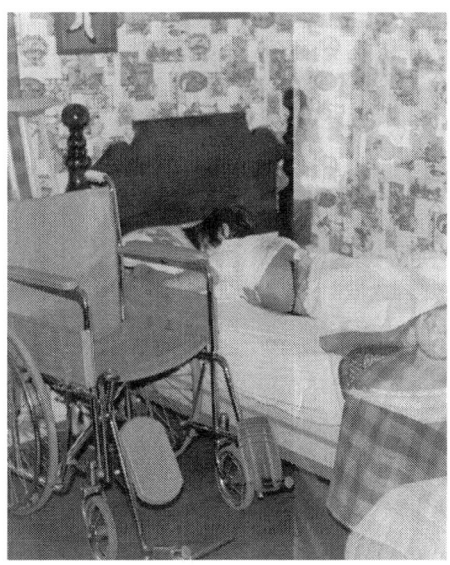

Crime-scene photos. Pictured above is the grotto that Butch DeFeo and Bobby Kelske conctructed. Above the grotto appears an open window. Here is where Butch entered the house to unlock the door, making it appear he had no key.

Pictured left: 12-year-old Marc Gregory DeFeo.

backyard and entered the house through the kitchen window, which had a broken latch. Although he would later claim he found his parents in bed, in reality, Butch simply unlocked the front door and exited. A few moments later, Butch had returned to the bar and carried on that he had found his parents shot. In a short while, the police would arrive at 112 Ocean Avenue, and things would never again be the same for Butch or Amityville.

CHAPTER SIX
Exposing Police Brutality

OVER THE YEARS, Butch DeFeo gained considerable notoriety from all of the sensational books and movies about the Amityville legend. Therefore, it is not surprising to see the Suffolk County Police Department and District Attorney's office bask in this same spotlight, boasting of their roles in bringing Butch to justice and solving the Amityville murders. What these agencies do not want revealed, however, is that the methods used to interrogate Butch were not only barbaric, but also criminal.

During the night of November 13, 1974, Butch did not want to cooperate with the homicide detective interrogating him. In fact, he repeatedly demanded to see his lawyer if the detectives were going to continue questioning him. Violating Butch's civil rights, the detectives continued interrogating Butch for more than 21 hours without the presence of a lawyer. During this period, Butch could not even use the restroom and was deprived of food and water.

Chapter Six

At his preliminary hearing, Butch described the brutal interrogation methods used on him. "I backed up into the wall, and before I could even get my hands up, they were all over me. I fell to the ground, and they started kicking me in the stomach. I remember one of them kicked me in the leg. Then I got up, and they told me to sit in the chair. And then they put a phone book on my head and took a blackjack and kept beating on top of the phone book with it for a good 10 minutes.

"By this time, I was crying. I was sick and I was hurt pretty bad. I couldn't take any more. I just couldn't. But I wasn't going to sign a statement saying I did it."

Because Butch refused to sign this confession, the prosecution had the difficult task of proving that Butch had, indeed, made an oral admission of guilt to the detectives. Because the detectives had not even tape-recorded the interrogation and the purported confession, the court had to decide which parties were more credible.

On October 1, 1975, after six days of preliminary hearings, Justice Thomas Stark sided with the police, saying their testimony was "basically accurate and credible."

He further stated, "No police officer used or threatened the use of physical force upon the defendant. The oral incriminatory admissions and statements obtained from the defendant . . . were not involuntary."

The ruling stood despite the fact that on November 18, 1974, just three days after his arraignment, Butch underwent a medical exam at the Suffolk County Jail. The physician's report, marked *Exhibit B* in the hearing, found Butch to have "a subsiding bruise on the abdomen, a subsiding bruise on the left leg, and healing abrasions of the spinal area." The report concluded that the injuries were between four and seven days old.

Although Butch's allegations against the homicide detectives were dismissed by Justice Stark, there was, in fact, ample evidence to indicate that something was out of the ordinary in Suffolk County. Affidavits, articles, official reports and testimony all support the fact that in 1974 the Suffolk County Police Department and the District Attorney's office were more interested in obtaining

121

convictions than with preserving the justice system they swore to uphold.

THE BRUTALITY ISSUE IN 1974

On Wednesday, October 20, 1974, Suffolk County dedicated an $8 million criminal courts building in Riverhead. An array of judges, police commanders, county executives and district attorneys were present. Also present were members of the Long Island Equal Justice Association (LIEJA), who held large banners in front of these dignitaries that read, "We demand prosecution for police brutality!"

The group also handed out leaflets to the crowd that described how the police department condoned harassment, illegal searches and seizures and police brutality. Listed on the leaflets were the names of the victims and the officers accused of the brutality. Instead of addressing the demonstrators' concerns, the dignitaries turned a blind eye.

On November 5, 1974, just eight days before the DeFeo murders, *Newsday* ran an article about police brutality in Suffolk County. It cited that over a 30-month period, 93 brutality complaints were filed against police officers. Not one officer, however, had ever been disciplined.

Helen Ackley, director of the LIEJA, accused the District Attorney's office of "not doing the job it should have been doing." In response to the allegations, the district attorney invited the association to meet with him to discuss the complaints. The meeting turned out to be ineffectual since the following January a new district attorney entered office.

* * *

Another group that was pivotal in exposing brutality was the Suffolk County Human Rights Commission (SCHRC). In 1974, the SCHRC suffered from its inability to take the necessary steps to insure complaints against the police were handled properly. Formed in 1963, the SCHRC was originally set up to conduct studies in the field of human relationships in the county. In 1972, Suffolk County

Executive Management Order #19-1972 allowed the commission the ability to report cases of police brutality, but stopped short of giving it the investigative powers it needed to insure appropriate action was taken against the police officers accused of these offenses.

This inability was described in a 1974 annual report issued by Lawrence Timpa, a human rights counselor, and James Taylor, senior investigator of the commission. Among the report's findings:

1. That Suffolk County "was not ready to recognize police conduct as a problem of sufficient proportions."

2. That Executive Management Order #19-1972 gave the SCHRC "the illusion of input" and gave its clients the "illusion of service."

3. That 60 percent of the Suffolk County Police Department's reports on brutality allegations "contain nothing more than a brief paragraph stating that no substantiation for a complaint can be found or the officer acted within the limits and scope of his authority."

4. That "no complaint referred via the Executive Management Order resulted in criminal action, indictment, or dismissal of any police officer."

5. That the Suffolk County Police Department found that 98.67 percent of the complaints lacked "sufficient cause for disciplinary action."

On November 19, 1974, just six days after the DeFeo murders, the SCHRC held a meeting with an agenda titled, "Meeting of the Task Force on Police Brutality." In response to its inability to investigate the reports of police brutality in the county, the SCHRC wanted some other policy established that would permit the fair and impartial processing of complaints made by the members of the general public in Suffolk County against police misconduct.

The recommendations made by the SCHRC would be ignored by the county leadership. Thus, the SCHRC would continue strictly as a reporting agency, hoping the prosecutor's office would eventually take action against police officers guilty of civil and human rights abuses.

THE AFFIDAVITS

To substantiate Butch's claims that he was tortured by the detectives interrogating him, a selection of affidavits taken from the SCHRC's files from 1974 reveal that the treatment Butch described was not isolated.

On February 7, 1974, at around 9:00 p.m. in the parking lot of a 7-Eleven store in Lindenhurst, John Palladino was sitting in his car with four other men, two of whom were undercover narcotics officers in the Suffolk County Police Department. "As the five of us sat in the automobile, three squad cars pulled into the parking lot and surrounded my car. Six officers, wielding pistols and shotguns emerged from the squad cars. I remember being dragged out of my car and thrown against the hood. I was then hit in the head with the butt of a gun. I was not hit once, but several times," explained Palladino in his notarized affidavit to the SCHRC.

Once at the Hauppauge precinct, Palladino told the SCHRC that he was subjected to a prolonged interrogation. As he sat handcuffed to the chair, he was ordered to provide the names of drug dealers and criminals known to him.

"During the course of the questioning, I was physically abused. On several occasions, a telephone book was placed on various spots on my head and face so that I could be hit with a club without leaving any bruises on my body to evidence a beating. One of the plainclothesmen hit me several times in the face and mouth with his closed fist. One of the blows he struck cracked four of my front upper teeth, and eventually necessitated their extraction."

When Palladino refused to answer the officers' questions or give them the information they sought, he was charged with the sale of a narcotic drug and sent to the Suffolk County Jail.

* * *

In a separate incident, Robert Meola said in his affidavit that on February 26, 1974, "Seven or eight officers of the Suffolk County Police Department broke into the Lavender Avenue address while I was sleeping . . . I asked to see a warrant. One officer showed me a small card saying that was it. I asked another officer who was looking in a money jar for a warrant. He turned and hit me."

Meola went on to state in his affidavit that he was arrested and taken to the precinct in Hauppauge. He also said that the officers took $55 from his wallet and gave him a receipt for only 15 cents. When he asked for the shield number of one officer, Meola said, "He hit me in the head three times with both fists and broke my glasses." At no time, according to Meola, was he ever informed of his Miranda rights.

* * *

At approximately 9:00 a.m. on May 24, 1974, Odell Collier was driving a stolen vehicle in the vicinity of Pinelawn. After being pursued by the Suffolk County police, he eventually abandoned the vehicle and took off running, but stopped when it became apparent there was no escape.

"Within a matter of moments, three officers approached me where I stood. I was instructed to put my hands behind my back. I did so and I was handcuffed. One of the officers tripped me, causing me to fall forward on my face," explained Collier in his affidavit.

Collier insisted that the officers continued beating him for the next several minutes, followed by their stripping him of his jewelry and money, which subsequently disappeared. Once at the First Precinct, Collier was taken downstairs to a private room. The detectives asked Collier several questions about the crime he had committed, but he refused to answer any questions without consulting an attorney first.

The detectives warned him to cooperate and provide the information about a string of burglaries they believed he had information about. "When I could not offer this information, one of the detectives punched me in the left temple. I was subsequently pulled by the hair, punched in the stomach, and kicked in the ribs and legs . . .

"I was asked if I was ready to talk. I could not take any further punishment. I begged not to be beaten again. I was told that a statement would be prepared for my signature." To end the torture, Collier signed the statement admitting his guilt.

* * *

On September 28, 1974, Sandra Wesley of Amityville went to pick up her 12-year-old sister and her sister's friends at a bowling alley off Route 110 in Farmingdale. After Wesley picked up the five girls, she began driving out of the parking lot. Suddenly, a squad car pulled behind her, flashing its lights. Wesley immediately pulled over to inquire what the problem was.

"When I asked the officer what was wrong, he replied that he was not going to stop me, but that he had changed his mind because of the smart remark one of my friends had made," Wesley told the SCHRC.

Even though Wesley tried to explain that the girls in the car were her sister's young friends, the officer demanded to see her license and registration. As Wesley reached behind her to get her license in her pocketbook, the officer grabbed her and placed her under arrest for no apparent reason. According to Wesley, the officer made no arrangements for the young girls and just left them sitting there as he hauled her off to the precinct.

Despite not feeling well, Wesley was detained at the station for two hours. She said, "My repeated requests for a tissue and the opportunity to go to the bathroom were continually ignored."

She eventually was charged with failing to yield to an emergency vehicle and driving without a license.

* * *

On October 7, 1974, Donald Terrell was approached by two undercover cops stating they were landscapers willing to hire Terrell, who was on probation at the time, for $30 a day. Five minutes into the drive to the supposed job site, the men identified themselves as police officers from a special unit involved with solving burglaries.

They then took Terrell to the First Precinct in Babylon simply because they assumed he was involved with something illegal. "At the precinct they asked me to tell them about any crimes I was involved in. Up to this point, no one read any rights to me. They told me that I robbed Moose's Bar, and I denied it," Terrell stated to the SCHRC.

According to Terrell, his feet were pulled out from underneath him, and he was repeatedly kicked and punched for 10 minutes as he lay on the floor. Eventually, Terrell was taken to another room where the beatings continued, uninterrupted. While Terrell's wrists swelled from the over-tightened handcuffs, the two cops ate pizza, telling him that it would give them energy to torture him more.

"The beatings continued for awhile, and then they took the handcuffs off. They let me rest for approximately half an hour, and then brought some papers for me to sign."

Finally, at 3:00 p.m. on October 8, 1974, Donald Terrell reached the breaking point, so he signed the confession the detectives wanted him to sign. He would later insist to the SCHRC that he was innocent of the charges against him.

* * *

On October 27, 1974, Daniel T. Simmons was relaxing at his home in North Amityville. The police entered his home and arrested him without cause or provocation. He was hit several times on the head, and to no avail, his wife and sisters attempted to come to his aid.

"At the precinct I was placed in a lineup. I was subsequently taken to a cell where I spent the night. When I awoke the next morning, I was not given any food or beverages," Simmons told the SCHRC.

Simmons insisted he was beaten repeatedly in his cell by officers who wanted to know the whereabouts of his brother and about a rash of recent robberies.

"I was then taken from the cell to a small room downstairs. I was accompanied by the same two detectives who had previously questioned me in the cell. I was ordered to disrobe completely; I was blindfolded with my shirt."

Simmons alleged that the officers struck him repeatedly in his face, head, chest and legs with belts, feet, fists and elbows. Simmons also claimed that one of the cops tried to make him perform oral sex.

"As I was totally exhausted and could no longer withstand this intense punishment, I had no choice but to sign a statement."

After Simmons signed the statement, he was transferred to the Suffolk County Jail.

* * *

These excerpts from the affidavits filed with the SCHRC are only a small sampling of the dozens of complaints filed against the Suffolk County Police Department in 1974. It is quite disturbing to think that these abhorrent tactics, reminiscent of Gestapo interrogations during Nazi occupation of many European countries, were permitted in modern times, let alone the United States. But, indeed, they continued to flourish as those in charge of Suffolk County have constantly ignored the problem.

Yet if the Suffolk County Police Department and District Attorney's office were still not clear on the scope of the brutality problem right under their noses, then they were aware of it after a special grand jury released its findings in a report from a special prosecutor appointed by then-Governor Nelson Rockefeller. The report, titled "Report Number Two of the Second Grand Jury of the Special and Extraordinary Trial Term of the Supreme Court," found:

1. The Suffolk County Police Department did not refer allegations of criminal misconduct of its police officers to the Suffolk County District Attorney's office, as it was supposed to.

2. An agreement in March 1976 was supposed to result in all future allegations to be referred to the Suffolk

County District Attorney's office by the Suffolk County Police Department.

Even the grand jury in its conclusion, however, realized that the agreement made in March 1976 would probably not be kept unless it was required by law. In the end, the grand jury was little more than a public slap on the wrist for those running Suffolk County.

A SCATHING ARTICLE

On Monday, June 11, 1979, an article titled "When Suspects are Abused" appeared in *The National Law Journal*. The article, written by Rafael Abramovitz, was a scathing exposé about police brutality in Suffolk County.

The article found that Suffolk County's homicide squad's 97 percent confession rate was much higher than the 35 percent confession rate of New York's Bronx County and the 20 percent rate in Brooklyn's Kings County for the same period of time. Many Suffolk County defense attorneys felt the confessions should not be taken seriously.

Commenting on his own difficulties with his new private practice, former Suffolk County District Attorney Henry O'Brien, the district attorney in office during Butch's trial, was quoted as saying, "I feel frustrated. I don't think there is anything to be done to change things. The homicide squad has a lock on things."

But O'Brien was not the only former prosecutor to speak out. In tape-recorded interviews, Abramovitz was told that prosecutors routinely heard how suspects were "beaten to a pulp; beaten for hours by homicide detectives." These same prosecutors felt they had to ignore these flagrant violations because they were on the same team as the cops.

Additional corroboration came from the Suffolk County Sheriff's Department, which confirmed that prisoners handed over from the county police often "exhibited signs of being abused."

Suffolk County Deputy Police Commissioner Charles Peterson, nevertheless, insisted that the rising complaints against his department were groundless. The deputy commissioner's stance was a clear indication that once again the Suffolk County Police Department was unwilling to rise to the level they were expected to.

Those in charge of Suffolk County may have claimed the cases were unfounded, but they could not ignore the fact that the police brutality complaints had too many similarities to be considered coincidences. It was found that telephone books were used as a cushion in beatings, blackjacks were used on the feet and other parts of the bodies, and genitals were often hit or kicked.

Between 1976 and 1978, at least six brutality suits brought against Suffolk County were settled out of court. Among them:

1. *Crite vs. Barry*, which was settled for $18,000. The plaintiff was taken to the basement of the station house where he was routinely tortured by being repeatedly hit with a blackjack and kicked in the groin by several police officers. After he refused to confess to a crime he did not commit, one cop put his service revolver to the suspect's head and threatened to kill him.

2. *Mills vs. Suffolk County*, which was settled for $5,000. After the suspect was driven to the police station, his hands were handcuffed behind his back and he was repeatedly beaten during questioning.

3. *Oqurndo vs. Suffolk County*, which was settled for $15,000. The suspect was hit in the eyes, mouth, back, legs and other parts of the body. Internal bleeding was apparent after the suspect vomited blood, twice.

4. *Phillie vs. Suffolk County*, which was settled for $10,000. While in police custody, the suspect suffered a fractured ankle after his legs were driven over by a police car.

The National Law Journal also reported the high number of reversals handed down from New York's higher courts. It should have been a clear indication for Suffolk County's leadership that there was a problem with their conviction methods, especially when the reversals were abnormally higher than other parts of the state. One such case involved William Maerling.

At 4:00 a.m. on Valentine's Day 1973, the police arrested Maerling at his Staten Island home for the murder of a "reputed" bookie. By 4:30 p.m. the next day, the police were exhibiting Maerling's three-page "confession," despite the fact Maerling could neither read nor write. The handwriting was that of Detective Dennis Rafferty, the same detective who allegedly had elicited a confession from Butch DeFeo.

During his preliminary hearing, Maerling testified about the admissibility of the confession. Of all the rigorous tortures the detectives employed, the most persuasive was their threatening to cut off Maerling's penis.

"[They] tied a piece of paper to my penis . . . two detectives picked me up and held me over this cutting machine in the file room and started cutting off the paper."

Maerling agreed to sign anything the detectives wanted him to, pleading for them to stop before they cut him. Once again, the Suffolk County justice system failed to act when the presiding judge sided with the officers, who obviously denied Maerling's story. The confession was ruled admissible in court, and Maerling was convicted of murder on January 3, 1974. The prosecutor who served on the case was none other than Gerard Sullivan, who would go on to prosecute Butch DeFeo.

Luckily, on December 21, 1978, the Second District Court of Appeals of New York ordered a new trial for Maerling. The court found that the police's informant in the case made statements that were "by no means to be accepted as reliable." The court of appeals also found that the defendant never offered a "valid" waiver of his right to counsel.

In a separate case, Suffolk County homicide detectives indubitably coerced a confession from the wrong man. In May 1976, William Rupp was picked up for questioning regarding the death of Walter Wallace, his former neighbor. As in the Maerling case, the next day homicide detectives had a signed confession in their possession.

Rupp stated to his attorney, Alex Chase, that he had been severely beaten and had signed the confession only to stop the beating. While in police custody, Rupp had to hospitalized for injuries to the head and neck. After they found pieces of gravel embedded into his scalp, doctors could confirm Rupp's allegations that he was hit with a concrete block.

Incredibly, these "experienced" detectives had overlooked the fact that Rupp's confession mentioned Wallace had been beaten to death. The medical examiner, however, had attributed Wallace's death to strangulation.

Eventually, the indictment against Rupp was dropped when a grand jury indicted Joseph Gurrier for Wallace's murder. At the time of his death, Wallace was set to testify against Gurrier for burglary. Not surprisingly, the homicide detectives had ignored an obvious suspect in favor of an innocent man.

THE SUFFOLK COUNTY BAR STEPS IN

In July 1979, the civil rights committee of the Suffolk County Bar Association was given the task of examining the allegations made in *The National Law Journal* concerning police brutality in the county.

The committee, at first, approached the issue cautiously, citing "the accused has much to gain by claiming police brutality and such claims are often viewed with skepticism by the courts and by the prosecutors . . . the accused, therefore, has a heavy burden to establish that he was beaten . . . and there seldom are any civilian witnesses present."

To determine the extent of the problem, the civil rights committee held public hearings in the county legislative auditorium in Hauppauge on September 17 and September 24, 1979. On hand were representatives from the Suffolk County Police Department, District Attorney's office, and the SCHRC.

From the hearings, the committee was able to ascertain a better understanding of the police brutality problem in Suffolk. The SCHRC told the committee, "The victims [of police brutality] are usually poor and powerless, or are perceived in that light. Often they are members of minority groups, or they are youth."

The SCHRC added that 75 percent of all complaints occurred in the First and Third Precincts and "persons in those areas often see the worst, rather than the best members of the Suffolk County Police Department."

Of the 311 complaints referred by the SCHRC to the police commissioner between 1972 and 1979, the Suffolk County Police Department found 97 percent of them to be unfounded, with no cause for any disciplinary action.

The civil rights committee also found that many cases of brutality were left unreported. Typically when suspects were injured while in custody, they were charged with assault in the second or third degree, depending on the severity of their injuries, in order to give the guilty officers legal justification for the suspects being injured. If no complaints were filed against the officers by the suspects, then there chances improved of resolving their cases without proceeding to trial. And it was clear that the Suffolk County courts usually protected the officers by siding with them even if there was incontrovertible evidence of wrongdoing by the police.

During the public hearings, Ernest Siegel, the police inspector in charge of internal affairs, stated, "Police attitudes, from the commanding officer level to the rank and file, need improvement in the area of the use of undue force."

In addition to the public hearings, the civil rights committee also reviewed several police brutality cases settled out of civil court and referenced in *The National Law Journal*. Appalled, the committee commented, " . . . neither the Suffolk County Police Department nor the District Attorney's office apparently undertook any investigation and/or disciplinary action following the settlements in these cases."

Another lawsuit that the committee reviewed was a 1976 class action suit that was filed in federal court in Brooklyn for 18 victims who were allegedly brutalized by the Suffolk County police. Judge

Jack B. Weinstein presided over the trial, but had to dismiss the suit because the law prevented a federal court from interjecting itself into the internal affairs of a state agency.

Before dismissing the claim, however, Judge Weinstein stated, "From 1970 to the present [1976], there have been a substantial number of cases where excessive physical force was used by some Suffolk police officers in arresting suspects, in questioning them to obtain oral admissions, and in punishing persons thought by some police officers to be showing what the police officers considered lack of respect or cooperation at the time of arrest or questioning . . . the frequency of the complaints indicate that they cannot be dismissed, however, as rare and isolated instances."

Regarding the overturned convictions by the New York Court of Appeals that were reported in *The National Law Journal*, the civil rights committee made a further determination. The committee stated, "The cases form a very strong line establishing the absolute right to counsel . . . the only time that an arrestee's right to counsel can be waived is if such waiver is undertaken in his attorney's presence . . . the cases do reflect, however, that counsel and family have not been afforded access to suspects taken into custody on criminal charges in Suffolk County."

One of the many recommendations the committee made was to establish an impartial panel to review police brutality cases. In addition, the committee also found that the police internal affairs unit invariably favored the police officers' versions of what happened.

Because the public was skeptical of the police department's ability to police itself, the committee recommended the establishment of a Law Enforcement Appeal Panel, or LEAP for short. It was recommend that the board be comprised of 13 members, six civilians and seven whom would be appointed by the police commissioner. Unlike the SCHRC, the civil rights committee wanted LEAP to have subpoena powers and the ability to conduct hearings about police misconduct.

Another important recommendation made by the committee dealt with recruitment of minorities and women officers to the police force. In 1980, the committee reported that 99 percent of the

Chapter Six

Suffolk County Police Department consisted of white males.

Of all the recommendations, the most logical was for the county police department to start videotaping its felony interrogations. This would have gone a long way to address the issue of brutality. Moreover, the committee recommended that an assistant district attorney be present at the earliest possible moment in the case, including the initial questioning of the suspect.

The committee, furthermore, felt it was its duty to remind the assistant district attorneys that they should stress to the police officers whom they closely worked with that any form of misconduct would not be tolerated. The committee stated, "Since the brutality issue is an obstacle to a successful prosecution, the tendency may be to ignore or disprove the brutality. In such instances, an assistant district attorney must be mindful of his ultimate duty, which is to administer justice. Should this conflict with his duty to obtain a conviction, the latter must yield."

The civil rights committee, however, found that the Suffolk County Bar also had failed to respond to the brutality problem. Only four of its own members were available at the time through the bar's lawyer referral service to handle police brutality cases. The committee wanted greater participation from the bar in this field of law.

On January 16, 1980, the civil rights committee completed its report on police brutality. On January 28, 1980, the committee's findings were released to the public after a 10-to-one vote by the directors of the bar. A copy of the report, titled "Report of the Civil Rights Committee on Allegations of Police Brutality in Suffolk County," was also sent to the county executives, the district attorney, the police commissioner, the leaders of the county legislature and the U.S. Attorney for the Eastern District.

In the end, the committee concluded that " . . . sufficient evidence is present to indicate that there is a serious problem with respect to police brutality in Suffolk County and the manner in which such complaints are investigated and resolved."

The civil rights report was the first of its kind because it officially pointed out the deficiencies in both the Suffolk County Police

Department and the District Attorney's office. Yet little was done by these departments to rectify the problem. Because the committee lacked the power to enforce its recommendations, those guilty of misconduct, corruption and brutality eventually returned to their old ways.

A MAN OF HONOR

Stuart Namm, the son of a plumbing supply store manager, had a passion for the law and hoped someday to rise to the bench. By day, he worked as an underwriter for an insurance company, but by night, he attended Brooklyn Law School.

In 1975, his lifelong dream was realized when he was elected district court judge in Suffolk County. After losing his re-election six years later, he was appointed by then-Governor Hugh Carey to fill a county court judgeship, which Judge Namm was able to extend to a 10-year term by winning re-election the following year.

In his early years, Judge Namm praised the Suffolk County Police Department and was considered by most to be a "hanging" judge. Many assistant district attorneys hoped for the chance to prosecute their cases in Namm's court.

But in 1985, Judge Namm presided over the first of two controversial cases that would not only open his eyes to deplorable conditions in Suffolk County, but also start a chain of events that would eventually cause the Suffolk County justice system to crumble.

On June 16, 1979, Archimedes Cervera, a prominent Suffolk County attorney, was murdered in his office. The initial investigation of the gangland-style execution went nowhere, and in 1982, Detective Dennis Rafferty headed up the case after the lead detective retired. In 1984, Michael Orlando, a police informant and known criminal, gave the police crucial information that led to the arrest of a suspect in the Cervera case.

On April 3, 1984, Peter Corso was arrested and charged with the murder of Cervera. In May 1985, Corso's trial began with Judge Namm presiding. Eventually, the jury acquitted Corso, reasoning that Orlando's credibility was in question as were the unprofessional investigative methods of the homicide detectives in the case.

Although Corso was acquitted of murder, the prosecutor still sought a guilty verdict for a cocaine possession charge that stemmed from his original arrest. Judge Namm, however, argued in his July 19, 1985 opinion that the possession charge "must be dismissed because of the lack of probable cause for his arrest on the murder charge."

Judge Namm cited, "Based upon the totality of the evidence presented: the nonexistence of reports and memoranda; the evasive nature of the testimony of the investigating detectives; the patent inconsistencies between the testimony of an independent witness with no apparent axe to grind and the testimony of the officers involved; and the almost cavalier attitude of the police in their testimony before this court; this court cannot, as a matter of law, conclude that there existed sufficient probable cause to arrest Peter Corso on April 3, 1984."

Besides all that, on May 19, 1984, the tape recorder and cassette found in Cervera's office the night he was killed was auctioned off at the police department's property bureau despite the defense's motion to preserve all tape-recorded messages. Outraged, Judge Namm wrote in his opinion, "Such action by agents of the Suffolk County Police Department constituted, at the very least, gross negligence, and its very worst the spoliation of evidence which might have been useful to the defense of Peter Corso."

Judge Namm, therefore, dismissed the entire indictment, including the drug possession charge. He said, "To do less would be to sanction police conduct which has been proven to be questionable at best, and which threatens the integrity of our system of justice."

In defense, Suffolk County District Attorney Patrick Henry said, "We had detectives who wound up being ridiculed by the judge, but I think they did an admirable job."

Judge Namm definitely took some heat for his comments in the Corso case, but he found himself alone after he presided over James Diaz's trial in September 1985.

Diaz was a 22-year-old drifter who had been accused of the brutal rape and murder of Maureen Negus, a mother of two, in her Port Jefferson Station home. The principal evidence against him consisted of a three-page written confession, which again was in Detective Dennis Rafferty's handwriting. This time, only the first page contained Diaz's signature.

The confession alleged that the murder weapon, a knife, was thrown in the woods nearby the house. Ten months after the murder, however, Negus's husband discovered the knife used in the murder only 15 feet from where her body was found.

Rafferty conveniently testified at Diaz's pre-trial hearing that Diaz had told him that he had never wiped the blood off the knife. This bit of information, nevertheless, was missing from the written confession and any police report or notes on the case.

The other part of the people's case was held together by a purported jailhouse confession made to Joseph Pistone, an informant and son of a cop. Regardless, the jury did not believe him. It was just as well because Pistone later recanted his testimony.

Like Corso, the jury acquitted Diaz, reasoning that the prosecution's witnesses, especially the police, were not believable. But by this time, Judge Namm had had enough. He now began publicly to scrutinize the police department, which led to a reprimand from the supervisor of the Suffolk criminal courts, Justice Thomas Stark, the same judge who presided at Butch's trial. Judge Namm felt as if he were all alone in his stand against a corrupt system.

THE STATE OF NEW YORK'S COMMISSION OF INVESTIGATION

On October 29, 1985, Judge Namm sent a letter to then-Governor Mario Cuomo, asking him to appoint a special prosecutor to investigate the misconduct of the Suffolk County District Attorney's office and the Suffolk County Police Department.

Judge Namm wrote, " . . . in two consecutive highly publicized murder trials, I have witnessed, among other things, such apparent prosecutorial misconduct as perjury, subornation of perjury, intimidation of witnesses, spoliation of evidence, abuse of subpoena power and the aforesaid attempts to intimidate a sitting judge . . ."

Because of Judge Namm's letter, on January 9, 1986, New York's State Commission of Investigation initiated a formal investigation into Suffolk County. Being a state agency, the commission had the authority to conduct any investigation regarding the faithful execution of the laws of New York, the conduct of public officers and employees and any matter concerning public safety and justice.

The commission was well aware of Suffolk County's track record. In its final report, the commission stated, " . . . despite over a decade of warnings — in the form of court decisions and grand jury and bar association reports — both the police department and the district attorney's office continued to ignore or to inadequately investigate and punish employee misconduct."

Prior to the governor's requesting the commission to step in, the commission had received many complaints about the Suffolk County Police Department and District Attorney's office, twice the number it received from any other county in the state.

The commission's main goal was nothing short of a major overhaul of the Suffolk County legal system to end the practice of gaining convictions by any means necessary. The commission cited then-District Attorney Henry as having "ignored the grave and demanding responsibilities of his Office." The needed areas of reform in the county the commission felt it could address were:

1. Misconduct and mismanagement in homicide investigations and prosecutions.

2. Illegal wiretapping by police personnel with the knowledge of the district attorney's office.

3. Misconduct, mismanagement and lack of oversight in narcotics investigations and prosecutions.

In April 1989, the state commission issued a 199-page report titled "An Investigation of the Suffolk County District Attorney's Office and Police Department." The commission spent more than three years investigating the county through every means possible, including conducting hundreds of interviews, holding private and public hearings, reviewing tens of thousands of documents, including trial and hearing transcripts, prosecution files, police reports and internal affairs files, and examining the files of the Suffolk County Human Rights Commission.

The commission also found several management failures in the Suffolk County homicide department. Since homicides tended to be high-profile cases, homicide detectives were considered elite personnel of the Suffolk County Police Department, often described as the best in the department.

Detective Lieutenant Robert Dunn, the detective who assisted Detective Rafferty in Butch DeFeo's interrogation, testified to the commission that 94 percent of homicide prosecutions in Suffolk involved confessions or oral admissions. The number was so high that the commission was highly skeptical, not to mention critical, of the rate.

The commission concluded that the homicide squad was more interested in obtaining a confession that relying on scientific methods and routine investigations, which included forensic studies, note-taking and crime-scene searches.

Regarding the lack of note-taking, officers in Suffolk County above the rank of patrolman were not required to take notes or memos. In his testimony to the commission, Detective Dunn said, "It must be dependent on the intuition and the intuitiveness of the detectives."

Detective Dunn further testified that even if a report was filled out, later it could be removed from the file undetected or simply lost.

The homicide detectives, moreover, did not fill out reports on all leads even if it meant a defense counsel would not learn about them.

The commission was flabbergasted to read a memo from a team supervisor in the homicide division to a detective inspector. The memo read:

> To the chargin of the defense counsel, homicide reports, historically, only reflect pertinent data as it applies to the successful prosecution of our cases . . . suffice to say that reports need not establish or prove our integrity. If reports support an investigation without losing sight of a successful prosecution then they are necessary. They need not be necessary if they will open up areas for scrutiny or loopholes in our cases.

The commission concluded that the lack of documentation was not a simple case of oversight or negligence, but rather a conscious decision by the homicide squad to avoid problems in obtaining successful convictions. This resulted, in part, from a lack of supervision.

This lack of supervision also overflowed into disproportionate salaries and overtime. High salaries were a strong incentive for detectives to remain in the homicide division. Detective Rafferty testified that he regularly logged more than 1,200 hours of overtime per year. The commission stated, "Part of the desirability for a great deal of overtime is that pensions can be greatly increased depending on the salary earned near the end of one's career, which was the case in certain homicide personnel . . ." In comparison, the Suffolk County police commissioner in 1985 was paid less than some of the homicide detectives.

Another inadequacy dealt with handling of crime scenes. Both Robert Genna, the supervisor in the crime laboratory of the medical examiner's office in Suffolk, and Lieutenant Dunn gave conflicting testimony about which party was in charge at a crime scene. Detective Dunn stated the medical examiner's office was in charge of a crime scene, while Genna stated that the homicide division was in charge.

The commission responded, saying, "When a supervisor in the medical examiner's office does not know that he is in charge, he cannot take appropriate steps to ensure that evidence is properly obtained and analyzed."

Also in the spotlight was the way certain veteran homicide detectives handled evidence, namely Detective Dennis Rafferty. In *People vs. Hamilton*, the homicide division's reliance on confessions proved once again to be its undoing.

Once the defendant's confession had been ruled inadmissible in trial, Detective Rafferty magically produced a .22-caliber bullet that tied the defendant to the crime. Detective Rafferty claimed that he had found the bullet on the defendant at the time of his arrest and placed the bullet into a file folder. Not only did he violate department procedures, but there was no paperwork or notes about the mysterious bullet's existence prior to the confessions being judged inadmissible in court.

The commission was astounded when Detective Rafferty, then a 17-year veteran and one of the most senior members of the homicide squad at the time, reasoned he had forgotten to label the bullet because he had no prior ballistics training. He brushed the criticism aside and reasoned, "Every black guy in Amityville has a .22."

For a number of years, the district attorney's office willingly prosecuted cases that should have never gone to trial. In addition, the district attorney's office also ignored the obvious signs of police brutality, misconduct and corruption.

"One of the most disturbing findings of the commission has been the systematic failure of the district attorney's office to investigate and take appropriate action where it has uncovered or been informed of misconduct," the commission said.

One such case involved David Woycik, an assistant district attorney. Suffolk County Police Officer Theodore Adamchak testified that Woycik had handed him an attorney's business card in an attempt to recruit him in a money-making scheme to refer cases to a private law firm. The firm was that of Gerard Sullivan and Thomas Spota, both former chief trial prosecutors in Suffolk. Furthermore, both Sullivan and Spota handled the prosecution of Butch DeFeo. In the end, not even a letter reprimanding Woycik was issued, and, as in previous cases, there was no further action

Chapter Six

taken by the district attorney to investigate the matter.

Throughout the commission's investigation, several police unions and benevolent societies in Suffolk County tried to hinder its investigation. In fact, District Attorney Henry even went to court to try to block the publication of the commission's report. Obviously, Henry had the most to lose since the largest portion of the blame fell on his shoulders because he allowed these corrupt and unethical practices to continue during his tenure as district attorney.

The commission's report, nevertheless, was published. The report rocked the pillars of the justice system in Suffolk County. District Attorney Henry called the report a "bastard child born out of the political rape of Suffolk County law enforcement." Yet the commission in its report made a strong case against Henry's department.

Thus, on March 14, 1989, Henry announced that he would not seek re-election. The commission, apparently happy that Henry was to be replaced, said, "The commission is certain that person [Henry's successor] will want to bring honor to this office."

Yet Patrick Henry would not remain out of the limelight too long. In 1991, he was elected to the Supreme Court of Suffolk County. Obviously, the voters did not care about his failure to be an impartial district attorney.

Commenting on the commission's report, Butch said, "The entire Suffolk County homicide squad was fired or forced to resign . . . the same cops who put me in prison with their lies."

Indeed, the entire Suffolk County homicide squad did resign, retire or get transferred to another department.

Even the police commissioner decided to resign before the commission's findings were released to the public.

Yet there were also negative consequences to the commission's investigation and subsequent report. Those police officers like Theodore Adamchak who felt it was their duty to testify honestly to the commission spent their remaining time in Suffolk County as "pariahs."

As for Judge Stuart Namm, his political career was virtually over. In 1992, he came up for re-election, a situation that normally required little effort to be renominated and then re-elected. Yet Judge Namm's own political party in Suffolk County abandoned him because he spoke out against the corrupt district attorney's office and the police force. When his term was up, Judge Namm and his wife of 38 years retired to North Carolina.

In a 1993 *Newsday* article, Judge Namm summed it up best when he said, "I hope that never again will another judge who is willing to challenge a corrupt criminal justice system be forced to pay for that fight with his judicial robes."

Martin Adelman, chairman of the criminal justice section of the state bar association in New York, said, "That kind of judging was considered remarkable, particularly in Suffolk County, where a lot of people thought there were injustices for a long time." Judge Namm was presented both with the Thurgood Marshall Award and the David S. Michael Award from the New York State Bar Association and the New York State Association of Criminal Defense Lawyers for his stance against corruption.

SUFFOLK COUNTY TODAY

The state commission report may have rocked the pillars of law enforcement in Suffolk County, but did it change the "good old boy" attitude that had been predominant in Suffolk County law enforcement ever since its consolidation in 1960?

The answer, disappointingly, may be no. As early as 1992, there were 749 complaints reported against the Suffolk County Police Department. According to *Newsday*, not one of those complaints resulted in a Suffolk County police officer receiving a reprimand. Representatives of Suffolk's chapter of the ACLU reasoned that the police force failed to conduct impartial investigations into the claims. They, too, wanted an establishment of a neutral civilian review board to oversee future reports of brutality. Once again, the police commissioner refused.

In early 2001, several Suffolk County highway patrol officers were under investigation for pulling female drivers over and forcing them to choose between stripping off their cloths and being arrested. This behavior is anything but new in a county that seems to have a scandalous legacy.

In fact, on June 3, 1974, the SCHRC and the board of governors of the Long Island Council of Churches sent a letter to the Suffolk County Police Department expressing their outrage that a woman, who was not a dangerous felon but only delinquent on a $15 traffic ticket, suffered a full internal and external body cavity search.

An excerpt of the letter read, "It is appears evident that this woman's case is not an isolated one, and that similar arrests and the indignities of such indiscriminate procedures are common practice."

Little did they know that these same indignities would still be occurring in Suffolk County in the 21st century.

CHAPTER SEVEN
Dissecting the Facts: A Close Examination of the Forensic Evidence

WHEN I DECIDED to write the *true* story behind the Amityville case, I knew I was faced with the daunting task of proving to the reader that the true account was not just another wild story dreamed up for entertainment purposes. I also knew that Butch DeFeo has told countless lies throughout the years and has often changed his story, sometimes for not getting his way. Thus, I felt I needed incontrovertible proof to back up the untold story. I found this evidence in testimony, interviews, affidavits and police reports.

Over the last two decades, there have been various parties, including Butch DeFeo, who have prevented the truth from coming out. Desires for money, fame, and secrecy were the main reasons behind the coverup. Along with Butch, the media and the Suffolk County Police Department are equally to blame for distorting the facts about exactly what happened on November 13, 1974.

The mystery and sensationalism surrounding the DeFeo murders only grew as time passed: from stories of a Mob hit to Louise DeFeo's being the true killer to disembodied voices ordering Butch to kill his slumbering family. Some of these versions, nonetheless, contained bits of truth in them. Such as:

1. *The mention of a second murder weapon.* In a 1986 *Newsday* article, Butch supposedly revealed how his mother, after killing her children, shot herself with a .38-caliber pistol. Although both Butch and Geraldine DeFeo disagreed with the article's content, they acknowledged that it revealed the presence of a second gun.

2. *Dawn DeFeo participated in the murders.* From day one, Butch DeFeo has insisted his sister had a part in the murders. During his trial, Butch offered a wild version of a phantom figure resembling his sister handing him his rifle and ordering him to kill.

3. *The Mob wiped out the DeFeo family.* Although it is widely known that both the DeFeos and the Brigantes had ties to organized crime, the fact was that the Italian Mob vehemently opposed the killing of children. Though far-fetched, there are those that still insist that the murders were part of a gangland hit gone sour.

4. *Butch and his friend were in the basement during the killing.* From the early days of his incarceration to his first parole hearing in 1999, Butch has insisted that others were in the house with him while his family was murdered. Even the then-Deputy Chief Suffolk County Medical Examiner theorized along the lines of multiple gunmen.

5. *The victim of police brutality.* At his arraignment on November 15, 1974, Butch indicated to his lawyer that the police had roughed him up. According to Butch, the homicide detectives fabricated evidence to use against him rather than build their case through legitimate investigative methods.

TIME OF DEATH

Often the simplest details can provide the most important clues in an investigation. During the week of November 13, 1974, *Newsday* published the local TV listings for all of Long Island. "Castle Keep," which aired on New York City's Channel 5, began at 11:30 p.m. on November 12, 1974 and had concluded by 1:45 a.m. on November 13, 1974, when the TV show "Combat" began. The police contend that sometime after the movie had ended, Butch DeFeo went upstairs to his bedroom, grabbed his .35-caliber Marlin rifle, loaded it, and then systematically killed each member of his family while they slept.

In contrast to this popular theory, Butch DeFeo swore to me that the murder of his parents occurred prior to the World War Two movie ending, and that he had nothing to do with the death of his younger siblings.

In fact, he was positive that the foyer clock read 1:05 a.m. as he ran by it charging after Bobby Kelske. What he was unsure of was the time Dawn killed the younger children.

A clue to the timeframe may lie in the recollection of Deborah Consentino, a local barmaid who knew Butch. Sometime between 3:30 a.m. and 3:45 a.m., on November 13, 1974, Consentino drove past the DeFeo house on her way home from work. She would later testify that she had not seen Butch's car, but only his mother's station wagon in the driveway as she passed his lit up house. Obviously, this corroborated Butch's story that Bobby Kelske and he did not return to 112 Ocean Avenue until approximately 4:00 a.m.

But the question of whether the neighbors heard any of the gunshots remained. Although *Newsday* was calling for occasional showers and wind for November 12 and 13, the weather was not extreme enough to mask the unmistakable sound of a high-powered rifle. According to Marlin, the gun manufacturer, the noise should have been audible at least a half-mile in either direction.

Since the DeFeo home sat only 50 feet away from either neighbor, the mystery why none of the neighbors heard the gunshots has endured. The prosecutor's theory was that the house acted like a castle, muffling the shots. Yet this seemed unlikely because the house, built in the mid-1920s, did not have adequate insulation to make it soundproof.

Seeking answers to my questions, I ventured to Amityville for the first time in June 1999. Accompanied by a fellow producer who would later serve with me on The History Channel documentary, we were put in touch with Rufus and Diane Ireland, the DeFeos' former neighbors.

Although the Irelands were now living on Enoch Island, located in the Amityville Creek, they agreed to an interview. As we rowed over to the tiny island, we could just make out the back of the DeFeo house.

At their kitchen table, Diane Ireland recalled the early morning hours of November 13, 1974. According to Mrs. Ireland, she had awakened sometime between 2:20 a.m. and 2:40 a.m. because she had wanted to go to the bathroom. While she was contemplating getting out of her warm bed, she heard what she described as rifle shots. Concerned, she awoke her husband. Unaware of the time, he told her it was probably duck hunters getting an early start or a tree branch hitting the outside window. Deciding to forgo the trip to the bathroom on the other side of the house, Mrs. Ireland settled back into bed.

When I asked Mrs. Ireland if she had ever reported this to the police, she insisted it was not until much later that she connected the two incidents. And because Butch DeFeo was already charged with the crime, she did not feel it was necessary to come forward.

As incredible as Mrs. Ireland's story may sound, there was a recurring theme to it. During my investigation, I discovered that individuals who had knowledge of the crime either refused to come forward or were threatened by the police into remaining silent.

After discussing the case with a former NBC reporter, I learned that other neighbors had also heard the shots. According to the former reporter, these neighbors were unwilling to go on record and wanted to remain anonymous.

Together, we theorized that they were reluctant to get involved because of the DeFeos' purported Mob ties. Even if they had, I felt that the Suffolk County police were not interested in statements from witnesses that would contradict their own theories. According to the homicide detectives, the murders occurred between 3:00 a.m. and 3:30 a.m.

In all reality, the exact time of death could never be determined. Proof of this resides in TV news footage from November 14, 1974.

Dressed in a tan trench coat to ward off the brisk morning air, the then-Suffolk County Chief of Detectives conducted a press conference in front of the DeFeo house.

Behind him, a lone light shined through the third-floor quarter-moon window. It was an eerie reminder that the home's occupants were not there.

Hordes of reporters surrounded the chief, who, like an old pro, dodged the questions he needed to avoid.

One reporter asked, "And you said they [the DeFeos] where dead at least 24 hours when they were found?"

The chief replied, "I never said no such thing. I said the best guesstimate by the medical examiner was 24 hours."

Another reporter chimed in, asking, "Twenty-four hours from when?"

"Twenty-four hours from when he examined them," the chief explained.

During the evening of November 13, 1974, Officer Kenneth Greguski, ordered to secure the crime scene, stood at the front door of the DeFeo house recording the time of arriving personnel. He noted that Dr. Howard Adelman, the deputy chief medical examiner for Suffolk County, arrived at 8:20 p.m.

After proceeding upstairs, Dr. Adelman performed a cursory examination of the scene. And from 8:30 p.m. to 8:33 p.m., the medical examiner officially pronounced each of the six victims dead.

Between 11:00 p.m. and 12:25 a.m., personnel from the medical examiner's office loaded the six bodies into the two van wagons from the medical examiner's office. They were then taken to the Suffolk County morgue where staff could conduct full postmortem exams.

On the afternoon of November 14, 1974, Dr. Adelman told reporters he was mystified how a single gunman could have perpetrated the crime. When asked about the position of the bodies, Dr. Adelman explained that the probability would rule against all six DeFeos being in the exact same position, lying face down in bed, at the exact same time. Later, at the DeFeo trial, Dr. Adelman again was asked if his theory about multiple gunmen had changed. He answered, "No."

Dr. Adelman's suspicions about multiple gunmen were later confirmed by an independent investigation conducted by Herman Race. Race, a licensed private investigator since 1968, had been a first-grade detective and supervisor at the New York City Police Department before retiring. More important, he was Michael Brigante Sr.'s friend.

Feeling that the Suffolk County Police were biased toward his grandson, Brigante retained Race to conduct his own investigation in September 1975.

Although all of the bodies were discovered in bed by the police, Race believed not all of the DeFeos were killed in their beds. Race also told the court that it was his professional opinion that Butch DeFeo had an accomplice. The discovery of partially burnt gun powder burns on Dawn DeFeo's nightgown only added credence to Race's testimony.

Race felt the powder burns on Dawn were a clear indication she had fired a gun the night of the murders. Geraldine said, "I was at the Brigantes' house in Brooklyn when Mr. Race came over to discuss his initial findings. After Mr. Race told Mike that he felt Dawn was definitely involved, Mike simply slid off the couch, onto the floor. All he could say was 'Not my Dawnie. Not my Dawnie.' He was in a state of shock the rest of the day."

Around 1980, Geraldine had gone to see Race at his office. "There, Mr. Race told me that he could no longer work on the case," Geraldine said. "In spite of my protests, he just handed me the check the Brigantes had just sent him. He wanted me to return it to them and tell them he had to resign. As far as I know, Mike Brigante never found out why Mr. Race suddenly quit."

The theory that some of the bodies had been moved was something that Gerard Sullivan, the assistant district attorney in charge of prosecuting the DeFeo case, was indecisive about. At trial, Sullivan theorized that Butch's father may have awoken, been shot, and then placed back into bed. Sullivan even entered photographic evidence, trial exhibit #35, which indicated that Big Ronnie's arm position showed he died out of bed. Yet in his own book about the murders, Sullivan openly questioned if any of the victims had awoken.

The position of Marc DeFeo's body was another indication that the family did not sleep through their own deaths. Marc usually slept on his back or side to avoid the pain of his football injury and not on his stomach because sleeping that way proved too difficult to get into his wheelchair. If this proved correct, then their killer, who, according to Butch, was Dawn, apparently ordered her brothers to lie face down before she shot them.

THE SUFFOLK COUNTY POLICE LABORATORY REPORTS

On the night of November 13, 1974, Suffolk County Detective Howard Sommers had the responsibility of photographing the entire interior and exterior of 112 Ocean Avenue. When he had finished, 11 rolls of film documented the DeFeo crime scene.

Crime-scene photographs are essential to any police investigation. And the defense felt that these photos were essential to its case. Although the defense wanted duplicates of the crime-scene photographs, they were denied them until shortly before the DeFeo trial was set to begin.

Combined with the photos, the Suffolk County laboratory

reports were more than enough to determine the validity of the true story that Butch DeFeo finally revealed to me. I am told that by the beginning of the DeFeo trial, there purportedly existed two sets of laboratory reports. The complete original set itemized every single piece of evidence, much of which implicated Dawn. The second set, which was deemed the "official" set, closely mirrored the prosecution's case.

Regardless, the laboratory reports analyzed several hundred pieces of evidence believed to have been connected with the crime. A brief summary follows.

Items #3 and #4 – Hand towels from the basement steps. Although the results of these items were never reported, the police felt they were significant enough to be "held for future comparison." If Butch's story is correct, then these were spare towels that Butch and Bobby Kelske used to clean with.

Item #11 – Tea bag and debris from the kitchen sink. According to Butch, he had to dump a full can of Maxwell House Coffee down the sink, so that Marc could use it to urinate in. These items were not the only articles taken from the kitchen. Because the medical examiner needed to test to make sure that the victims had not been drugged, various items from the sink and dishwasher were taken in for examination.

Item #13 – Hairbrush from foyer on first floor. A photograph showing a girl's baby-blue hairbrush lying on the marble tile of the foyer was taken by police during the initial hours of the investigation. Its presence corroborated the story Bobby Kelske told about Dawn's throwing her hairbrush at him because he refused to help her kill the children. Regarding the analysis of the item at the police laboratory, the brush was "to be held for future comparison."

Item #16 – Powder particles from Dawn DeFeo. In the report, the analysis of item #16 read, "The pieces of powder are partially burnt particles of Nitrocellose *(sic)* gunpowder." It was Herman Race's belief that this was indication enough that Dawn DeFeo had to have fired a gun during the murders.

Item #18 – Fiber from third floor east side [Dawn DeFeo's] bedroom. Item #19 – Piece of cloth from entrance to southeast [Allison

DeFeo's] bedroom. Item #20 – Piece of cloth from inside southeast [Allison DeFeo's] bedroom. Because Butch was heartbroken over Allison's death, he claimed he sent Bobby to clean up any incriminating evidence in her room. According to Butch, after Bobby was finished in Allison's room, both of them went upstairs to arrange Dawn and clean up the blood and brain matter on her wall and headboard. These three items, tied together in the lab reports, helped substantiate the fact that someone had cleaned up the mess in the two rooms.

Item #25 – Two dishes and four spoons from radiator in master bedroom. According to Butch, his mother, father, and the younger children were in his parents' room eating ice cream prior to the murders. A crime-scene photograph seemed to corroborate this. Next to a hairbrush on the radiator in Big Ronnie and Louise's bedroom sat two dessert bowls, one on top of the other, with four spoons lying inside.

Item #26 – Stain from outside master bedroom floor. According to Butch, this was where his father had fallen after being shot a second time. Although the analysis officially stated "gross examination of the chemical tests failed to reveal the presence of blood," a source involved with Suffolk County law enforcement told me otherwise.

According to this person, the homicide detectives even tested the portrait of Marc and John DeFeo, item #30, hanging on the staircase, for the presence of blood. On a supplemental report, the results were broken down into the minutest detail. The lab technicians concluded that it was a simple meatball stain.

This source, who asked to remain anonymous for concerns about his safety, explained, "Item #26 was just listed as inconclusive. In all actuality, #26 was a bloodstain, and this is what led the detectives to believe that Big Ronnie did get up out of bed. Because the prosecution was unsure of their strategy at trial, the analysis was left out of the final report even though it had appeared in the initial reports.

"Because the prosecution eventually decided to make Butch the sole perpetrator, the lab reports had to mirror this. So many of the original reports were lost or destroyed. The original command report from the lab stated that it was more than likely that a few of the victims had gotten up."

In November 2001, I finally was allowed access to certain records, photographs and trial transcripts in the possession of the Suffolk County District Attorney's office and Police Department. There, I found further proof to corroborate what this source said.

Incredibly, one of the crime-scene photographs showed two shoes, one a Fruit of the Loom tennis shoe, the other a girl's black dress shoe, with splotches of blood on and around them. What is unclear is whether Butch DeFeo's lawyers had any knowledge of this photograph's existence. After all, the "official" set of laboratory reports made no mention of the shoes or the blood.

More important, the blood on the shoes had not dried at the time the photograph was taken. Therefore, one likely scenario was that the bloodstains were made while Butch and Bobby cleaned up the crime scene in the late afternoon of November 13, 1974.

Item #31 – Flashlight from second-floor hallway.

A crime-scene photograph showing a military-type, angled flashlight located on a brown recliner in the second-floor hallway was taken by the police photographer during the investigation. Since Butch DeFeo had such poor eyesight, it would be next to impossible for him to have aimed and fired his rifle in the dark. Therefore, a flashlight was needed to illuminate the targets.

In an supplemental motion to the courts, Jacob Siegfried, Butch's attorney during the early days of his incarceration, stated the obvious when he said, "Conclusion that Ronald J. DeFeo Jr. could not fire the Marlin rifle, hold a flashlight and a revolver at the same time.

"That Ronald DeFeo Sr. did leave his bed and that Louise DeFeo did wake up and turn bodywise sideways before she was shot a second time. Obtained by diligent inquiry is the fact that lighting in the DeFeo master bedroom was poor and flashlight was used for better sight."

Item #33 – Expanded bullet from box spring of victim (Louise DeFeo) second-floor bedroom. This particular item in the lab reports was probably the most significant to prove that Butch DeFeo was not the only shooter. Although the police insisted that this bullet came from the Marlin rifle, the microscopic tests results read, "Failed to display a sufficient quantity of identifying striae to ascertain if it had been fired in item #82 [the .35-caliber Marlin rifle]." After a bullet is fired from a gun, it will have striae, which are channels or grooves made from the barrel. If Butch's story is correct, then this obviously was the bullet fired from Bobby Kelske's Colt Python.

According to the affidavits signed by Roger and Linnea Nonnewitz, Suffolk County Detective Dennis Rafferty came to their house during the investigation to inquire about a .38-caliber handgun, and to see if Butch had ever been seen with one. Since Kelske's handgun was a Colt Python, it could fire both .357 Magnum and .38 special caliber bullets. But the police wanted to connect Butch with his own .38-caliber handgun.

In the course of my investigation, Butch and Geraldine DeFeo gave me a few of the affidavits and legal motions that Jacob Siegfried had purportedly written. Wanting to validate the documents in question, I contacted Siegfried's son, who had taken over his father's practice. On October 29, 2001, I received verification that the signatures on the documents were those of Jacob Siegfried. Siegfried's son, however, was unable to locate his father's file on the case. None of the affirmants could be located to verify the affidavits.

According to Siegfried's motion, Suffolk County Detective Sergeant Ernest Klug was approached by Steven Hicks during the late hours of November 13, 1974. The motion stated, "Sgt. Klug, on 11-13-14-74, makes a report to homicide to detain Robert Kelske. He has obtained information from Steven Hicks . . . that Robert Kelske showed him a Colt Python revolver. Sgt. Klug's reports Robert Kelske, the second suspect, did a good job of dodging around the questions."

Item #64 – Piece of rag from trash basket at foot of Coles Avenue, Amityville. Coles Avenue intersects with Ocean Avenue one street to the south of the DeFeo house and ends at the foot of the Amityville Creek. At the edge of the water sits a small landing where village residents can sit on a bench and enjoy the view. Since 1974, very little has changed. Behind the bench, near the street, sat a wire-mesh trashcan, where the white rag was recovered.

Since Butch and Geraldine DeFeo insist that Bobby Kelske was the one who disposed of the rifle, it is probable that Kelske had every intention of discarding it into the water at the small landing's edge. However, because the landing was so close to adjacent backyards, Kelske may have had second thoughts and decided not to chance someone's seeing him. Nevertheless, the rag was discarded in the Coles Avenue trashcan.

After leaving Coles Avenue, I theorized that Bobby drove south on Ocean Avenue to the Richmond Avenue dock, a large dock facing the entrance to the greater bay. Concealing the rifle, Bobby made his way to the end of the dock to throw the rifle in the water.

Wanting to see if this theory was plausible, I ventured to the dock for another look on a late afternoon in July 2001. The Amityville dock had not changed much over the years. As in 1974, a large pole sat on the northernmost end, and a bench sat roughly in the middle. Because it was raining, not a soul was in sight. It was not hard to imagine the dock's being just as deserted on a cool November afternoon.

Taking note if anyone had seen me, I walked slowly out to the most secluded part of the dock, which was behind the large pole. Once there, I was out of sight from any prying eyes from behind. I now had an unhindered view of the large bay. I was sure this had to be the spot where the weapon had been thrown off the dock.

The police report regarding the recovery of the weapon proved my assumption correct. According to the report made by Suffolk County Detective Robert Schomacker, shield #501, Nassau County diver Melvin Berger discovered the Marlin rifle "approximately 30 feet from the northerly side of the dock, and approximately 25 feet east of the adjacent bulkhead."

The northern and easternmost points of the dock were precisely where I was standing: behind the large pole, hidden from view. Like a discus thrower, Kelske must have flung the rifle out as far as he could.

In addition to the official reports, I decided to try to contact Bobby Kelske, even though I was warned that he refused to talk

Richmond Dock.
Bobby Kelske drove south on Ocean Avenue to the Richmond Avenue dock (above). Concealing the rifle, Bobby made his way to the end of the dock to throw it in the water.

Dawn's headboard.
This crime-scene photo (below) is enough indication that Dawn's headboard had been cleaned up prior to police arrival.

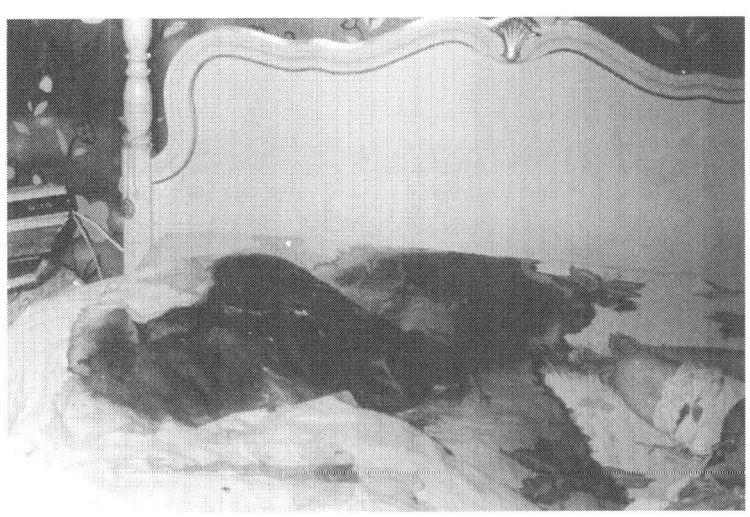

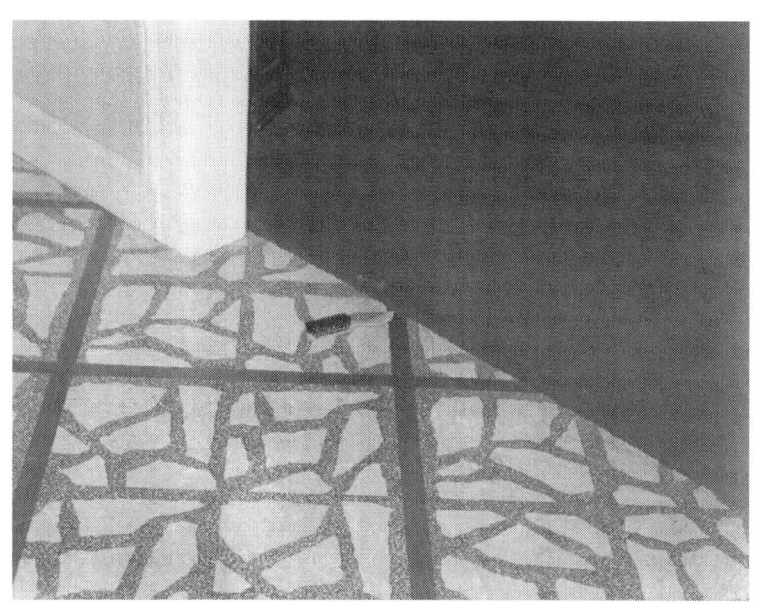

Brush on foyer floor.
Above, a baby-blue brush sits on the foyer of the DeFeo home.
According to Butch DeFeo, this is where Dawn had thrown her
hairbrush at Bobby Kelske.
Blood droplets around shoes (below).

about the DeFeo murders. I was told by several Amityville residents that there had always been suspicion about Kelske's involvement with the murders. So, through a relative of his, I forwarded Kelske a letter asking him to speak with me.

Kelske denied my request, but stated that he had an interest in viewing my Web site if he would not see any of the DeFeo children's pictures. Although Kelske shot only Louise DeFeo, allegedly out of mercy, he did not prevent the deaths of the younger children by stopping Dawn DeFeo, most likely because he did not feel Dawn was serious.

It is my belief that Kelske has been burdened ever since by the guilt of knowing he was partly responsible for the children's deaths. His statement seemed only to lend support to my conclusion.

Another individual I tried to contact was Augie Degenaro. From the onset, I was told Augie was a very elusive character. In fact, he refused to even list an address in an alleged affidavit he made for Butch DeFeo in front of Jacob Siegfried in 1974. Nevertheless, I was hopeful that he could be found.

During my conversation with former Brooklyn Assistant District Attorney John Christopher Fine, I asked him about Augie. Although Fine stated he had known Augie Degenaro, he said he was unable and unwilling to provide me with any information more than that, citing it was a confidential matter.

Although Fine's unwillingness to help me locate Augie was a disappointment, I found it fit a pattern. I had heard from sources tied to organized crime that Augie Degenaro, at one point, had either turned state's evidence and was under some form of witness protection, or he was dead. For all intents and purposes, he had completely disappeared.

POSTMORTEM EXAMS

At 1:00 a.m. on November 14, 1974, Doctors Rappaport and Adelman of the Suffolk County Medical Examiner's office began a postmortem exam of the DeFeos. Representing the Suffolk County police was Detective Robert Schomacker, shield #501.

Chapter Seven

At approximately 1:15 a.m., Dr. Rappaport began examining the body of Allison DeFeo. The official report submitted by Detective Schomacker stated, "Postmortem lividity [discoloration] was present in the front portion of the body. Rigor mortis had set in . . . The victim had an entrance wound on her left cheek. This wound was ringed by multiple fine pockmarks of an approximate area of 3-3/4 inches x 3 inches."

The cause of death, according to Dr. Rappaport, was a bullet wound to the head and brain, which caused massive hemorrhaging.

Allison's wound gave a vital clue to identity of her killer. It is my belief that because a sibling rivalry existed between Dawn DeFeo and her younger sister that the wound was meant to disfigure Allison's beauty. Additionally, the pockmarks found in the postmortem exam, known as stippling, would also be discovered on the backs of Marc and John DeFeo, but were not present on the bodies Big Ronnie, Louise, and Dawn DeFeo.

At the DeFeo trial, Detective Alfred Della Penna, chief of the Suffolk Police Department's firearms identification section, testified that stippling was "caused by the burning particles of powder which have not fully burned as the bullet was passing down the barrel. It strikes the flesh and ruptures the capillaries."

When asked the distance for its occurrence, Detective Della Penna replied, "Stippling can be produced anywhere a distance of less than two feet."

Presumably, the same person who had killed Allison had also shot Marc and John. This would also appear to corroborate Butch DeFeo's claims that he did not kill the children, but only his parents and Dawn.

At 2:40 a.m. on November 14, 1974, Dr. Rappaport began the examination of Dawn DeFeo. The exam found that all of Dawn DeFeo's clothing was bloodstained. As with her sister, rigor mortis and lividity were present. Dawn's entry would was at the base of her skull in the back of her neck. Examination of her skull found several fractures, some of which were directly along the path of the bullet. The cause of death was a bullet wound to the head and brain, which caused massive hemorrhaging.

In *High Hopes*, co-authored with Harvey Aronson, DeFeo prosecutor Gerard Sullivan wrote, "Dawn's wound was the most terrible to look at. The killer stood about two and a half feet away and fired at the back of her neck . . . she had been menstruating, and her sheets were sodden with blood beneath the pink blanket."

And at the DeFeo trial, Sullivan had the chief medical examiner explain why there were fractures in Dawn DeFeo's skull. Dr. Adelman said, "The whole portion of the left side of her face was concave and had collapsed under the explosive effect of the wound."

In the basement of the DeFeo home sat two giant-size bottles of Clorox bleach. According to Butch, he and Bobby Kelske had cleaned up Dawn's room, so as to fit in with their plan to make the murders seem part of a robbery that had gone wrong. If Dawn's wound was as explosive as Dr. Adelman had testified to, after all her clothing was drenched in blood, then clearly her white headboard would have been covered in blood and brain matter. Since Dawn's head was right up against the headboard, something suspicious in itself, there could be only one possible reason why the "explosive" wound had not sprayed it red: It had been cleaned prior to the police's arrival.

Additionally, the crime-scene photographs showed that Dawn's hair, which had been drenched with blood, had been allowed to dry prior to Butch and Bobby's moving the girl into her final position. Therefore, Dawn's hair, which was clumped together, did not flow evenly as it should have if she already had been in that position.

Moreover, the photographs showed Dawn wearing a stiff, cuff bracelet that one would normally take off before going to bed. And her autopsy photos showed her nose swollen, an indication that a violent struggle for the rifle had possibly taken place as Butch DeFeo claimed.

Finally, Sullivan suggested in his book that the copious amounts of blood on Dawn's sheets were because she was menstruating. However, the blood on her sheets stopped around her waist line, so it could not have resulted from her menstruation. Unless, of course, Sullivan was referring to her position prior to Butch and Bobby's arranging her into bed.

Chapter Seven

Dr. Adelman began the postmortem exam of Ronald DeFeo Sr. at 2:42 a.m. The official cause of death was "bullet wounds of the chest and abdomen."

Dr. Adelman noted that "the heart had been shattered and the spleen had been lacerated." Dr. Adelman found that Big Ronnie's body contained three wounds: two entrance and one exit. The one bullet that did not exit the body was later recovered during the autopsy.

Wound #1, which Butch insisted to me Dawn had inflicted, was located in the middle of the back to the left of the backbone and 51 inches from the right heel. After Big Ronnie had struggled to his feet, he charged his attackers like a bull. Butch claimed he then shot his father, who was hunched over possibly due to the first wound in his back, in his chest.

The photographs taken at the crime scene and morgue showed that wound #2, which the medical examiner labeled an entrance wound, was located at the lower left back flank and 47 inches above the left heel.

Prior to the autopsy, each wound was measured with a card, which had a two-inch ruler printed on it. The card was then photographed next to the entrance and exit wounds of each victim as a visual means of measurement. The official autopsy report certified by Dr. Adelman, which Michael Brigante Sr. had obtained through his police contacts, stated the measurement for wound #2 in Big Ronnie's back was one inch by half an inch. But the measurements that appeared in the crime-scene and postmortem-exam photographs were approximately two inches in height and two inches in width. But whether this was an exit or an entrance wound is still debatable.

However, according to Ronald Singer, Laboratory Director of Tarrant County Medical Examiner's Crime Laboratory in Forth Worth, Texas, the "jagged, gaping hole" that appeared in the postmortem photographs of Big Ronnie may not be an accurate depiction of the initial wound since the wound may have been excised for closer examination prior to the photograph's being taken.

According to Butch and Geraldine, Michael Brigante Sr.

claimed that Big Ronnie's entrance and exit wounds were purposely mislabeled in order to support the homicide squad's case against Butch. Later at the DeFeo trial, the prosecutor would suggest that the trajectories of each bullet were different, so there was no precise way of knowing Big Ronnie's location when he was shot.

The other hole located in Big Ronnie's back, wound #1, also listed in the autopsy report as an entrance wound, was a half an inch by a quarter inch. The ruler shown in the photograph seemed to corroborate this.

In the official autopsy report, the measurements of the chest wound found on Big Ronnie read one inch by three-eighths of an inch. But, in the photograph depicting the wound with a small ruler next to it, the wound measured approximately three-quarters of an inch by half an inch. In no way does the wound extend an inch.

Whether this was a simple miscalculation on the examiner's part remains unclear. According to Ronald Singer, the apparent differences could be due to a number of things, including the position of the body at the time of the measurements.

In spite of all of these inconsistencies, the "official" police theory was that Butch DeFeo, the purported sole gunman, had stood at his parents' bedroom door and fired two shots into his father's back while his father lay in bed. However, at Butch's trial, prosecutor Gerard Sullivan was not totally convinced himself that this was accurate and even hinted at this in his opening statements to the jury. Furthermore, Sullivan informed the court that testimony would corroborate the fact that Big Ronnie "was put back in bed after he received one shot," and even entered photographic evidence that he felt supported this theory.

Sullivan's statements tend to support Butch's claims that his father died out of bed. Since even the prosecutor tended to lean toward that possibility, this meant Butch DeFeo would have needed help placing the 270-pound man back in bed to the position in which he was found.

At 11:40 a.m. on November 14, 1974, Dr. Adelman began the postmortem exam of Marc DeFeo. Adelman found "an entry wound in the lower left middle of the back with powder burns around the wound."

The official cause of death was a bullet wound penetrating the heart, liver, diaphragm, pericardium and ribs. There was nothing out of the ordinary with Marc's postmortem reports. The boy, who apparently was ordered face down by Dawn, died within seconds.

At 1:22 p.m., Dr. Adelman began the exam of Louise DeFeo. In his report, Detective Schomacker wrote, "Further examination of the victim discloses an entry wound, number one, on the right posterior side, 46 inches over right heel. And a second entry wound, number two, on the upper front right posterior side. There were three exit wounds: number one, between the breasts in the middle of the chest, 50 and a half inches above the left heel; number two, over the left nipple; number three, to the left of the left nipple, 50 inches over the left heel. In addition, there was a 'through and through' wound (two holes) on the inside of the left wrist. Dr. Adelman noted that this wound (in wrist) aligns with exit wound number three when the elbow is flexed . . . Dr. Adelman noted the cause of death to be massive internal and external hemorrhaging due to the bullet wounds of the chest and abdomen penetrating the liver, diaphragm, lungs, heart, ribs, sternum, breast and left wrist."

After Big Ronnie had been shot, Louise raised up, clutched her gold chain, and turned toward the doorway. Not only did the postmortem exam confirm that Louise was clutching her chain at the time she had been shot, but so does the crime-scene photograph of her lying in bed. With a death grip, Louise must have held onto her chain even after the bullet had penetrated her wrist.

Interestingly, the crime-scene photographs showed Louise in a different position from the one she had been shot in. The position of the blood splatter on the bed and headboard also suggested that she had been moved.

Another photograph of the master bedroom showed Big Ronnie lying uncovered on the bed. More important, the photo showed his right foot partially hanging off the bed as if he had been hurriedly placed there. Unlike her husband, Louise was face down underneath her blanket and neatly tucked away. It was corroboration that Butch, in a last gesture of love, rearranged his mother, so that she appeared to be sleeping peacefully.

At 2:50 p.m., Dr. Adelman began the last examination on John DeFeo. Afterward, he ruled the cause of death to be massive hemorrhaging of the liver, diaphragm, lung, heart, vertebral column, spinal cord and thymus. John's wound was 36 inches above the right heel and one inch to the right of the middle of his back. The killer may have chosen to kill John first since Marc, who had suffered a football injury, would have never had enough time to climb into his wheelchair, grab his crutches, or even crawl away. In fact, Marc would have needed assistance to turn over on his stomach, a fact that even Gerard Sullivan acknowledged at the DeFeo trial.

THE SEVENTH VICTIM

During the final stages of my research in November 2001, I finally was allowed by the Suffolk County Police Department to view the negatives of the DeFeo crime-scene photographs. Although I already had more than a 100 DeFeo crime-scene photographs that I previously helped acquire for a TV documentary, I wanted to find out if there were any photographs of *Item #26*, which was listed in the Suffolk County police laboratory report as a "stain from outside master bedroom floor." Because Herman Race had testified that he had found portions of the DeFeo floors bloodstained, I wanted to obtain a photograph of *Item #26* for further analysis.

The process was an arduous one at that. For more than three hours, I examined hundreds of negatives. Although the clerk was quite helpful, even offering me an extra-large magnifying glass for viewing the negatives, she showed me only one negative or strip of negatives at a time. This tight control was needed since all that existed of the DeFeo crime-scene photographs were these negatives.

Interestingly enough, it was at that time I uncovered the photo depicting the blood on the shoes. Although there was no photo of *Item #26*, I discovered an additional photo that opened up a whole new can of worms.

I began to grow distressed while viewing the negative the clerk labeled *20B2*. Ever since I had acquired the DeFeo crime-scene photographs, I had spent untold hours reviewing them for clues. Hence, I knew every detail of the DeFeos' bedrooms and beds. I slowly realized while viewing the negative that I was staring at a seventh body in a sixth bed.

Moreover, the surroundings of this mystery body resembled the DeFeo basement with its wood paneling. Since I was not sure if this was just a red herring or something extraordinary, I simply ordered a reproduction of the photo. A couple of weeks later, it arrived.

By that time, however, I was putting the finishing touches on the first edition of my book. Obviously, there was little time to have the photo scrutinized. In fact, I originally felt the body in the photo was that of Dawn DeFeo.

After I began work on the second edition of my book, I contacted Christopher Berry-Dee, a renowned British criminologist and author. Berry-Dee, who had interviewed Butch DeFeo in 1994 for a TV documentary series called "The Serial Killers" and for a chapter in his book, titled *Talking with Serial Killers*, was the director of operations for the prestigious Criminology Research Institute. Christopher Berry-Dee's background was impressive, to say the least.

I sent Christopher Berry-Dee several DeFeo crime-scene photographs, including a photo of the DeFeo basement. Understandably, Berry-Dee was initially skeptical about this "mystery" photo, believing, as I originally had, that it was a "red herring." Berry-Dee and his team of criminologists, nevertheless, agreed to examine the evidence I sent.

His interim report of May 28, 2002 read, "We have examined this material as a team, and for the interim period, I would like to give you our immediate thoughts. Ric, in cases such as this, especially where much hype and notoriety are attached, it is easily forgiven if one gets lost in the 'ripple effect,' where the waves on the pond lead away from the initial splash. Therefore, I would concentrate your mind on the 'splash' – where the stone hits the water. In other words, the initial crime scene and the implications of what we can believe to be true.

"We are, collectively, of the belief that you have seven corpses in the DeFeo residence. That you have brought to light the 'mystery body' does you much credit. We feel that the odds against this body being found shot, in another room, which is identical or almost identical to the DeFeo basement, are all but impossible. We take into consideration your integrity here and the circumstances of how this photograph came to light."

Christopher Berry-Dee's report went on to hypothesize that this seventh victim may have been the catalyst that led to the murders, even causing Ronald DeFeo Sr. to leave his bed to investigate a commotion. Events could have escalated, according to Berry-Dee, and from then on, "there could be no living witnesses."

This expert criminologist went on to write in his report, "There were very powerful influences at work once the police arrived. Mafia linked with police contrived to 'tidy' this mess up. DeFeo had his 'confession' beaten out of him; the states' attorney played his role, while making the occasional slip of the tongue en route. And you have one of the most dishonest judges known to man manipulating the American justice system. But why?

"Your answer lies in the seventh victim, Ric! Who was she? Why was she there? Why was her body never identified and this murder made public? Who had inquired about their missing daughter? Who really wants to know? There, colleague, is your can of worms."

Ever since uncovering this photo, I have heard rumors that the Suffolk County police had been seen bringing in a large garbage bag full of something into the DeFeo house the day after the murders. In spite of the fact that these rumors have yet to be substantiated, they also have yet to be refuted completely. The possibility that this seventh victim was one of the DeFeos who was returned to the crime scene in this garbage bag—for whatever reason—has not been entirely ruled out.

Indeed, I do not feel the body in this photo was that of a seventh victim, but rather one of the DeFeos repositioned. Yet the CRI's findings regarding the location of this photo matching the DeFeo basement is a significant fact. While viewing the DeFeo crime-scene negatives, I noted that there were three negatives of the mysterious victim in two different strips: twice on negative 17B1 and once on 20B2. I compared my notes with the police clerk's order sheet and found that both matched. On the same strip of negatives were other images of the crime scene at 112 Ocean Avenue, including shots of Dawn DeFeo lying in bed. This fact alone suggested the photos were taken at approximately the same time.

Regardless of the identity of this mystery body, the existence of this photo proved that Suffolk County's investigation was, in itself, negligent. If this person was a DeFeo, then the photo proved that the police tampered with evidence. If, however, this person truly was a seventh victim, then the coverup and ensuing corruption are unprecedented. This victim's identity and the reason he or she was placed in the DeFeo basement remains to be learned.

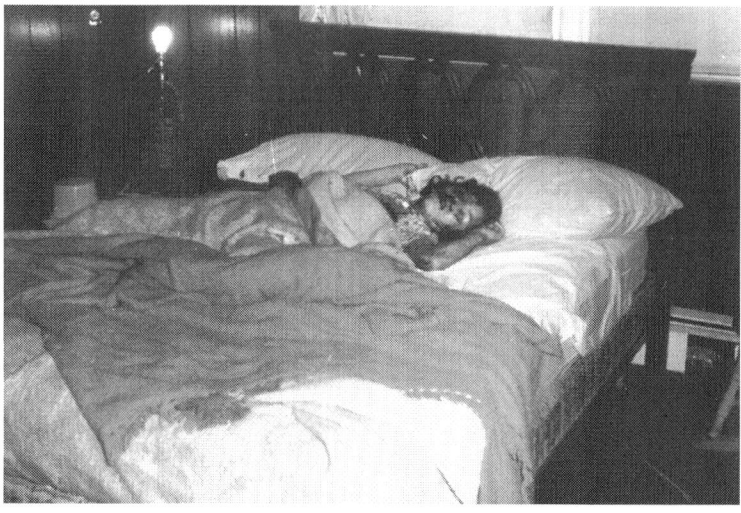

Pictured above is the "seventh" body.

Pictured above is a close-up of Louise DeFeo in bed. The pattern of blood splatters helped police determine the woman had been shot as she sat up in bed. This image also supports Butch's claims that he tucked his mother's body in with love.

Pictured below is the laundry area located in the basement of the home where Butch washed his soiled clothing after the murders.

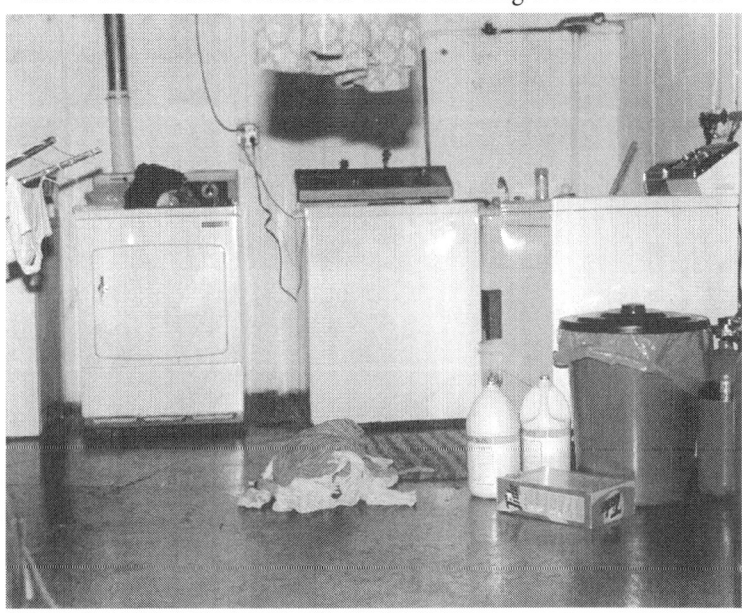

CHAPTER EIGHT
Guilty Until Proven Innocent

AFTER PUTTING ON a convincing act for the bar patrons at Henry's Bar, Butch DeFeo and Bobby Kelske returned with the bar owner and three others to 112 Ocean Avenue. The Amityville Village police then were notified that a homicide had taken place on the quiet street. First on the scene was Amityville Police Officer Kenneth Greguski, who would shortly request the presence of the Suffolk County detectives.

During the next few minutes, several uniformed and plainclothes officers arrived. Among them were Amityville Detective Sergeant Pat Cammaroto and Suffolk County Detective Gaspar Randazzo, shield #410. A year before, Sergeant Cammaroto had helped arrest Butch for grand larceny because he was in possession of a stolen outboard motor.

One of the first things that Detective Randazzo did was post Greguski at the front door to secure the scene. Because Shaggy was still barking uncontrollably, Butch was asked to take the dog outside. Butch obliged and put the sheepdog into the back of his car.

Police overrunning 112 Ocean Avenue (above). Dozens of police officers and detectives took over the DeFeo residence and the Ireland house in order to investigate the crime. Pictured below: The DeFeo kitchen, where Father McNamara consoled Butch.

The Ireland house (above).
Although the Irelands no longer live next door to the infamous Amityville house, their memories are quite fresh.
The DeFeo headstone (below) as it appears in December 1974.

Shaggy would stay there until later that night when animal control would take it to the Babylon Town Animal Shelter, where it would remain until friends of the family rescued it a few days later.

While Detective Randazzo was upstairs examining the crime scene, Butch and Bobby were sitting in the kitchen at the nook with Father James McNamara of St. Martin of Tours in Amityville. Father McNamara immediately came over upon hearing about the incident. He would later recall his shock to a reporter by commenting that the DeFeos seemed "like an average good family."

Although Butch was still crying, Father McNamara, unaware of Butch's involvement in the crime, consoled him with prayer. During their conversation, Father McNamara made him promise not to take any action against the people who killed his family. Afterward, the Catholic priest went upstairs and performed final blessings on the deceased DeFeos.

Upon Detective Randazzo's return to the kitchen, he immediately began questioning Butch about his family's purported connections to the Mob. It was obvious to the detective that a service manager's salary could have never afforded the Ocean Avenue house or its expensive furnishings. "Randazzo kept talking about the mob angle," Butch said. "So Bobby volunteered the name of Tony Mazzeo while sitting with the cop at the kitchen table."

By 7:15 p.m., the Suffolk County homicide detectives from the First Precinct started to arrive. Realizing that too many individuals were entering the crime scene, the supervising detective ordered all nonessential personnel to vacate 112 Ocean Avenue. At this point, the police needed to use the house next door. So Rufus and Diane Ireland allowed their house to be used as the base of operations for the ongoing investigation.

After Detective Randazzo transferred Butch from the DeFeo kitchen to the Ireland's sunroom, he continued the questioning. Contrary to simple logic and the most fundamental procedure of any investigation that nobody can be ruled out as a suspect, the Suffolk County detectives insisted that Butch DeFeo, at that time, was not one. Of course, this insistence that Butch was not a suspect from the onset was only a cover story, which, subsequently, the

Chapter Eight

unsuspecting public believed.

At approximately 7:30 p.m., Sergeant Gerard Gozaloff, shield #526, took over the questioning. According to Butch, the attitudes of the police changed after Detective Gozaloff's arrival. And it was at that time that Bobby was ordered to leave his friend's side.

Butch said, "Gozaloff told me, 'Listen, you got to come down to the precinct to give this statement.' I was crying and I was upset and I told him I wasn't going. I was standing up at that time, and Officer Gozaloff took his hand and he pushed the side of my face and pushed me down. And then he said, 'Listen, I told you we are going down to the police station. It'll be better for you down there.' He then unsnapped his gun, grabbed my arm, and we left the house."

After Bobby left the Ireland's sunroom, he spotted Rocco DeFeo and Vincent Procita standing nearby. Earlier, over police objections, Rocco had gained access to the downstairs of the DeFeo house. Although he demanded to see the bodies of his son and daughter-in-law, the police refused and forced him out.

At around 8:00 p.m., Butch was led out of the Ireland house by Detectives Gozaloff and Joseph Napolitano, shield #486. Upon seeing his grandson being taken away, Rocco ordered Bobby Kelske to find out where the detectives were taking him. Obeying the order, Bobby Kelske approached the two detectives who were walking on either side of Butch, forcibly leading him by the arm.

"Where are you taking Butch?" Bobby called out to them.

"Don't worry about it," one of the detectives replied, waving Bobby off as they continued leading Butch to an unmarked police car.

As they were walking down the driveway, Butch said, "I got a couple of cartons of cigarettes, I think, in my trunk. Can I get a pack or two out?" The detectives refused to release their grip on Butch and denied his request.

Butch's claims, however, about cigarettes in his trunk proved true. After his vehicle was impounded on November 13, the police searched his trunk and found 10 cartons of Lark cigarettes. According to Butch DeFeo, his attempt to grab cigarettes was nothing more than a ploy to get rid of the .25-caliber pistol he had on him. He allegedly had to discard the small gun in the back of the unmarked police vehicle when the detectives were not looking.

* * *

Meanwhile, in Brooklyn, Michael Brigante Sr. received a call from a police officer in Suffolk County. The officer told Brigante that his daughter "had just had a terrible tragedy."

"Now wait a minute," Brigante demanded. "What is it?"

"Your daughter and her family are all murdered. They are all dead. Will you come out?" the officer asked.

Michael Brigante agreed and arrived after 9:00 p.m. Immediately upon his arrival, Brigante approached the commanding officer and demanded to be allowed access to his daughter's home, citing he was an active member in several police benevolent associations. The officer refused, and Brigante went berserk and needed to be restrained by several officers.

Later that evening, Detective Gozaloff would return and ask Brigante if he thought that his grandson could have had anything to do with the murders. Of course, this is despite the Suffolk County homicide squad's insistence that Butch was not a suspect until the next day. Insulted by the question, Brigante gave a dirty look to the detective and replied, "He is a wonderful grandson."

After Detective Gozaloff shot off a few more questions, Rocco DeFeo approached and shouted to everyone, "Don't tell these bums nothing. This is family." After Rocco said that, Detective Gozaloff would not get the time of day if asked.

Before the night was over, Brigante would send Richard Wyssling, his nephew by marriage and a practicing attorney, to find out the whereabouts of Butch to represent him in these critical hours. Because the police were uncooperative, Wyssling failed in his attempts to find and represent Butch that night.

At 8:50 p.m., Detective Lieutenant Robert Dunn of Suffolk County's Organized Crime Unit arrived at the crime scene. The police were concerned about the DeFeos' alleged ties to the Mafia. Earlier, before being kicked out of the crime scene, Rocco placed a call to his brother, Peter DeFeo, who was a reputed hit man in the Vito Genovese crime family.

Although arrested several times for crimes ranging from murder to attempting to obtain illegal kickbacks from a teamsters union, Peter DeFeo was never convicted. This, of course, did not stop police from figuring in the "Mob" connection as a possible reason for the murders.

In fact, according to Detective Sergeant James Barylski, shield #358, at 7:45 p.m. that evening, a man who identified himself as Mr. Lee called the DeFeo residence. Recalling the incident at the DeFeo trial, Detective Barylski said, "The phone rang at the DeFeo residence. A man identified himself as a Mr. Lee, who was a friend of the family. He heard something was happening at the DeFeo residence and wanted to know what was going on." Although Barylski refused to discuss the matter over the phone, he would later learn that Mr. Lee was allegedly connected with Carlo Gambino.

Regardless, it was not too long before the police decided that the DeFeo murders did not fit the typical pattern of a gangland hit. Besides, they knew the Mob would not condone the killing of children, and it seemed they had already decided in their own minds that Butch and Bobby were the guilty parties.

By 11:00 p.m., the bystanders in the street realized the scope of the tragedy when the medical examiner's staff began to remove the bodies. Doug Spero, a reporter for WNBC radio, recalled, "When the smaller body bags started to come out, people's hearts dropped because you knew those were children."

Just when the onlookers thought it could not get any worse, one of the body bags accidentally opened, spilling out the young body of John DeFeo before it could be placed in the coroner's van. Although the medical examiner's staff tried quickly to cover the body, dozens of spectators had witnessed the grisly site. It was a scene, and a night, that the people of Amityville would never forget.

Earlier in the evening, Geraldine DeFeo had been told by a neighbor that the late TV news was reporting a mass murder in Amityville. Concerned over Dawn's attempted stabbing of Big Ronnie the previous night, she had the neighbor watch her children while she proceeded to Amityville.

Speeding the entire way, Geraldine drove the 90 miles in record time, arriving close to midnight, just in time to see the body bags being carried out. "Words cannot describe the surreal atmosphere. It was like a dream. The people in the body bags were my family. I was so sure that Butch was dead," Geraldine said.

After joining the other relatives, Michael Brigante Sr. assured Geraldine that Butch was alive and that he had been taken in for questioning. Although she would later try to see her husband, the police refused access to him, reasoning that he had not finished giving his statement.

JOEL MARTIN'S SCOOP

On November 13, 1974, reporter Joel Martin was not only the news director for Babylon's WBAB radio, but he also was the Long Island correspondent for United Press International.

At 7:00 p.m., Martin was about to leave WBAB for the day when a call came into the newsroom from UPI's Manhattan news desk. "They told me there had been a terrible mass murder and that a number of people had been killed," Joel Martin recalled.

After getting directions to 112 Ocean Avenue, which was only minutes away from WBAB, Joel Martin proceeded to the scene with tape recorder in hand. His proximity to the story gave him a jump on the city reporters, who were still in transit.

"Police were everywhere. It was like a movie set. Initially, they [the police] kept people behind barricades and were saying very little. I recognized someone I knew from the police department, somebody I knew well. I went over to him and asked if he could tell me what was going on. Off the record, he told me that six people in the DeFeo family had been murdered. As far as they could tell, it appeared they had all been shot. Frankly, I think the police were just as overwhelmed and as surprised as everyone else," Martin said.

But Joel Martin's local ties not only offered him a jump on his colleagues, but also afforded him a chance to enter the crime scene. "It was a beautiful house," Joel Martin said. "I couldn't get in very

Chapter Eight

far because there were so many emergency personnel there that you could not do very much. Everyone was very quiet. It was surreal. It didn't feel chilling at all."

Later, while the city reporters were huddling together trying to figure out what county they were in, Joel Martin wandered through the neighborhood looking for information. Near the Coles Avenue dock, Martin came across a group of kids who recognized him from his radio show.

Joel Martin said, "I asked them what they thought happened. They told me the DeFeos were nuts. They were always fighting. The kids didn't seem scared, interestingly enough, because everybody knew about Ronnie [Butch]. The kids said, 'Ronnie did it, man.' These kids seemed to know. One neighbor told me he heard a dog bark some time between 3 a.m. and 3:30 a.m."

Joel Martin's discovery regarding the time of the barking would later serve as the basis of the time of the murders, even though the medical examiner never set an exact time of death.

As far as Butch DeFeo's being a suspect, Joel Martin learned, through officials at the crime scene, that they had zeroed in on Butch almost immediately. Pertaining to Bobby Kelske and Dawn DeFeo's involvement, Joel Martin said, "Bobby Kelske's name came up from friends and people who knew the family. And the thing about Dawn came up almost immediately also. Bobby Kelske and Dawn's name were there from the very beginning. There is no question about that."

Having heard of Augie Degenaro and being familiar with the allegation that Augie may have been involved with the crime, Joel Martin explained, "There was a story that someone had kept lookout [during the murders]. I heard this story, too, from the [neighborhood] kids."

On Saturday, June 22, 2002, I had the opportunity to sit down with Joel Martin at the Nautilus Diner in Massapequa. Accompanying me was Geraldine DeFeo.

At first, Mr. Martin was skeptical of Geraldine's claims regarding her marriage to Butch and her connections to the DeFeos and Brigantes. In the years proceeding the DeFeo murders, Michael

Brigante Sr. contacted Joel Martin to thank him since he was one of the only reporters not to disrespect the memory of his daughter. Because he had spoken to him several times, Joel Martin was no stranger to the mannerisms, language and nuisances displayed by Michael Brigante Sr.

Over lunch, Geraldine was slowly making progress by explaining why there was no record of her marriage to Butch DeFeo. Of course, it helped that Geraldine knew all of Brigante's favorite terminology. But the remainder of Joel Martin's skepticism vanished after she pulled out her old photo ID.

A few days later, in a tape-recorded interview, I asked Joel Martin to go on record and recall if he had seen Geraldine at the crime scene on November 13, 1974. He explained, "I remember seeing her. I can't remember what time I saw her. She looked so familiar to me. When I saw the old picture, I didn't know that was who she was since she had been so sick [in recent years]. I looked at the picture and I said, 'I know her.' I did a double take, and I said, 'I recognize you.' She must have been in some part of the story since I don't doubt that she was there.

"You see, when they first talked later on about Ronnie's being married, there was a lot of skepticism. I think the skepticism was because there was nothing ever said about it publicly. It was never revealed. Nobody ever knew it. If it happened, it was a secret, and nobody understood why. When details about the marriage did surface, [Butch] was already locked up. So it was assumed that if there was a relationship that it was common-law."

As for Geraldine's authenticity, Joel Martin commented, "There is no reason to think that she wasn't one of his girlfriends. Now whether they were legally married or not, unless a document is produced, I suppose you could argue it either way. She seems to know a tremendous amount about the story and about the people involved. And she has got those ID cards. I do remember that face back then, but I just cannot place who she was. I am not sure what she has to gain from lying.

"A stubborn skeptic would say that some people would like to latch onto these stories because it gives them a moment of fame or a moment of attention. It puts them in a spotlight, where otherwise they might not be anybody.

"But Geraldine seems to know too much, and she has too many details. Clearly, there was some kind of relationship [between Butch and Geraldine]."

Since Joel Martin had spent several days in front of the DeFeo residence covering the ongoing investigation, I decided to show him the photo of the "seventh" body during our meeting. Although Joel Martin believed the body in the photo looked like one of the DeFeo children, I had wanted to learn if this veteran reporter had heard the rumors about the police bringing in a large garbage bag to the DeFeo residence the day after the murders.

Regarding the rumor about the garbage bag, Joel Martin explained, "I didn't see anything like that. But I had heard some strange stories about that. I don't know what that was about. I don't know if they were bringing something in or something out. Yeah, I heard the rumor, too. I just never could make any sense out of what it was. I could never find out the details.

"Frankly, I don't know why they would have needed to do anything since they had so much evidence against [Butch]. If any mistake was made by the police, in hindsight, they may have been overeager, or maybe they made mistakes in the homicide investigation because they had never had anything like this to deal with in this enormity with this kind of publicity and amount of attention. I don't have any question that they got the right guy."

THE NIGHTMARE BEGINS

After Butch was forcibly removed from the Ireland's house, he was taken to the Amityville precinct. However, fearing his relatives would come and get him, the police took Butch farther away, to the Suffolk County First Precinct in nearby Babylon.

After arriving at the Babylon precinct, Butch was seated at a desk in one of the precinct's two interrogation rooms. Over Butch's repeated protests, the detectives administered a paraffin test. The results, of course, came back negative because Butch had taken so many showers over the course of the day, and because he had used an extensive amount of bleach on his hands during the cleanup of the crime scene.

Immediately after being given the paraffin test, Butch said, "I demanded to call my attorney, Richard Hartman, who had represented me on a previous case. They told me, 'Don't worry.'" According to Butch, none of the officers ever informed him of his Miranda rights.

Knowing he was going to be there for awhile, Butch requested to use the bathroom and asked for a drink of water. Butch recalled, "The detectives told me that if I drank any water, then I would have to piss worse. Then we went on with questions, and they were asking me about guns, a lot of other things. They were trying to accuse me, asking me a lot of questions about myself and Robert Kelske."

Detective Harrison then arrived to take over the questioning as Detective Gozaloff returned to the crime scene. Before Gozaloff left, Butch again said, "I want to go back to my house to see my family, my grandparents and my uncle." Even though Butch had not yet been charged with any crime, he was not allowed to leave the precinct.

Because word had reached the detectives that an attorney was looking for Butch, the decision was made to move him to the Fourth Precinct in Hauppauge. "As they were taking me out, I saw Robert Kelske in another room out there, you know, through a hallway . . . and I tried to tell Kelske to tell my grandfather to get me out of here, get me out of the precinct, get me away from the police, and they grabbed me and we went to the Fourth Precinct," Butch recalled.

It was close to midnight by the time Butch arrived at the Hauppauge Precinct. There, Butch was informed Bobby Kelske had told his interrogators that he had been shooting heroin earlier in the day.

According to Butch, Detective Harrison then continued talking about his grandfather's purported connections with the Mob and his gun collection. Butch told the detective, "I don't know what you are talking about. But, man, I got to go piss, and my mouth is dry.

Can I get some water?" According to Butch, Detective Harrison responded, "Butch, if you drink that water, you'll only want to go the bathroom more."

Sometime before 1:00 a.m., the interrogation was moved downstairs into the basement. Butch would later learn the reasons behind the move: Richard Wyssling had arrived at the same precinct, demanding to see him.

THE EIGHT-PAGE STATEMENT

Despite the severity of the homicide investigation, a tape recorder or an assistant district attorney was suspiciously absent from the interrogation of Butch. Yet the police insist Butch offered his full cooperation with them, giving them an eight-page statement.

Butch, admittedly, told the police several fabrications that appeared in his official statement. The rest of the statement, Butch alleged, was improvised without his cooperation. After Detective Gozaloff had returned, he continued writing the statement. The main points were:

1. Before work, Butch had gone to Saul's Luncheonette, as usual, to have his egg cream and muffin.

2. Butch was supposedly early to work on the 13th because he had stayed home from work on the previous day.

3. Since Butch was the boss's son, he left work at 1:00 p.m. on the 13th and had another employee punch him out.

4. After leaving for work, Butch went to meet Mindy Weiss.

5. At around 3:00 p.m., Butch went to Bobby Kelske's house. The statement read that Kelske was asleep, so Butch told his friend he would meet him at Henry's Bar at around 6:00 p.m.

6. Butch then went to Henry's Bar and had several vodka and 7-Ups.

7. When Butch left the bar, he went to Patty Geiger's house to score some heroin.

8. After returning to the bar, Butch told its patrons he had to break a window at his house because nobody was answering the phone or the door. In his statement, Butch also said he did not have a house key that day.

9. Butch concluded with some additional information about Tony Mazzeo and one of Carlo Gambino's men named Mr. Lee.

Regarding what is true in the statement and what was concocted by the detectives, Butch explained, "I gave the cops some stuff that went into it. I didn't tell them about Mazzeo; Bobby did. As far as I was concerned, Mazzeo was a 70-year-old man who couldn't get his dick up. But I went with it and told them a lie about Mazzeo and my father having an argument.

"I lied about the timeframe because I was so tired because I hadn't slept the night before. I told the cops the lie about the missing house key, but I never went over to Mindy's house that day like they said. I was through with Mindy and was trying to fix her up with a friend.

"However, I really did force the kitchen window open. But whoever wrote that stuff about the skunk vodka is full of shit. I had a Coke to drink because you can't mix heroin and alcohol, and I hate vodka."

At about 2:30 a.m., Butch was still holding out, opposed to signing the eight-page statement, which was in Detective Gozaloff's handwriting. "I told them, 'I want to go back to my house. You people either charge me or let me go,'" Butch said. In order to leave, the detectives told Butch, he had to sign the statement.

INVESTIGATING BUTCH

Contrary to what the Suffolk County police contended, Butch was considered a suspect from the outset. Therefore, it comes as no surprise that the police needed to verify his whereabouts that day. So at 11:00 p.m., on November 13, 1974, Detective Edward Simmons, shield #312, visited Vito D'Iorio at his home.

In his report, certified by his supervisor, Captain Daniel Mueller, Detective Simmons repeated what he was told by D'Iorio, a Brigante Buick employee. In addition to confirming Butch's early arrival, Detective Simmons wrote, "Ronnie Jr. went about his day's work in a normal way. Mr. D'Iorio stated he had his lunch in his office at about 12:30 p.m. and Ronnie Jr. came into the office and hung around for awhile. Mr. D'Iorio stated that at about 2:00 or 2:30 p.m., Ronnie Jr. told him he was going home and at that time he left." D'Iorio's statement presented a different picture from Butch's. D'Iorio's claims were later corroborated at the DeFeo trial by Lucy Burkin, another Brigante-Karl employee, who said Butch had been in her office at 2:30 p.m. using the phone.

At 2:30 a.m. on the 14th, while Butch was undergoing an intense interrogation, Detective John Shirvell, shield #429, discovered two rifle boxes in Butch's room. In his rush to discard incriminating evidence, Butch had forgotten about them. Although the police stated they were out in plain view, Butch insisted the boxes were in his closet. If, in fact, the boxes were in Butch's closet, this would serve to explain why Butch had forgotten to get rid of them earlier, along with the other incriminating evidence.

The box labels indicated that they were originally cartons used to ship two Marlin rifles, one of which was the .35-caliber rifle used in the murders. The other one, a .22-caliber rifle, had already been accounted for in Butch's room. Since the .35-caliber Marlin was slowly becoming suspect as the murder weapon, and because it could not be located at the DeFeo house, the detectives felt this was an indication that Butch knew more than he was saying. Another piece of incriminating evidence would come from Steven Hicks's house.

Hicks was part of the same crowd that Butch ran with, so during the hunting season of 1973, Butch lent him the .35-caliber Marlin rifle to go deer hunting. Because Hicks was not sure how to load the weapon properly, he asked Barry Springer for assistance.

On the witness stand at the DeFeo trial, Hicks recalled, "Barry loaded the gun, and he had pointed it down to the floor, and he cocked it a few times. A few bullets ejected without firing, and then, bang, one went off."

The bullet was eventually recovered beneath Hicks's floor and sent to the police lab for analysis. That afternoon, when the lab results came back, it confirmed what the detectives had already concluded. The bullet recovered in Hicks's house matched those found in the victims, all except, of course, the .38-caliber slug in Louise.

FROM THE FRYING PAN INTO THE FIRE

Even though the Suffolk County homicide detectives had very little evidence to tie Butch to the crime, they believed they could elicit a confession from him. After signing the prepared statement, Butch accompanied Detectives Gozaloff and Harrison.

"The three of us, me, Detective Harrison and Detective Gozaloff, left the Fourth Precinct," Butch said. "Now I had thought they were taking me to Rocco DeFeo's house. We got in the car; I was in the middle. I don't remember who was driving, but I know I was in the middle. And the next thing I know, they're taking me to a white house.

"I said, 'What's this? What's going on here?' They said, 'Come on. You are coming in here now.' And I told them, I said, 'I thought you guys were going to take me to my grandfather's house.' And they said, 'You can't go there.'"

Chapter Eight

The white framed house that Butch was taken to was the homicide building, which sat a thousand yards away from the entrance to the Fourth Precinct. In order for them not to raise suspicions, the detectives drove Butch around to the rear of the complex rather than to the lighted area in the front. It was imperative for the time being that only homicide squad personnel knew he was there.

Butch was led into a nine-by-12 room, which contained filing cabinets, two chairs and a window positioned high up. Completing the interrogation room was a two-way mirror along the wall. For the next six hours, Butch would be subjected to continuous questioning. It did not matter that he was thirsty, hungry, exhausted, or in need of a bathroom. The detectives wanted one thing: a signed confession.

According to Butch, Detective Harrison kept telling him to make it easy on himself and confess. Although the situation was growing increasingly desperate, Butch continued to demand his lawyer. After a fruitless attempt to convince Butch to admit to the murders, alternate methods were employed. It was 9:00 a.m., on November 14, when the torture began.

Knowing he would make it worse for himself if he fought back, Butch could only lie still while he was repeatedly kicked, punched and stepped on. After this did not gain them the results they were seeking, members of Suffolk's homicide squad switched to their tried-and-true method of a blackjack and a phone book. For 10 minutes, a phone book was held to Butch's head and then repeatedly struck with a blackjack. The phone book would act as a buffer, preventing an excessive amount of bruising on Butch.

"By this time, I was crying. I was sick. Now I was hurt. I was hurt pretty bad. I couldn't take anymore. I just couldn't. But I wasn't going to sign a statement saying I did it," Butch said.

After the phone-book technique did not work, the officers placed a paper bag over Butch's head and rammed it into the filing cabinet several times. Butch might have been in pain, but he would never sign a confession. And the detectives must have been stunned by this perseverance, not realizing Butch had been conditioned by the years of abuse inflicted by his father.

Changing their tactics, Detective Dennis Rafferty and Detective Lieutenant Robert Dunn took over the interrogation at 10:30 a.m. In fact, Detectives Rafferty and Dunn were a specially trained team, called in on special assignments to interrogate suspects.

By this time, Butch had been in police custody for 14 and a half hours, and still was not given any food, water, access to a restroom or a lawyer.

"I had my head down in the chair, and Rafferty came over and said, 'Are you all right? I'm not like the other guys. I'm not an animal. I'm going to try to help you, you know, so you can leave here. Let's go over your statement again.' I blew up, stood up and said, 'I have been over this statement 200 times at least. You go ahead and read it; I'm not going over it again.' Detective Dunn then pushed my shoulder into the filing cabinets in the room, and told me to sit down. Detective Rafferty had, you know, his handcuffs. He put one cuff on my hand and hooked the other end of it to the handle of the filing cabinet where I was sitting in the chair so I couldn't do that again, get up like that," Butch said.

For the next seven hours, Detectives Rafferty and Dunn questioned Butch about his story. According to Detective Rafferty, Butch offered several different versions of events throughout the day until he finally broke down. "At that point, he started to cry the heaviest he had cried all day," Detective Rafferty explained later under oath.

According to Detective Rafferty, Butch started his oral admission by saying, "Once I started, I just couldn't stop. It went so fast." Over the next hour, the adept interrogator apparently was able to obtain a complete oral confession from Butch, including the location of several pieces of incriminating evidence.

But it should be noted that Butch never signed any form of a written confession or statement regarding the murders. The detectives reasoned it was because Butch was afraid of his grandfather, Michael Brigante Sr., who had close ties to several police organizations and was reputedly connected to several crime families. Incredulously, neither the interrogation or oral confession was ever

Chapter Eight

tape-recorded.

Contrary to the detective's version of events, Butch said, "I never made any oral confession to Rafferty. Rafferty made his own confession. The only thing I said to Rafferty and Dunn was 'fuck you, eat me, and suck my dick.' If they have a statement saying that, then I said it."

According to Butch, the beatings continued throughout the rest of the day. "In between the beatings, Rafferty would tell me how the murders went down. All kinds of shit how I shot my two brothers and sisters. He grabbed two chairs and positioned them like Marc's and John's beds and stood between them. Then he said, 'Bam! Bam! That's the way it was, right, Butch? You did it all with that no-account Kelske. Your partner ratted you out, so you may as well tell us it all, Butch.'

"Again, I told Rafferty to fuck off. He left for a few minutes and then returned with a written confession ready for my signature. Rafferty kept telling me, 'Sign it; get if off your chest.' I never confessed. Rafferty said how it went down, not me," Butch said.

With regard to Detective Rafferty's statement that Butch cried on his shoulder, Butch countered, saying, "I wouldn't cry on no dick-smoking cop. He's a liar."

It was up to the courts, however, to decide whose version of events to believe: Detective Rafferty's or Butch DeFeo's, an accused mass murderer. In 1974, the entire Suffolk County judicial system was plagued with corruption and favoritism. This being the case, Butch's purported confession was accepted while the stories of police brutality were rejected.

Wanting further corroboration of Butch DeFeo's claims about his beatings, I contacted Christopher Berry-Dee, a British author, producer and criminologist. In 1994, he helped produced a 30-minute documentary about Butch DeFeo, entitled "The Serial Killers."

Although Berry-Dee readily admitted the show did not turn out quite like he expected, he did have a chance to interview Detective Dennis Rafferty. In an E-mail to me, Berry-Dee wrote, "I can confirm that I interviewed Detective Dennis Rafferty at

Yaphank on 27 September 1994. I asked him about DeFeo's claim that his statement was beaten out of him, to which the detective replied, 'Sure. Of course, we did a good job on him.'

"I was also shown the physical evidence: the 35 Marlin [rifle], [Dawn DeFeo's] nightdress, etc. When interviewed, I asked Detective Rafferty about a re-examination of the clothing. He replied, 'Not a chance in hell. This stuff [the clothing] will never be looked at again. We'll make sure of that.'"

With regard to the clothing, it was Herman Race's assertions that Dawn's nightdress could prove she participated in the murders. As Detective Rafferty admitted to Christopher Berry-Dee, officials in Suffolk County would do everything in their power to prevent Butch DeFeo, as they did in 1974, a chance to prove his case. In fact, my own requests to view the evidence were adamantly denied.

COVERAGE OF THE DEFEO MURDERS

There was no ifs, ands, or buts about it. The DeFeo murders were the biggest news story at that time: a family of six found in their beds, in sleeping attire, systematically murdered.

Journalists and reporters battled over interviews, shoving microphones and tape recorders into the faces of interviewees. Anyone who had knowledge of Butch DeFeo or his family was a worthy subject.

One such interviewee was the bartender who was tending bar at Henry's during the time Butch came in pleading for help. He told reporters, "He [Butch] had two drinks, left, had a soda, left and came back saying his parents had been shot."

Two youths in the street explained how Butch was not one for starting fights, although he would never back down from one. "He," they said, "never looked for trouble."

A neighbor, who was friends with Louise DeFeo, had this to say about the DeFeo's eldest son: "He was Louise's pride and joy; she adored him."

That evening, Amityville residents were shocked when the Suffolk County police announced that Butch DeFeo was charged with the crime. Butch's arrest report read, "On 11-13-74, at about 3:30 a.m., the defendant did shoot and kill his mother, Louise DeFeo, his father, Ronald DeFeo Sr., his brothers, Marc and John DeFeo, and his sisters, Dawn and Allison DeFeo, in their bedrooms at the aforementioned residence."

Reacting to the arrest, Butch's long-time friend, Glenn Hoffman, told *The New York Times*, "I can't believe it even if they say it's true. He could have been set up for it. You don't know what's involved . . . I was just talking to [Butch] just recently how proud he was of his brother playing football. He'd never kill his brother."

Stacy, Geraldine's daughter, explained, "I couldn't believe they were all dead. I don't know if I really understood it back then, but I thought Butch could never do any of that. And the people that said he could were all liars."

Overall, the media vilified Butch, claiming he had drugged his family and then killed them all for the $200,000 of life insurance money his father had taken out on them. Yet the chief of detectives admitted that such a policy might not have even existed, and the medical examiner conclusively stated the family was not drugged. At a news conference in front of the DeFeo house, even the Suffolk County Chief of Detectives told reporters they had no idea what the motive was. Disregarding fact, irresponsible reporting took over as Butch became labeled an inheritance killer, mass murderer, and psychotic.

BUILDING THE CASE AGAINST BUTCH

One of the few things Butch did reveal during the brutal interrogation was the whereabouts of the Brooklyn sewer and the items he had placed inside. On the afternoon on November 14, the detectives recovered the pillowcase and its contents.

Because Butch's clothes were bloodied after the police beat him up, they were later added to the sewer evidence. The police would later contend that the blood on the clothes was from Allison DeFeo. Overlooking the fact that Butch was meticulously clean, Detective Rafferty stated Butch wiped his hand on his clothes after accidentally dipping his hand into a pool of his sister's blood to retrieve a spent shell casing. However, no trace of blood was ever found on any of the rifle casings.

The homicide detectives might have recovered the sewer evidence, but the two crucial pieces of evidence they needed were the missing murder weapons. Because Butch claimed he did not know where Bobby had thrown the rifle, he could not give the police any clues as to its whereabouts, even though he insisted they beat him profusely to reveal its location. Of course, the detectives would later insist that Butch had been the one to dispose of the weapon and had been the one to lead them to it by making diagrams of its purported location. Butch, however, claimed he only signed blank pieces of yellow paper to avoid any further torture.

During the course of shooting footage for NBC news, a cameraman captured an interesting conversation behind the DeFeo house between one of the divers and a detective on the police boat. After just surfacing from the bottom of the Amityville Creek, the diver told the detective, "I didn't see anything stirred up like anything had gone into the mud. Do you think this would be the area that they threw it at?"

The detective replied, "Well, we would think they threw it [off] the dock, going out."

The word "they" certainly is an interesting choice of words. Since both Butch DeFeo and Bobby Kelske were taken in for "questioning," it stands to reason that it is likely the police were referring to them.

Further support of Butch's claims that he had no idea where the rifle was thrown can be found in a supplemental police report made by Detective Robert Schomacker, shield #501. In his report, Detective Schomacker wrote, "On 11-15-74, the undersigned [Schomacker] was assigned to be present while a search for the murder weapon was conducted at the canal at the rear of the scene at 112 Ocean Avenue, Amityville . . . this search met with unsuccessful results.

"At about 1100 hours, the search team was moved to the Amityville Village dock at the south end of Richmond Avenue,

Chapter Eight

Amityville . . . at about 1148 hours, the weapon was found by one of the five divers."

Later, at the DeFeo trial, this same diver had admitted, under oath, to witnessing the Suffolk County police drawing diagrams right on the police boat.

On November 15, prior to his arraignment, Butch was picked up at 7:30 a.m. at the Suffolk County Jail by Detective Harrison and Detective Barylski and taken back to the Amityville Creek. They had wanted Butch to point out the location of the murder weapon and any other weapons he may have discarded.

Although Butch has remained adamant about not being the one to dispose of the rifle, he informed author Christopher Berry-Dee in 1994 that he told the police the weapon was near the dock after being taken from his jail cell because he did not want to be beaten up anymore. It is clear by this slip of the tongue that if Butch was not the one who disposed of the rifle that he at least knew of its general location.

In Butch's favor, however, is the fact the he had told the detectives about the Brooklyn sewer during his brutal interrogation. Therefore, it can be argued that Butch would have told them the exact location of the rifle's whereabouts if he knew. The divers, nonetheless, would not have taken until 11:48 a.m. on the second day of searching to retrieve the rifle if they had an exact location the first day.

So the question is, did Bobby tell the police the location of the rifle? Geraldine said, "Bobby wanted me to give Butch a message in jail. He told me to tell Butch that he didn't tell the cops where he threw the rifle."

Regarding Bobby's interrogation, Geraldine added, "Bobby told me that the cops told him, 'One of you son of a bitches are going to confess.' Bobby was called 'the brick' for a reason. You could hit Bobby, and he would barely flinch. The only way they got Bobby to cooperate with them was by threatening him with jail time. Knowing Bobby, to save his own neck, I believe he told the police the whereabouts of the rifle."

On Butch's arrest report, it was stated that the time of the murders was approximately 3:30 a.m. This was contrary to the fact that the medical examiner could only give a broad timeframe of death: not over 24 hours from the time the bodies were discovered.

Yet the Suffolk County police interviewed a 15-year-old neighbor, John Nemeth, who told police in his statement that "he awoke at about 0300 hours and he heard the DeFeo dog barking for about 15 minutes, but heard nothing else." However, at the DeFeo trial, Nemeth testified that he heard Shaggy bark more than once that night.

In her statement to the police, Mrs. Anderson, another neighbor, said she reported hearing dogs barking at about 0300 hours. She got up to quiet her own dogs, but they would not stop barking.

So was it responsible police work to infer that a 15-year-old boy, who was two houses away from the DeFeos', was able to distinguish between the neighborhood dogs well enough to pick out Shaggy's bark? Let alone, was Shaggy's bark sufficient indication that a murder was going on inside 112 Ocean Avenue?

Regardless, the police built a large portion of its case on Nemeth's statement. In fact, Nemeth's later testimony would indirectly serve to corroborate Butch's so-called confession that the Suffolk County Police fabricated.

THE ARRAIGNMENT

November 15, 1974 was the scheduled date of Butch's arraignment at the First District Court in Hauppauge. Prior to going before the court, Butch finally got a chance to meet with his counsel, attorney Leonard Symmons. Symmons was an attorney who specialized in criminal law in the law office of Hartman and Alpert. Butch's former attorney, Richard Hartman, referred the case to Symmons because he was once an assistant district attorney in neighboring Nassau County.

Symmons's only strategy was a defense based on mental defect, better known as an insanity defense. Prior to the arraignment, Symmons sat down with Butch to inform him of the process. Although Symmons never asked about the specifics of the crime, he did present Butch with a copy of his eight-page statement.

During this time, Butch had not been able to relay word to his grandfathers that the ledgers his father had kept were destroyed. The crime families mentioned in the ledgers could not take a chance that Butch would rat them out to save his own neck. On a police surveillance tape later given to the prosecution, a Mafia capo, in a conversation with Michael Brigante Sr., addressed this concern, saying, "This kid can hang everybody." Although Butch had no intention of doing this, a hit was commissioned nonetheless.

Later that day, Butch went before Judge Donald L. Auperin, who had moved the arraignment proceedings to the jail's chapel for extra security since the Suffolk County police got wind of the hit. Dressed in blue overalls reminiscent of a mechanic's, Butch calmly stood before Judge Auperin as he was read the charge against him. To simplify the process, Butch would be arraigned only on Marc's murder.

During the hearing, Symmons pointed out that Butch had swollen lips and a cut above the left eye. Symmons, therefore, requested a medical exam. In addition, he wanted Butch to undergo a psychiatric exam to help prepare the insanity defense. Although Judge Auperin denied Symmons's request for a psychiatric evaluation, he did approve the medical exam. Judge Auperin also denied Butch's request for bail and set a felony exam for the following Monday.

After the proceedings, Leonard Symmons made himself available for an interview with NBC TV on the steps to the courthouse. When asked why he wanted Butch to undergo a psychiatric exam, Symmons replied, "Based upon two factors. One upon a conversation I had with the defendant, Ronald DeFeo Jr., this morning. And based upon the nature of the charge and that he is alleged to have taken the lives of six members of his family."

When asked about his request to have a physical exam for Butch, Symmons explained, "Yes, the defendant appears to have sustained an injury to his left eye, to his lips and various parts of his body that are not visible to me."

In spite of Symmons's attempts, Butch did not like the young attorney. According to Geraldine, Butch called Symmons "Hippy Dippy." Because Butch refused to plead insanity, Symmons was soon replaced.

After Butch's arraignment, he was transferred to the Suffolk County Jail. Finally out of the hands of the homicide squad, Geraldine got her first chance to see her husband since his incarceration. "He walked out, and I almost didn't recognize him," Geraldine said. "He walked with a limp, and his face looked like it had been a punching bag. After he sat down, I asked him to take off his shoes so I could see his feet. Those bastard homicide cops beat his feet! They were black and blue and so swollen Butch could barely put his shoe back on."

During their visit, Butch recounted to Geraldine some the events of November 13, 1974, insisting he had nothing to do with the death of the children. Butch also gave his wife a message for his grandfather, Michael Brigante Sr. "He wanted me to tell Mike that he had taken care of the ledgers," Geraldine said.

It was not until later that Butch found out that Bobby Kelske purposely had not told Brigante the ledgers were destroyed. "Bobby knew we destroyed the ledgers, but he still went to the house with both of my grandfathers pretending to look for them," Butch said. Butch was beginning to see a different Bobby, one he could not trust.

On her way out of the jail, Geraldine met up with Rocco DeFeo and Michael Brigante Sr. She recalled, "Immediately upon seeing me, Mike and Rocco pushed me into a phone booth. They told me I had to be careful and that I had to stop being Butch's wife. When I asked why, they told me their connections informed them that the cops had realized that it was an impossibility that Butch could have killed everyone alone. They had felt that a female had to have kept the kids quiet, so they were beginning to feel they needed to find an accomplice. Big Mike and Rocco did not want to risk the cops implicating me, so they told me I no longer existed as Butch's wife."

Geraldine claimed that both men had a soft spot for her and her children. Because Shea Marie was barely three months old, they did not want Geraldine to be implicated in the murders.

Chapter Eight

According to sources who wish not to be identified, there was a meeting that took place at a race track between representatives of the Colombo and Genovese crime families. Since the Genovese family had the best hit men around, it is reported that the Colombos wanted to use one of these hit men to kill Butch. Although the request was denied, the Genovese family agreed to assist with getting rid of any trace that Butch and Geraldine had been married. After all, Geraldine's family and friends were concerned about her safety as much as Michael Brigante Sr. was.

This alleged meeting fit perfectly with what my Suffolk County deep throat source told me. He said, "Money and power can make anything disappear."

* * *

On Monday, November 18, 1974, hundreds of mourners gathered at St. Martin of Tours in Amityville to say goodbye to the DeFeos. Graveside services were held later that day at St. Charles Cemetery in neighboring Pinelawn. Although scores of relatives from both the Brigante and DeFeo sides showed up, the service was almost inaudible because of the airport across the street.

While the DeFeo family was laid to rest, the Suffolk County Grand Jury issued an indictment citing six counts of second-degree murder against Butch. Defying logic, Butch was now alleged to have done the impossible: In the span of a few seconds, and on two different floors, Butch killed all six members of his family while they slept.

Because the Suffolk County justice system wanted this case behind it, possibly because a new district attorney would be taking office in January 1975, the felony hearing originally set for the 18th was replaced with the grand jury proceedings.

Amidst the shock he was feeling with knowing his entire family was gone and he was now considered the lone killer, Butch was examined by a jail house physician for the injuries he had reported at his arraignment three days earlier. The report found "a subsiding bruise on the abdomen, a subsiding bruise on the left leg, and healing abrasions of the spinal area." The physician found the injuries to be between four and seven days old.

ENTER JACOB SIEGFRIED

By the end of November 1974, Rocco DeFeo and his brother, Peter, had agreed with certain elements in the Colombo family that Butch was a liability and needed to be taken care of. Also around this time, Michael Brigante Sr. finally received word that the ledgers Big Ronnie had kept had been destroyed. In his wisdom, Brigante devised a plan to keep his grandson alive.

First, Brigante had to appease Rocco. To do this, he made Butch relinquish administration rights of Big Ronnie's estate. Next, Brigante used all of the pull he had with the Colombo family to call off the hit on his grandson. It worked. "In return for a favor," Geraldine said, "and after Big Mike gave his word Butch would never turn into a rat, his life was spared."

Brigante, however, was not finished bartering with Butch. Because the Brooklyn D.A.'s racketeering squad was turning up the heat on the dealership, Brigante had planned for months to close it. The DeFeo murders, nonetheless, worsened the situation, and Brigante was forced to close his business faster than expected. In addition, his police contacts in Nassau County were threatened by elements in Suffolk County and told to stay out of the DeFeo investigation. Nevertheless, Brigante's contacts got word to him that his grandson would take a hard fall.

For Geraldine, this confirmed what Bobby Kelske told her. Geraldine said, "Bobby told me that Butch was the perfect fall guy: a braggart and a loudmouth kid who used drugs." Over the years, Geraldine's suspicions that the Brigantes did not want Butch out of jail because of his big mouth grew.

On November 19, 1974, Brigante sent his attorney, Alexander Hesterberg, and another attorney named Jacob Siegfried to have Butch sign over administration rights to Louise's portion of the estate. This was partly done because he wanted to handle the money wisely and partly because of the rivalry he faced with Rocco. Butch accepted, and in return, his grandfather retained attorney Jacob

Chapter Eight

Siegfried to replace Symmons as Butch's lawyer.

Verifying that this meeting occurred, criminologist Christopher Berry-Dee wrote in an E-mail to me, "Jail records show that this meeting took place on 19 November."

Therefore, right around the beginning of December 1974, Jacob Siegfried officially took the case. Unlike Symmons's insanity approach, Siegfried wanted to deal with the facts, so he immediately asked Butch for details about his movements on November 13, 1974.

Although Siegfried already had a general idea of who was interviewed, he approached the district attorney's office for any statements taken during the course of the police investigation. "Siegfried was referred to the homicide squad," Butch recalled. "Then he received a memorandum back stating no statements were taken from Franklyn Boyd, Allen Espasita, Jaylor Germol Nestor, and Robert McKinta. This is how Siegfried found out their correct last names."

After getting his first memorandum, Siegfried had Frank Boyd put him in touch with the others. After verifying with the individuals that they did, in fact, give a statement to the homicide detectives, Siegfried submitted another request to the district attorney's office for their statements. "Siegfried then got another memorandum from the D.A. saying that his request was denied because the statements weren't pertinent to the defense," Butch said.

Feeling otherwise, Siegfried had the individuals in question attest to the statements they had given to the Suffolk County homicide detectives in front of him. He then planned to depose himself and enter an affirmation of the suppressed statements into the court.

In his statement, Franklyn Boyd told Siegfried how he was awakened in the early morning hours of November 13, 1974 by Bobby Kelske, saying:

> Upon arrival at 800 Coney Island Avenue, Brooklyn, New York [the address to Brigante-Karl Buick dealership], and entrance to the building,

Affirmation of Testimonial Not Entered

Please take notice that in the office of Jacob Siegfried came before me

Augusto Degenaro

Given Address - areas around New York City

That in the beginning of the summer months the sister of Ronald J DeFeo, Dawn DeFeo had begun talking with him (Degenaro) about wanting a gun that was clean (no markings) and to have him assist her in the crime of killing her father she (Dawn DeFeo) knew he (her father) had money hidden and if he (Degenaro) helped her she would find it and give him half. She (Dawn DeFeo) also wanted him to get her heavy duty sleeping pills – that would not taste bad and that her brother Butch was going to be in on this plan so he could get away from the crazy family too.

Note that Degenaro states these kind of conversations continued up until the events of the killings of the DeFeo family November 13, 1974

Mr Degenaro states he will make no further comments on the events of November 13, 1974 other that he was in his car a 1973 Cadillac in front of the deFeo him the night the crime occurred and had nothing to do with the murders

Mr. Degenaro further makes statement he will not discuss if any conversations took place with himself and Ronald Joseph DeFeo concerning the murders.

Sworn to by

        Augosta Degenaro

Affirmed December 12 – 1974

JACOB SIEGFRIED

Affidavit from Augie DeGenaro

In the above affidavit, Augie DeGenaro reportedly confirmed the fact he had been outside the house on November 13, 1974. DeGenaro could not be located to authenticate the affidavit or substantiate the claims that he was fronting the DeFeo home. However, Jacob Siegfried's son informed author Ric Osuna via a fax that the signature of his father appeared authentic.

Chapter Eight

> Robert Kelske unwrapped a revolver that was wrapped up in a white handkerchief with initials RJD in one corner. The handkerchief was marked with large splotches of what appeared to be blood. Kelske then gave Boyd instructions to melt the pistol down in the melting pot on the property along with a bag containing clothing . . . On or about November 15, 1974, Franklyn Boyd was questioned by detectives of the homicide squad of Suffolk County. Mr. Boyd was informed that any testimony relevant to the case was to be used for the prosecution only and, therefore, he would not talk with defense counsel.

Jaylor Germal Nestor's affirmation to Jacob Siegfried, though shorter, added further corroboration that Butch did not act alone in the murder of his family. Nestor's affidavit read:

> That in the month of October 1974, Dawn DeFeo spoke with him about a gun and drugs. The gun to kill her father with. The drugs to put to sleep her whole family, so she, Dawn DeFeo, could commit the crime of killing her father. Dawn DeFeo further stated if she had to kill them all to get out, she did not care, especially her rotten older brother, Butch, who wouldn't help her. She hated him, too.

Both Robert McKinta and Allen Espasita's statements to Siegfried verified Butch's movements on November 13, 1974. Instead of stopping there, Siegfried went a step further and got two affidavits from Augie Degenaro. In the affidavits, Augie confirmed the fact he had been outside the house on November 13, 1974, and how Dawn had previously offered him money to help him kill Big Ronnie, and how she wanted him to get heavy-duty sleeping pills that would not taste bad.

Augie's affidavit went on to state that "he knew Ronald DeFeo

Sr. had attempted to confine his son in certain matters and a scare tactic was used by cutting DeFeo's [Butch's] brake line in his car to convince DeFeo [Butch] to cooperate with him."

On January 15, 1975, Siegfried made a notice of motion in the courts. In his motion, Siegfried requested to inspect the grand jury minutes upon which Butch's indictment was based; copies of admissions or summaries made by Butch during his interrogation; an order to suppress all evidence, oral or tangible since Butch did not have access to counsel during his interrogation; the right to examine and copy the original notes of the homicide detectives together with statements of various witnesses.

Siegfried further argued that he felt that the only reason the prosecution presented the evidence straight to the grand jury, circumventing a preliminary hearing, was because it had no legal evidence except an alleged confession obtained without Butch's attorney present.

Two days later, in a supplemental disclosure request, Siegfried motioned the court to allow the affirmations. Siegfried wrote, "In that the prosecutors withheld testimonial evidence that could help the defense by pointing to the involvement of others in the act. Clearly this evidence could support the facts that are questionable surrounding the case. There is some indication that the court is attentive to the prosecution case and considers the defense low standards, and weighs defense evidence lightly."

In his supplemental motions, Siegfried cited *People vs. McMahon*, misc. 2d 1097, to remind both the courts and the prosecution that "they first must seek justice not conviction."

The court rejected Siegfried's supplement disclosure request, but allowed his original motions. And on March 11, 1975, Judge John J.J. Jones ruled on Siegfried's January 15th motion. Judge Jones approved a preliminary hearing regarding the admissibility of Butch's purported confession. Furthermore, the court found that the evidence was legally sufficient enough to support the grand jury's indictment, but allowed Siegfried access to the minutes of the proceedings.

The court, however, denied Siegfried's request for the police department's reports, stating, "The reports of the police department requested, to the extent they constitute documents made in connection with the investigation of the defendant, are exempt from discovery under §240.10 (3) CPL. Defendant has made no showing that any of the police reports include routine factual information filed in the normal course of police activity, which is material to the preparation for his defense."

§240.10 (3) CPL, translated into layman's terms, meant section 240.10, paragraph 3, of New York's Criminal Procedure Law. However, the only item exempt under that section of the law is an "attorney's work product" and not police reports. Judge Jones's ruling was a small victory for the prosecution.

"At this point, Siegfried was feeling very aggravated," Geraldine remembered. "So he wanted to petition the Chief Justice in Washington, D.C., for a change of venue. Butch wouldn't allow him to because another inmate had told him how he had tried a similar motion. The inmate told Butch that when his request was denied that the Suffolk County justice system got its revenge for seeking help outside the county."

On May 15, 1975, with no other alternative, Jacob Siegfried filed a notice of defense of mental disease or defect. Geraldine explained, "At that point, Siegfried told Butch he had to plead insanity because no matter what he did, even if he submitted the bible, they would tell him it wasn't pertinent."

Butch refused and took out his frustrations on Siegfried by threatening him with physical harm. His grandfather was very displeased and told Siegfried he had done all he could for his grandson.

Although Butch apologized and admitted in court that he was in error, on May 27, 1975, Siegfried formally withdrew from the case. His grandfather's disapproval meant Butch would now have to use assigned counsel.

PART FOUR:
A MOCKERY OF JUSTICE

CHAPTER NINE
A Losing Strategy

ON JULY 7, 1975, William Weber was assigned to be Butch DeFeo's counsel by the court clerk of Suffolk County. Prior to being officially assigned, Weber received an inquiring phone call from the presiding judge, Honorable Ernest L. Signorelli, to see if he would be interested in taking the case.

It was no accident that Judge Signorelli called Weber. In the past, Weber had supported Judge Signorelli's ongoing campaign for a seat on the surrogate court. Concerned over the implications, Judge Signorelli said, "I assigned him [Weber] because I have the greatest confidence in him, and his ability to give this defendant the best possible defense he knows of."

Immediately, Weber faced the same problems that had plagued Jacob Siegfried: lack of cooperation from the prosecution and the inability to obtain certain reports. By the time of Weber's arrival, it had seemed that the prosecution had decided on prosecuting Butch solely for the crime. This left Weber with one strategy: the insanity defense.

So on July 29, 1975, Weber announced in court that he had planned to go ahead and use the "defense by mental defect" filed by Jacob Siegfried. However, Weber stressed that the defense had the right to withdraw it "after future investigations of the case."

"Butch was still up in arms about pleading insanity," Geraldine DeFeo said. "But Bill Weber was faced with a dilemma. He knew Butch did not commit the crime alone, and he knew the Suffolk County police were covering up the truth. So his hands were tied."

According to Butch, Weber finally got him to agree to an insanity defense because he promised him that they were all going to make a lot of money.

Confirming this, Barry Springer said in an affidavit, "During my meetings with William Weber, he told me that people approached him to write a book and that it was to be based on the trial, which had not started at the time he mentioned the book to me."

The money and book idea aside, Butch knew he had little choice but to go along with the insanity defense. His grandfather was no longer footing the bill for an attorney, and the Suffolk County justice system made it abundantly clear that it would do everything in its power to prevent Butch from getting a fair trial. So Butch gave Weber the okay and decided to feign insanity.

ENTER GERARD SULLIVAN

With regard to attorneys, William Weber was not the only change in the starting lineup. "In the early days of the case," Geraldine said, "Michael Brigante Jr. warned me that the word on the street was that there was this young, hotshot prosecutor who really wanted the case. That being Gerard Sullivan. This was another reason why the Brigantes, with the help of their attorney Alexander Hesterberg, had to make sure I did not legally exist as Mrs. DeFeo. Rumors had it that Sullivan believed a female had kept the kids quiet. Since I had intimate dealings with the family, the Brigantes were afraid that he would implicate me in the crime."

Chapter Nine

In *High Hopes*, a book Sullivan would later co-write with Harvey Aronson about the DeFeo case, Sullivan said, "When the DeFeo murders occurred, I was assigned to the rackets bureau . . . There was going to be an unprecedented murder prosecution, and it was passing me by. From the beginning, I wanted to prosecute the man who had blasted away six lives. I wanted a piece of that case. And I couldn't see my way clear to getting it." Sullivan, nonetheless, would eventually get his wish.

Although the DeFeo case was initially assigned to veteran prosecutor Edward W. Connors, Sullivan was willing to maneuver to get it.

Regarding Connors, Sullivan said in his book, "I was a tyro out of law school when I came to the district attorney's office, and I had learned a great deal by watching Eddie Connors. Where we differed was that Eddie felt it was up to the police to do all the investigating; he would work with what he had in front of him. I felt prosecutors should be innovative. I believed in thorough investigation, and I thought the prosecutor's job started with it."

Feeling he was a better candidate to lead the prosecution of the DeFeo case than his predecessor, Sullivan finally convinced Connors to trade cases. In *High Hopes*, Sullivan wrote, "I am an extrovert—I have a definite ego need, which trial work satisfies."

Gerard A. Sullivan, a graduate of St. John's Law School in Brooklyn, had begun working for the Suffolk County District Attorney's office in the spring of 1970. For Sullivan, successful prosecution of a murder case would help advance his career. And since, at that time, the DeFeo murder trial would be the biggest in Suffolk County's history, Sullivan wanted it. But Sullivan faced one problem: Judge Ernest Signorelli.

In 1971, Sullivan was cited by Judge Signorelli for not following his orders and for impugning his impartiality. To sum it up, Sullivan stated, "His honor did not like me; I did not like him."

More important, Judge Signorelli was very cautious about police testimony and critical of policemen as witnesses. This was a grave concern for the young assistant district attorney since his case relied heavily on testimony from Suffolk County detectives, who had allegedly elicited a confession from Butch.

BUILDING A CASE FOR INSANITY

Weber's strategy was to get Butch institutionalized for two to three years rather than receive a life sentence in a state prison. To do this, Weber had to convince a jury that the defendant was insane by bringing up examples from Butch's past, even if it meant fabricating them. Regardless, the question of guilt was no longer an issue.

On September 30, 1969, Butch DeFeo registered for the draft. Although it was the height of the Vietnam War, Butch was able to avoid, and eventually beat, the draft altogether.

According to Maria Dascole, executive to the local Selective Service board in Bay Shore, New York, Butch had been found unfit for military service on January 19, 1971 because of neurological and psychiatric problems arising from his habitual drug use.

According to Butch, his grandfather had informed him that to avoid being drafted, he would have to act crazy and tell the board he was a drug user. But in all reality, there was every indication that Butch's grandparents paid $5,000 to certain political figures to insure Butch would not be drafted.

Weber expanded and used the incident to begin building his insanity defense. After all, if the military would not take Butch during the height of the Vietnam War, then it was possible to convince a jury that Butch was truly insane.

But Weber needed more testimony to convince a jury that Butch was insane. Consequently, he decided the best way was for Butch's own friends to testify falsely that he often acted irrationally.

In an affidavit, Linnea Nonnewitz wrote, "Weber attempted to rehearse me to testify to facts which were not true in reference to state, '[Butch] beat the children up.'" In her affidavit, Linnea also insisted she informed Weber that Butch did not want to pursue an insanity defense and that she would not testify falsely.

Expanding on this, Barry Springer said, "Weber advised me that he was utilizing an insanity defense for DeFeo at the trial, and wanted me to testify about incidents between myself and DeFeo that I

Chapter Nine

and he were directly involved with to make up an insanity defense for the jury. I advised Weber that [Butch] was not crazy nor insane in any way. Weber then told me that he could not use me at the trial unless I testified his way."

Many years after his trial, Butch tried to get the United States Attorney General to look into the wrongdoings of his case. His then-attorney, William L. Shaffer, wrote to the civil rights division, saying, "William Weber of Suffolk County, State of New York, deliberately fabricated the defense of insanity, and conspired during the process of representing plaintiff in criminal court to write false books . . ."

According to Butch and Geraldine DeFeo, Weber had found a couple who would buy the DeFeo house and move into it to corroborate Butch's fabricated story.

Geraldine said, "Weber wanted Butch to begin saying he heard voices in his head, which had supposedly drove him to kill his family. He told Butch and me that he had found this couple who would move into the house and say that they also heard voices. Then Weber and the couple would write a book and give Butch a percentage. Weber boasted that Butch was going to be out in two or three years, and be filthy rich."

The most preposterous event that was fabricated for the insanity ploy was that Butch had taken a loaded shotgun, placed it to his father's head, and pulled the trigger, twice. After the gun failed to go off, Big Ronnie believed it was a miracle and found religion.

Yet not one defense witness could ever recall Butch's defending himself against his father's constant abuse, let alone striking him. In spite of that, Butch was convinced it was in his best interest to testify as if the incident were true. Today, the incident is the most widely recognized event in the DeFeo story, even though it never occurred.

Another humorous fabrication was that Butch's favorite song was "I Shot the Sheriff." Butch explained, "Weber just wanted me to say this because it made me look even more out of control."

CONFLICT WITH BOBBY KELSKE

Despite being in jail awaiting trial for the murder of his family, Butch purportedly wanted his friend to smuggle him in drugs. Geraldine, who told Bobby about Butch's request, said, "Bobby refused to do it because he was afraid he would get caught. This put even more strain on Butch and Bobby's friendship. Butch felt that Bobby owed him because Bobby should have been in jail right along with him."

Although Kelske informed Geraldine that he would not smuggle in drugs for Butch, Kelske gave her a message to tell Butch to "shut up about the veranda doors."

Butch's cover story was that he had entered his locked home through the kitchen via a window that had a broken latch. In reality, after cleaning up the crime scene, Butch exited the house through the veranda doors because the doors could be locked inside and then shut from the outside.

If the Suffolk County detectives in charge of the case had conducted a more proficient investigation, they would have learned that Butch could have entered the front door to the house, even though he claimed he did not have his house key.

Geraldine explained, "The DeFeos always kept an extra key on the side of the house underneath the trashcans. Besides, every member of the household had their own key. The only way that Butch could have convinced the police he really entered through the window in the kitchen was by throwing his key away."

This was later confirmed by Linnea Nonnewitz, who stated to me that she had, on one occasion, used an extra key in the little shed by the kitchen door.

Regardless, from day one, the police had suspected Bobby Kelske's involvement with the murders. Kelske's cover story was that the first time he had seen Butch on November 13, 1974, was at around 1:00 p.m., even though two Brigante-Karl employees put Butch at work until 2:30 p.m. that day. Although Kelske was still afraid that he would be prosecuted along with Butch, he had helped the detectives with their investigation. According to Butch, Kelske was hopeful that if too many facts, like the veranda doors, did not arise, then he could avoid a similar fate.

Gerard Sullivan, nonetheless, tried to point out in the preliminary hearing that Butch and Kelske did everything together, including burglarizing a house on Ocean Avenue and burning Big Ronnie's boat. Sullivan even brought up the canal murder. In an attempt to corner Kelske, Sullivan asked, "Did you not take money from his wallet before throwing him into the Amityville River." Kelske's obvious reply was, "No, sir."

Butch explained that certain elements of the Mob wanted Kelske dead. Knowing he was in danger, Kelske purportedly wrote a letter that contained incriminating evidence about the Mazzeo fire, which supposedly implicated Carlo Gambino and Michael Brigante Sr. Therefore, if something was to happen to Kelske or his family, the letter would find its way into the hands of the authorities.

Even private investigator Herman Race told Brigante to beware of Kelske. "I was at the Brigante house in Brooklyn," Geraldine said, "when Mr. Race told Mike that he should have nothing to do with Kelske because he had found evidence that Kelske had a role in the murders. But Mike always believed in keeping your friends close, but your enemies closer. So until his death, he kept a tab on Kelske, even inviting him over for an occasional dinner."

I also was informed by a relative of Bobby Kelske's that Kelske had "dealings" with other crime figures. Once in a hospital to receive treatment for his drug abuse, it was alleged that Kelske was forced to jump out of a window in order to avoid an attempt on his life. Although Kelske may have been worried for his own safety, this did not prevent him from checking up on his children. Estranged from his wife, he would often sit across the street from their home, watching them closely to make sure they were safe.

PREPARING FOR TRIAL

Hoping that Judge Signorelli would grant him the police reports, crime-scene photos, and other necessary material to prepare a real defense, William Weber submitted a supplemental omnibus motion to Jacob Siegfried's on July 22, 1975. In his five-page affirmation, Weber said, "Since affirmant has been assigned to defend the defendant only two weeks ago, and prior defense counsel being unavailable to turn over his file or to discuss this case, it is respectfully requested that the court consider these facts in determining the various requests for relief herein."

Assistant District Attorney Gerard Sullivan, and his superiors, opposed Weber's new omnibus motion, citing, " . . . the notice of motion seek matters which appear to have been already moved for and denied by Judge Jones in . . . his March 11, 1975 decision."

On August 1, 1975, Weber got the break he was looking for when Judge Signorelli ruled in his favor, granting him copies of all photographs, the names and addresses of all prosecution witnesses, and the approval of a preliminary hearing prior to the jury trial beginning. In addition, Weber received a set of laboratory reports.

In his ruling, Judge Signorelli also precluded Sullivan from entering into evidence any additional oral statements made by the defendant, the right for Weber to hire a private investigator at the county's expense, and the ability for the defendant "to order transcripts of all court proceedings at county expense . . ."

Weber's request, however, for an expert criminologist and a polygraph examination of all police officers present at the time Butch made his written statement and alleged oral admissions was denied.

On September 15, 1975, the defense was struck a devastating blow when Judge Signorelli announced in a hearing, "I deem it advisable to disqualify myself from the case, and I am going to ask the administrative judge to reassign the case."

Although both the prosecution and defense originally expressed confidence in his ability to preside impartially over the case, Judge Signorelli abruptly felt his relationship with Weber had become an issue. Not wanting anything to jeopardize his bid for a surrogate court seat, Judge Signorelli resigned. It was a calculated move because on Tuesday, November 4, 1975, Judge Signorelli won his election to the surrogate court.

Nevertheless, it was clear. The powers that be in Suffolk County had threatened Judge Signorelli because he had sided with Weber on the omnibus issue and because there was a real danger that the prosecution's case could be thrown out in the upcoming preliminary hearing.

On the same day that Judge Signorelli announced his decision, Gerard Sullivan requested "an additional one-week's time to prepare for the conduct of the hearing in this case." According to Sullivan, he was behind a week because of an intervening matter. Even though he was forced off the case by Sullivan, Judge Signorelli still granted the request.

On September 18, 1975, the case went before Judge Frank L. Gates to be reassigned. According to Judge Gates, there was no available trial date in the county court, so he asked Judge Arthur Cromarty, the administrative judge for all courts in Suffolk County, to refer the case to the Criminal Term of the Supreme Court of Suffolk County.

In his book, Sullivan explained that even though he stated for the record that he had no objections against Judge Signorelli's presiding over trial, he believed everyone knew how he really felt. Sullivan also openly admitted that he had an active role behind Judge Signorelli's dismissing himself. Sullivan wrote, "But I had not finished maneuvering. I was about to engage in a time-honored strategy that defense lawyers and prosecutors have honed into an art form. Some called it 'judge shopping.'"

Sullivan helped pressure Judge Signorelli from the case in order to get the judge he wanted. His wish came true because the DeFeo case was rescheduled to begin on Monday, September 22, 1975, at 9:30 a.m., with Justice Thomas Stark—Sullivan's choice—presiding over it.

In 1994, Justice Stark was interviewed by British criminologist Christopher Berry-Dee. Regarding his interview, Berry-Dee wrote in an E-mail to me, "Shortly before the trial started, the prosecutor, ADA Gerard Sullivan, asked Judge Signorelli to remove himself from the case, which he did. In turn, and quite illegally, Sullivan handpicked Thomas M. Stark. I interviewed this judge in his office in 1994. He dismissed the matter with a wave of his hand, saying, 'In hindsight, this was quite wrong, but things were different back then.' I also spoke to Sullivan, who refused to comment on the matter."

Since 1969, Justice Thomas M. Stark had served as a Suffolk Supreme Court judge. On top of that, he had an additional six years' prior experience as a county judge. Suffolk County District Attorney Henry O'Brien agreed with his subordinate's decision that Justice Stark was the right pick for their case. The odds were now tipping even further in the prosecution's favor.

CHAPTER TEN
Impeaching the DeFeo Trial

PRIOR TO JURY selection, a preliminary hearing, originally granted by Judge Ernest Signorelli, was scheduled to begin. Its purpose was to assess the alleged statements and evidence obtained from Butch's purported confession. Weber wanted the preliminary hearing to suppress the oral admissions alleged to have been made by the defendant.

Against Weber's wishes, Butch insisted on testifying at the hearing because he wanted everybody to know the truth. Butch described his plight at the hands of the Suffolk County police to Justice Stark, who would decide if Butch's rights had been violated.

Butch told Justice Stark, "I'd say within an hour afterwards at the First Precinct, they took a paraffin test on my hands. I didn't care for that too much because I felt that I was being accused of committing this crime as soon as they did that because I knew that my family had to be shot; they already told me they were shot. Then I demanded to call my lawyer Richard Hartman, who was my attorney with another case. And they said, 'Don't worry.'"

Regarding the beatings, Butch testified about being threatened with death if he did not sign a confession. Describing Detective Harrison's threats, Butch said, "He told me I better sign this statement . . . And he told me there was three officers outside the room. He said, 'They want to come in here and kill you.' I said, 'What do you mean they want to come in here and kill me?' He said, 'They want to come in here. They are going to kill you.' He said, 'You better sign this.'"

Butch went on to describe the beatings he had suffered while in the custody of the homicide department. Detective Harrison, who was present in court, grimaced noticeably while Butch testified. Although Weber objected, Justice Stark found Detective Harrison to be conducting himself properly.

Another crucial witness for the defense was Richard Wyssling, an attorney-at-law. On the evening of November 13, 1974, Wyssling was asked by his mother-in-law, Angela Brigante's sister, to go down to Amityville to see if her sister was all right. Upon arriving, he was asked by the Brigantes to represent Butch.

At the crime scene, he was informed by Detective Randazzo that Butch was at the First Precinct in Babylon. Once at the precinct, Wyssling approached the desk and said, "I am the attorney for Ronald DeFeo. I understand he's being charged with six counts of murder."

"I presented my card and said, 'I demand to see him. And if there is any questioning at any point, I want it stopped . . . 'The patrolman or sergeant, as I say, I don't remember, called up on his intercom and told me that there was no one by the name of Ronald DeFeo there. And I said to him, 'We are not talking about a petty larceny situation. I would think that you would want to go into the back room and find out whether he's there.'

"At which point he got up, and he went to the back area, or he left me and he started walking towards the back area of the precinct. He returned in about 20 minutes, and he said, 'There is no one here by the name of Ronald DeFeo.' So I said, 'Was he ever here?' And he says, 'Well, I'm not really sure.' And I said, 'Well, if he's not here, where is he?' And they made another phone call at that point, and they, the patrolman, told me that he was at the Fourth Precinct."

After getting directions, Wyssling arrived at the Hauppauge police precinct more determined than ever not to experience another runaround.

Under oath, Wyssling recalled his experience at the Fourth Precinct, saying, "I then went to the desk, and there were two patrolman on duty. And I asked them, I told them, that I was the attorney for Ronald DeFeo. Again, I presented my business card, which is in evidence, and I told them that I wanted to see him now. And, if they were taking any testimony that I wanted it stopped."

After getting the runaround for another 20 minutes, Wyssling was again told that nobody by the name of Ronald DeFeo was there.

Wyssling continued, saying, "So at this point I think I became a little boisterous in terms of 'I demand to see him.' I said, 'You guys have pushed me around all night long, and I demand to see him now.'"

A supervising officer approached Wyssling and told him he doubted that he was an attorney. Under oath, Wyssling recalled his response, saying, "What do you want me to do, quote the law to you? And so he paused at that point, and then he left the room. He returned in 15, 20 minutes, and he said, 'Ronald DeFeo is not here.'"

Despite the response, Wyssling pressed for more information, well aware of Suffolk County's need to keep Butch DeFeo isolated. At 1:50 a.m., Wyssling gave up the futile attempt to see Butch. For evidence of his visit to the police station, Wyssling offered his phone bill showing a collect phone call to his wife made from the Fourth Precinct.

Needing to destroy Wyssling's credibility, Sullivan went on the offensive. Sullivan brought up that Wyssling harbored personal resentment toward certain personnel in the Suffolk County District Attorney's office. Furthermore, Sullivan pointed out that Wyssling had been indicted on several unrelated offenses, including perjury. But when asked if his testimony in the DeFeo case was colored by any resentment, Wyssling answered, "Absolutely and unequivocally no."

On October 1, 1975, after six days of testimony from 20 witnesses, Justice Stark issued his ruling regarding the hearing. It was no surprise that he ruled in favor of the prosecution.

In spite of the fact that during the interrogation of Butch DeFeo no tape recorder was used and no assistant district attorney was present, Justice Stark found the officers "accurate and credible."

Regarding Richard Wyssling's testimony about his conversations with the various officers at the two police precincts, Justice Stark found it "not worthy of belief."

Justice Stark said, "This witness's hostility towards and bias against the prosecuting authorities of this county was clearly evident." Wyssling's past infractions with the law, which he would later receive three-years probation for, offered Justice Stark the convenience to disregard his testimony that clearly indicated the detectives refused Butch DeFeo's right to an attorney.

With regard to Butch DeFeo's testimony, Justice Stark said in his ruling, "I find many factors which demonstrate the unworthiness and fabricated nature of this interested witness's testimony."

THE POST-HEARING CONFERENCE

Out of the approximately 7,000 pages of transcripts detailing both the preliminary hearing and trial, the post-hearing conference between Justice Stark, Gerard Sullivan and William Weber provided the most penetrating insight into the "true" details of the crime.

At the outset, in an attempt to nail Weber down on his defense, Justice Stark asked, "At this time, Mr. Weber, are you prepared to continue our discussion as to the matter of the defendant's intentions of raising the defense of mental disease or defect?"

Weber replied, "Your honor, I am not able to answer you on that point, at this time."

Still needing a definitive answer, Justice Stark continued pressing Weber on the issue. Whereas Weber replied, "Your honor, at this point, the only thing I could ask the court to consider is my application for an adjournment of the trial."

Weber went on to explain to Justice Stark his need for the 60-day adjournment. Because he had been retained as an attorney only since July, Weber needed more time to prepare his case. Although Judge Signorelli had granted Weber's omnibus motion on August 1, Weber had not received any paperwork from the district attorney until August 27.

Weber insisted, "That was the first date which I could effectively start acting in behalf of the defendant."

Weber then argued that the county's $300 allocated to him for hiring a private investigator was far too low to find a competent investigator. Weber explained to Justice Stark that this caused him a significant delay since it was not until September 22, 1975 that Herman Race was officially retained by the DeFeo estate and Michael Brigante Sr.

Regarding the laboratory reports, specifically those pertaining to the alleged clothing found in the Brooklyn sewer, Weber said, "We have determined, basically, through Mr. Race's pointing out to me certain facts, that not all laboratory reports have been turned over to me."

After hearing Weber's arguments, Justice Stark pressed prosecutor Gerard Sullivan to warrant that every report was turned over to the defense. Naturally, Sullivan insisted that the Suffolk County District Attorney's office had complied with the August 1 ruling and turned over every report.

At that point, Justice Stark asked Weber, "Well, assuming that the district attorney's office has provided you with copies of every document from the laboratory in regard to examination of these items, is there any other reason that you seek to delay the trial of this indictment?"

Weber answered, "Based upon the preliminary investigation that Mr. Race has conducted, he is prepared to testify as why he needs additional time to enable me to prepare an adequate defense."

After being granted permission to address the court, Herman Race said, "Your honor, I can say with almost a reasonable certainty there is more than one person involved in this. There is more than one gun been used. And I would say with a very reasonable certainty there is another party involved in this. When I say, 'another party,' more than one, I say, your honor."

Rather than have the public hear Race's findings, all parties agreed that it was best to clear the courtroom for the remainder of the conference. Afterward, Weber explained their position to Justice Stark. He said, "I believe that when the prosecutor asks certain good faith cross-examination questions of the witness Robert Kelske, plus the information that we have, indicates us to believe—we knew all along that no one person could possibly have committed this crime, your honor.

"I don't think there is any investigatory agent or person in the county, or anywhere, that's going to say that one person committed this crime. But based on certain questions that were asked of Mr. Kelske, which indicated the type of witness we were dealing with because we didn't get any cooperation out of him, whatsoever, when Mr. Race went over to see him.

"In fact, we got adverse cooperation, if, I could use that word, from him. That, coupled with the information that we have, plus certain inconsistencies that are in the laboratory report itself, which Mr. Race has pointed out to me, we feel that we could very well substantiate that another person engaged in this killing; yes."

Race added, "Your honor, we have very good reason to believe that all of the bodies that were found in bed were not shot in bed."

"What's the basis of that?" Justice Stark inquired.

Race responded, "The basis of that is I do find there is one and possibly two were shot in another room and put into bed. I might add, Mr. Weber has shown me quite a number of photographs, but I don't recall seeing any photographs of the floors of the other rooms, which I believe were bloodstained."

After finally being afforded an opportunity to speak, Sullivan said, "I want to first point out, Judge, that an assumption that was made by the defense that the prosecution would rely, as a theory, as it were, upon the final version of the events of that evening being given to the interrogating detectives by the defendant is an erroneous assumption."

"There is nothing inconsistent in the defendant's guilt as we will present it to the jury with a theory that an accomplice was present and, in fact, participated . . . the fact that there is no accomplice present or there is no other accomplice under arrest does not diminish the criminal liability of this defendant."

Although Sullivan agreed that it was likely that Butch DeFeo did not commit the crime alone, he argued that Butch was still liable for his involvement and pressed Justice Stark to proceed with trial.

Weber maneuvered once again. He argued that the presence of an accomplice might assist Butch in an emotional strain defense rather than a mental defect one. If an emotional strain defense was used, and successful, then the charge against Butch would be reduced from second-degree murder to first-degree manslaughter.

After hearing additional arguments from both sides, Justice Stark took a recess before issuing his ruling. Finding the reasons for the adjournment insufficient, Justice Stark denied Weber's request and ordered jury selection to commence on Monday, October 6, 1975.

After several days of jury selection, 12 jurors and four alternates were sworn in on Thursday, October 9, 1975, at 4:08 p.m. The trial portion was scheduled to begin on Tuesday, October 14, 1975.

THE OPENING STATEMENTS

Gerard Sullivan was first to address the jury with his opening statements, which would later prove somewhat contradictory to the case he presented, and, subsequently, wanted the jury to buy.

Offering an explanation of the proceedings to the jury, Sullivan said, "The law requires that the prosecution render an opening statement to the jury for the purpose of making known what it intends to prove in support of each and every count of the indictment against this defendant. It is meant to give you a broad outline, a preliminary view of what will be proven by the evidence upon the people's case.

"Ladies and gentlemen of the jury, each of you will be changed to some degree by this case. You will leave this courtroom after rendering a verdict, perhaps a month from now, carrying with you an abiding memory of the horror that occurred in that house at 112

Ocean Avenue in the dead of night 11 months ago."

Referencing the murders, Sullivan said, "I tell you now that although the people will prove beyond a reasonable doubt that each of these six human beings were murdered in their bedrooms between 2:00 and 4:00 a.m. on November 13, 1974, when all evidence in this case is known to you there will still be unanswered questions as to certain details as to what went on that house that night."

Concerning Butch DeFeo, Sullivan explained, "On Tuesday, November 12, 1974, Ronald DeFeo Jr. didn't go to work ostensibly by reason of stomach pains. The people will offer proof that on that day the defendant's relationship with his parents, and particularly with his father, had so deteriorated that that day, November 12, was a day of climax."

Contradicting himself, Sullivan suggested, "that sometime after 3:00 a.m., on November 13th, Ronald DeFeo pointed the death weapon at his father's back and fired it . . . and there is no definite proof as to where precisely Ronald DeFeo Sr. was at that point in time his son fired the first shot into his back."

Sullivan even explained how the trajectories of each bullet in Big Ronnie were different. Because of this and other evidence, Sullivan told the jury that they may "conclude that this defendant first shot his father after he had gotten up from his bed, and thereafter, the body of his father was placed back into bed to be found later by the police."

Obviously, Sullivan neglected to mention that Big Ronnie weighed 270 pounds, which would have resulted in Butch's needing assistance to put his father's body back into bed.

Sullivan's description of the murders continued with the killing of Louise. Moving onto Allison, he told the jury how after Butch had shot his sister, he ejected the spent cartridge into a pool of her blood. Regarding Marc and John DeFeo, Sullivan said, "We will offer evidence that Marc, the 11-year-old boy, suffered from a football injury to his hip and could only move about with a wheelchair or crutches, and that the same injury limited his ability to move about in his bed. He needed assistance to turn over in his bed, and, indeed, was most likely to have slept on his back. When this corpse was found by the police, he lay on his stomach, his head buried in a pillow. Ronald DeFeo fired almost point blank into the boys' backs from a position standing alongside, somewhat to the rear of their beds."

Sullivan continued with his description of Butch's killing his sister Dawn, and then his attempt to conceal and discard incriminating evidence, including dumping the pillowcases into the sewer in Brooklyn. Regardless, the most baffling statement Sullivan made was regarding what Butch allegedly told his interrogators.

Sullivan said, "You will learn that ultimately DeFeo never did tell the complete truth to the police. After hearing all the evidence in this case, you will find that the failure to ever relate a complete truthful account of the killing requires us to rely upon the other independent evidence in the case to fill the voids . . ."

In contrast to Sullivan's opening statement, Weber's was extremely short. Weber first reminded the jury that nothing he or Sullivan said in their openings could be considered evidence, and that the burden of proof rested on the prosecution and not the defense. He suggested that the statements were more or less of a bird's eye picture of what this long and lengthy trial was going to be about.

Weber said, "The evidence that Mr. Sullivan told you he was going to produce, admittedly, came as a result of certain alleged oral statements made by Ronald DeFeo approximately 20 to 30 hours after he was held by the police in custody, intentionally deprived from seeing or speaking to any members of his family; intentionally deprived from consulting with an attorney; intentionally deprived, in essence, of his constitutional rights."

Throughout the DeFeo trial, William Weber pursued a twofold strategy: prove Butch's constitutional rights were violated and have the jury find Butch not guilty by reason of insanity. Interestingly enough, Weber never even touched upon the insanity issue in his opening.

THE PROSECUTION'S STAR WITNESS

There was no doubt about it. Detective Dennis Rafferty was the prosecution's chief witness. After all, he was the detective credited with eliciting a confession from Butch DeFeo. In order to sell the jury on the alleged oral confession made by Butch DeFeo to Detective Rafferty, a reason had to be concocted as to why Butch DeFeo, who was supposedly very cooperative with the police, would not sign a written confession.

When questioned why he had not been able to get Butch to sign a written confession, Detective Rafferty said, "I asked him if he would reduce that to writing, if we could take the whole statement, and put it in writing, and he said, 'No.' I said, 'Why not?' And he said, 'Because if I put that in writing, my grandfather will see it.'"

The severity of the crimes Butch was alleged to have committed dictated that at least an assistant district attorney should have been present during the questioning. Weber pointed out this blunder, when he asked Detective Rafferty, "At any time during the six and a half hour period of questioning, Detective, did you ever call for an assistant district attorney to be present in that room?"

Detective Rafferty responded, "No, sir, I did not."

Weber pressed, "Did you ever ask for a stenographer to be present in the room."

"No, sir, I did not."

"Did you ever take any notes as you were questioning Ronnie?"

"No, not while I was questioning him."

After comparing Detective Rafferty's testimony given at the preliminary hearing and the trial, it became evident that the police and the prosecution had not ironed out all of the details of their stories.

During the trial, Gerard Sullivan would allege that Butch got the bruises on his face not while he was in police custody, but, rather, from a fistfight with his father two days before the murders. This was in light of the fact that all of the defense witnesses testified that Butch never hit his father even in the face of extreme adversity.

At trial, Weber exploited the prosecution's mistake when he asked Detective Rafferty whether he noticed any marks on Butch's face during the interrogation.

Weber asked, "Did he have any marks on his face at this time?"

"Not that I can recall. No, sir," Detective Rafferty answered.

In fact, every other police officer who came in contact with Butch testified that they also had not recalled seeing marks on his face. It was not until November 18, 1974 that a jailhouse exam discovered that Butch had suffered a brutal beating of some sort, which the detectives obviously had given him.

Another crucial prosecution witness was Detective Rafferty's interrogation partner, Detective Lieutenant Robert Dunn. Like Detective Rafferty, Detective Dunn failed to take any notes of the intense and lengthy interrogation. In fact, at one point, Weber tested the officer's memory by asking a simple question.

Weber asked, "What, if anything, do you recall Ronald to be wearing during this interview?"

Detective Dunn answered, "Well, my recollection is casually dressed. It could have been dungarees. It could have been something — I'd have to say casual. I'd have to describe it as casual dress, very casual dress. Work clothes, semi-work clothes, something like that."

However, regarding the needle mark on Butch's arm, Detective Dunn found it to be on the wrong arm for a dope addict. Something he considered "extraordinary."

During their interrogation of Butch DeFeo, Detectives Rafferty and Dunn had allegedly asked Butch DeFeo to cooperate with them by drawing diagrams of 112 Ocean Avenue. Of course, they insisted that Butch DeFeo cooperated, even though there is evidence indicating Butch may not have drawn any diagrams, but only initialed them after he was beaten.

For obvious reasons, Detective Dunn stated under direct examination by Gerard Sullivan that he was never in 112 Ocean Avenue.

On cross-examination, Weber asked Detective Dunn, "Is it your testimony that you were at the crime scene for three hours and at no time did you ever enter the DeFeo residence or the Ireland residence?"

Detective Dunn responded, "That's absolutely correct, Mr. Weber. Never entered either one."

Weber went for the kill. He pointed out to Detective Dunn that Officer Kenneth Greguski had recorded his entering the DeFeo residence at 8:50 p.m. on the night of November 13, 1974. In fact, in his own testimony elicited earlier, Officer Greguski was asked by Weber if he had "personally observed all of these individuals coming in at the hours indicated [on his log]?"

"Yes, sir, I did," Officer Greguski replied.

Detective Dunn was caught in a lie as it became increasingly evident that he had the motive and means to draw the diagrams himself.

Incredibly, Detective Dunn testified that prior to the interrogation ending, he had left before Butch DeFeo had made the alleged confession. Weber asked, "Did you hear Ronald DeFeo state during the interview that he committed the crime?"

"No, I did not," Detective Dunn answered.

Weber delivered his final blow to the interrogating team's testimony when he put Frank Boyd on the stand to discuss his own experience with the detectives. Boyd testified that Detective Rafferty told him, "If you tell me one thing, I'll let you go home in 15 minutes. Tell me, didn't Butch DeFeo tell you he was going to kill his whole family?" Refusing to sell out Butch, Boyd turned down the offer. Sullivan, nevertheless, was outraged at Weber's line of questioning.

FACT VS. FABRICATION

At the DeFeo trial, and later in Gerard Sullivan's book, it had been alleged that Dawn DeFeo's alarm clock had been ringing when the police arrived. Detective Gaspar Randazzo described, under oath, Dawn's room. He said, "The alarm clock was on the night table. It was still going. It was set to 7:15 a.m."

Weber did an excellent job of pointing out that Detective Randazzo was either lying or confused. During his testimony, Detective Randazzo erroneously stated that he was the one who led Butch DeFeo and Bobby Kelske to the kitchen. Once more, Amityville Police Officer Kenneth Greguski's testimony and report

Butch DeFeo's bedroom (above).
Two gunboxes discovered in Butch's room, according to the police, caused detectives to view Butch as a suspect. Butch claimed the boxes were in his closet and not where they were later photographed.

```
2000 HRS.    DR. ADELMAN      M.E. OFFICE
2030 HRS.    D.C. INSP. CAPLES + INSP. SHERIDAN
2035 HRS.    INSP. DOPP
2050 HRS.    DET. LT. DUNN    ORG. CRIME UNIT
2125 HRS.    DET. FITZGIBBON  #216  LAB UNIT
2128 HRS.    DR. FLEMING      DEP. M.E.
2155 HRS.    Following men present at scene from Special Investigation Service
             DET. GENNING     #371
             DET. VOGUL       #556
             DET. SGT. LEE    #375
2204 HRS.    Following men present from M.E's OFFICE
             RODRIGUEZ        #2
             ED FRANK                          WAGON #'s 774, 775
             MORRIS           #65
2220 HRS.    DET. DAGUANNO    #628   I.D. UNIT
2226 HRS.    CAPT. PROBECK            I.D. UNIT
2236 HRS.    INSP. W. MCBRIDE   Commander 1st P.T.
2240 HRS.    P.O.'s CARROLL #2691, BALFOUR #2601, REGULA #1581.
2305 HRS.    MR. BILL MCKEAN: REP. FROM COMM. KELLY'S OFFICE, Also MR. GINAS
```

Two crucial documents to the author's investigation: Officer Greguski's police report (above) and Herman Race's testimony (below).

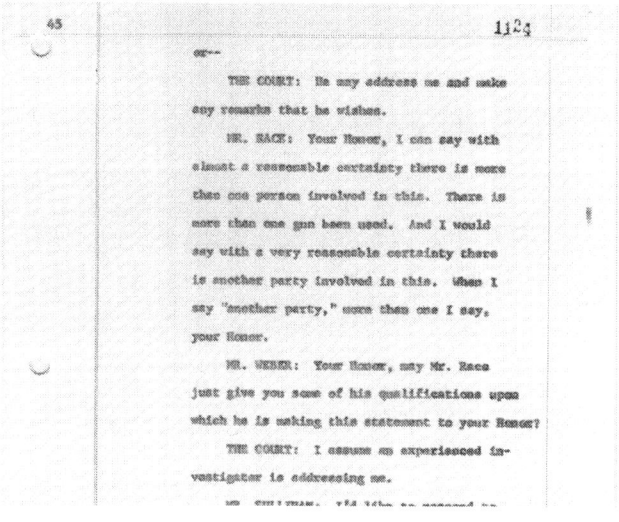

Chapter Ten

proved otherwise.

Weber also made it a point to impeach Detective Randazzo's testimony by comparing it with his testimony from the preliminary hearing. In other words, Weber pointed out to the jury that Detective Randazzo had given an entirely different version when he testified at the preliminary hearing in September.

Going back to the alarm clock, Amityville Police Officer Kenneth Greguski, who was the first police officer on the scene, noted nothing about a ringing alarm clock in his report.

Regarding the discovery of Dawn DeFeo, Officer Greguski wrote, "Upon checking the third floor of the house, reporting officer found another female lying in bed face down, and she also had apparently been shot."

When asked under oath if he had heard an alarm clock when he was in the house with the other bar patrons, Bobby Kelske answered, "No, not that I remember."

Another item Kelske testified about was the rifle boxes, which led the police to suspect Butch's rifle was the murder weapon. The homicide detectives stated the boxes were discovered in a small alcove in Butch's room on November 14, 1974. According to detectives, it was this discovery that caused them to focus on Butch DeFeo as a suspect.

Butch, however, insisted that he would not have forgotten to discard them if they were not in his closet. Weber, wanting to establish this fact, asked Kelske, "Had you observed guns in the bedroom?"

Kelske replied, "Yes."

"Where did you observe these guns?"

"They were hung up on a wall."

Pointing to the rifle boxes on the evidence table, Weber asked, "Did you ever observe these boxes in Ronnie's bedroom?"

"No," Kelske said.

Incredibly, several detectives testified that Butch DeFeo's room was not considered part of the crime scene until the next day, even though a spoon with residue was found in Butch DeFeo's dresser and entered into evidence on the evening of November 13, 1974.

This was in addition to the fact that the rest of the guns in Butch's room were examined that evening to determine if any of them had been used in the commission of the crime.

It was an absurdity that the detectives were arguing that Butch's room was not part of the crime scene during the initial hours of the investigation. To illustrate his point that everything and every room in the DeFeo household was considered part of the crime scene, Weber produced a crime-scene photograph taken on November 13th showing a fiber on the kitchen floor. Regrettably, Weber's implication that the detectives had taken out the rifle boxes from Butch's closet and had lied under oath fell on deaf ears.

With regard to Butch's face, Bobby Kelske stated that during the day on November 13, 1974, he had seen no unusual markings on Butch DeFeo's face. Kelske also testified about being taken into police custody from the Ireland's house.

Kelske said, "They called me over by the car, and I think Detective Caples was there. And they said, 'We want to talk to you. Will you take a ride with us down to the precinct? We want to ask you some questions,' or something. And I got in the car with Detective Harrison, and we took a ride down to the First Precinct."

Like Butch, once at the precinct, Kelske received a paraffin test. Because of this, Weber wanted to establish for the jury that by that time on November 13, 1974, both Butch DeFeo and Bobby Kelske were the prime suspects. If he could impeach the detectives' testimony that Butch was not a suspect until November 14, then Weber had a good chance of impeaching the alleged confession as well.

Seeing where Weber was heading, Justice Stark said, "All right, I'm going to require you to step up to the bench and advise me of the nature of this potential testimony."

Weber explained, "Your honor, the nature of this testimony to be elicited will show that at this point the police were accusing both the defendant and Kelske of giving inconsistent statements."

Not wanting the jury to hear Weber's comments, Sullivan quickly interjected, "Keep your voice down."

As usual, Justice Stark ruled in the prosecution's favor. According to Justice Stark, he ruled that Bobby Kelske's testimony could not be elicited if he did not know the name of the detective who questioned him. Justice Stark said, "Unless you are able to pin this down to a particular police officer, the most I could permit would be Kelske's testimony as to what he, Kelske, said to some police officer."

After a few minutes of recounting his experience, Bobby Kelske said, "He [the detective] came in there, and he said, "One of you two — ."

Objecting, Sullivan quickly cut off Kelske's answer.

After Bobby Kelske was admonished for not following Justice Stark's ruling, he was asked again to repeat only what he said to the detectives.

Kelske replied, "I told him to go fuck yourself."

If Kelske had been permitted to finish, the jury would have heard him recount what the detective had said to him: "One of you two sons of bitches are going to confess."

But as much as Bobby Kelske tried to help Butch, even testifying falsely that Butch was often irrational, Kelske also damaged the defense's case.

In *High Hopes*, Sullivan wrote, "When we reopened the investigation, Kelske and another man were under indictment for promoting gambling. It was a penny-ante sports-betting operation, but it was enough so that at one point, we considered offering Kelske a deal. However, we never had to. Kelske would testify for the defense at the trial, but he would help me more than he would Weber."

During his interrogation, Kelske had helped the police because, according to Butch, he had been threatened with jail time. Kelske not only told the police that Butch had masterminded a break-in robbery at his grandfather's dealership, but he also told them that a few months before the murders, Butch had been interested in finding a silencer. Since everything Bobby Kelske had told the police about Butch surfaced at the trial, these comments would later, according to Butch, "hang him."

In fact, after the trial, Kelske had nothing further to do with Butch and Geraldine DeFeo. On one occasion in Manhattan, Geraldine approached Bobby Kelske, whom she had encountered unexpectedly in the street.

Geraldine said, "I went to Bobby and said hi, and I was almost floored by his response. He told me that he didn't know me. At first, I thought Bobby was just kidding around, but he repeatedly insisted that he had never met me in his life. He even ignored my daughter, who was quite fond of him and who was pulling on his pant leg."

Geraldine's claims were later verified by a relative of Bobby Kelske's, who confirmed the story, saying Kelske had spoken of the encounter. Since he was afraid of reprisals from the Suffolk County police, Kelske made it a point never to discuss the DeFeo murders ever again.

Testimony about the break-in robbery at the Buick dealership added further credibility to Sullivan's motive, which, it seemed, he concocted himself. At the outset, Sullivan knew he needed a concrete motive. Thus, he implied that Butch had killed his family over money.

By bringing up Butch's past conviction of grand larceny, Sullivan was able to marry the two together. Sullivan would theorize that valuables and at least $100,000 were kept in a box located in a secret hiding place underneath the sill of Big Ronnie's closet.

Sullivan said, "Members of the jury, people don't make hiding places like that to keep some insurance papers or some letters, or a few hundred dollars. But I do suggest that it supports an inference that there was a great deal of money, something very valuable kept in that box."

Not only was Sullivan's theory flawed, but Sullivan was well aware that it was inaccurate. First, it would practically be impossible to store "several hundreds of thousands of dollars" in the box because it was much too small. Next, the box, which was found free of any fingerprints, had the key taped to the top of it. So why would Big Ronnie tape a key to the top of it, if there were money and valuables inside it?

Furthermore, there was an additional envelope found in the master bedroom that contained several hundreds of dollars in cash. And if Butch was so interested in killing his entire family for money,

Chapter Ten

then why only a few days after the killing did he grant full control of the estate to his grandfathers? Not to mention, he would eventually renounce all of his rights to the estate.

At the DeFeo trial, Detective Gerard Gozaloff recalled for the jury his discussion with Butch regarding insurance money after Butch had already allegedly confessed. Detective Gozaloff said, "At this time he asked me did I think that he could collect insurance. There was about 60 or $70,000 worth."

Sullivan asked, "What did you reply?"

"I told him I didn't know, that I didn't think so, but that if he was crazy that he might be able to collect it," Gozaloff explained.

Gozaloff's testimony, however, was the complete opposite of Detective Sergeant James Barylski's. At the preliminary hearing, Detective Barylski recalled having the same conversation with Butch DeFeo in the presence of Detectives Harrison and Gozaloff.

Detective Barylski said, "I asked him at that particular time, I said, 'Ronnie, do you know how much insurance there is on your mother and father?' And he said, 'About 60 or $70,000 worth.' I says, 'Well, you know, you are never going to be able to collect it.' He says, 'Well, why not?' I said, 'If you are found guilty of a crime whereas you may be a beneficiary in an insurance policy, you cannot collect.' He then says, 'Well, if I'm found not guilty, can I get the money?' I said, 'Yeah, you will probably have to sue for it, but you would get it.'"

But the most definitive evidence to discredit the prosecution's theory that valuables and money were the reason for the murders comes from a bank safe deposit inventory made after the murders for the DeFeo estate. The DeFeo family's jewelry collection, which totaled more than $10,000, was kept in a safe deposit box in a bank. Furthermore, the estate inventory showed that the DeFeos had had several checking and savings accounts that were worth several thousands of dollars.

But it was clear that Gerard Sullivan did not want the jury to know that none of the jewelry was missing. Before Weber could elicit the testimony from Roger Nonnewitz, who was prepared to prove this, Weber was called up to the bench by Justice Stark.

Weber explained to Justice Stark, "Your honor, on this Sunday, members of the district attorney's office, or some detectives, made an appointment with the Nonnewitzes to go examine the jewelry that was taken out of the safety deposit box and the jewelry that was taken out of the house in order to determine whether or not any jewelry was missing. And the detectives cancelled the appointment."

Incredibly, Justice Stark asked, "I want to find out what the relevancy of this is."

Taken back, Weber replied, "The relevancy?"

"Yes. To what issue in the case does it go?"

"The motive of robbery."

After a few minutes of debating, Justice Stark once more ruled in the prosecution's favor. Out of the entire trial, it probably was the clearest example of favoritism exhibited for the prosecution's case.

In his ruling to Weber, Justice Stark said, "Based upon the statement made at the bench, I'm satisfied that the witness cannot give any relevant testimony on a particular issue. You may withdraw him."

The next obstacle that the prosecution had to overcome was the fact that Butch had been brutalized while he was in police custody. To combat this, the prosecution found John Donahue, a 10-year-old who was purportedly friends with John DeFeo.

Sullivan made it a point to insist that Donahue wore his school uniform while he testified in order to present a more sympathetic picture to the jury. Beginning his questioning, Sullivan asked the boy when he had last seen John DeFeo.

Donahue replied, "On Monday."

"What Monday was that?" Sullivan asked.

"I don't remember," the boy replied.

Leading his witness, Sullivan said, "Was it the Monday before he died?"

Donahue replied, "Yes."

Donahue went on to testify that he saw Big Ronnie hit Butch, in the mouth, in the basement, during a heated argument. In spite of the fact that on the witness stand none of the police officers could recall seeing any marks on Butch's face prior to his interrogation,

Chapter Ten

Sullivan now claimed that any bruises Butch had sustained resulted from the fistfight with his father that Donahue allegedly had witnessed.

Regarding Donahue's testimony, Weber told the jury, "Boys of that age are very, very open to suggestion. Well, what happened? Well, back at the hearing, young John testified, initially, he said he was on the top step. But when I asked him to draw the mark at the hearing as to what step he was on, he said he was on the third step. Then I said, 'John, where did the fight occur? Can you draw a mark on the diagram?' This was back at the hearing. And he drew a mark over here.

"Now, Mr. Sullivan knew as well as I know, and I was about to prove to you if it became necessary, that just by looking at these photographs, the steep steps, the low ceiling, it was impossible for that boy to have seen a fight.

"So, what happens now? He comes in during the trial, the morning before, and he spent time up at the district attorney's office. And he told the district attorney that the fight happened near the couch. You heard him say on direct examination the fight happened near the couch. But when the district attorney shows him a picture that, in my opinion, obviously, he had to have been shown this before, he puts a mark as to where the incident occurred: nowhere near the couch, which is on the other side of this wall. But more so than putting the mark on this picture, I showed him the very same diagram that I showed him in September. And I said, 'John, will you put a mark on the stairs that you were on when you say you saw the fight?'

"And now he's down to the fifth or sixth step. He started out at the first. He then marked third. And now, here in November, he is down to the fifth or sixth step."

The final blow to the credibility of Donahue's testimony came from Lucy Burkin's testimony. Burkin, who worked for Brigante-Karl Buick, testified that both Big Ronnie and Butch had left work amicably on the Monday prior to the murders at 5:45 p.m. By the time they got home, John Donahue would have returned to his own home. Therefore, he could have never witnessed a fistfight in the basement between Big Ronnie and Butch.

Sullivan, nevertheless, was not through. He also put a corrupt cop by the name of Bortan "Burt" Borkan on the stand. Borkan, who allegedly had been friends with Big Ronnie, had said he had heard Butch make a death threat against his father only days before the murders. Big Ronnie evidently told Borkan that his son was "a devil on his back." In his book, Sullivan wrote that Borkan "made no secret of his disdain for Ronald Jr."

When asked if his father had ever said that he had a devil on his back, Butch DeFeo said, "I have never heard my father say that in his life, to me or to anybody else."

Regarding Borkan, Weber told the jury, "Doesn't it make you wonder why Burt Borkan turns around on that one issue to help the district attorney, nearly a year after the incident, never told anybody about it, but now at a time when he's in trouble before the Brooklyn Grand Jury, he volunteers this information to Mr. Sullivan after speaking with Detective Rafferty."

Even Sullivan admitted to the jury that Borkan was a "dirty cop." Moreover, Borkan was quoted as saying in the November 15, 1974 issue of *Newsday* that Butch "was like any kid today. They want to be on their own." It is doubtful that Borkan ever heard Butch threaten his father or saw any bruises on Butch's face, especially since Borkan was obviously trying to gain favor in his own case.

Additionally, it came out at the DeFeo trial the timecards for Brigante-Karl Buick for the week of the DeFeo murders had been confiscated by the police. Not only would these have substantiated the fact that John Donahue's testimony was fabricated by the prosecution, but also show that on November 13, 1974 Butch left work around 3:00 p.m., and not 1:00 p.m. as the police stated.

In fact, *The New York Times* reported on November 15, 1974 that "Mr. DeFeo Sr. reported for work on Tuesday morning [November 12] along with his son Ronald Jr." The sources, according to the article, were several associates and employees from the dealership.

To support his theory about the motive, Gerard Sullivan insisted that Big Ronnie had left work early on November 12, 1974, to confront Butch about the phony robbery. Yet Michael Brigante Jr., Big Ronnie's boss, testified differently. He said, "He [Big Ronnie] was telling me that he was going home; that he felt the family was in danger of being killed."

In her testimony, Lucy Burkin, a cashier at Brigante-Karl Buick dealership, also verified that Big Ronnie, her supervisor, had told her that he had been receiving threatening phone calls and that he was worried. Furthermore, when asked if Big Ronnie had ever told her that he thought Butch had committed the robbery, Burkin replied, "No."

Although Big Ronnie was known to be paranoid and delusional, even believing he had the gift of E.S.P., there may have been some merit to his claims.

At 11:30 p.m., on November 13, 1974, Nassau County Police Officer William Cotumaccio, shield #2540, received a phone call while on desk duty at the Eighth Precinct. The caller, who refused to identify himself, stated that on November 12, 1974, he was at a bar in North Massapequa and was told by someone that he was going to kill the "whole DeFeo family." Although the Suffolk County Police apparently had several leads on the person who allegedly made the threat, there was no other information in the report except that this individual possibly had ties to Big Ronnie. This report, combined with Burkin and Brigante's testimony, lent credence to the fact that Big Ronnie was, indeed, threatened by individuals outside his family.

One of the most difficult hurdles for the defense was the alleged diagrams that Butch DeFeo purportedly had drawn of where he had discarded the Marlin rifle. To this day, Butch insists that he did not know where Bobby Kelske had discarded the rifle.

Regarding the diagrams, much of the testimony given by the police officers seems to contradict the fact that Butch DeFeo had drawn any diagrams, even though he may have been physically forced later to initial some.

In fact, Nassau County Scuba Diver Melvin Berger, the diver who recovered the Marlin rifle, testified about the alleged diagrams.

He recalled that the Suffolk County police were "drawing them on the Suffolk County Marine boat."

Even James Caples Jr., the Suffolk County Deputy Chief of Organized Crime Control Bureau, who was responsible for the crime scene, testified differently than Gerard Sullivan probably would have liked. When asked why on November 15, 1974, he had moved the search from behind the DeFeo house to the Ocean Avenue/Richmond dock, Caples explained it was because the lead Nassau County diver told him they had only one hour of air remaining.

Caples explained, "I then asked him if he would proceed back to the Ocean Avenue dock where we had searched the day before. He informed me he would."

Yet Sullivan not only wanted the jury to make a giant leap of faith, but he also needed to repair the damage done by Berger's testimony. In his book, Sullivan explained, "The source of the confusion was that Butch DeFeo had made two diagrams showing where he dumped the rifle. He drew the first for Rafferty and Dunn, and it was right on target. Later on, however, in an apparent attempt to mislead detectives, DeFeo made a second diagram, changing the location to the canal behind his home."

Expanding on this idea, Sullivan asked Caples if he compared the "correct" diagram that Butch allegedly had drawn with the location at which the divers recovered the rifle. Caples said, "The result of the comparison was that it was the approximate location where the weapon was found . . ."

But Weber was not about to give up so easily. He asked Caples, "Before they went into the water, do you recall any particular diagram having been shown to the divers?"

"No, sir, I do not," Caples answered.

In contrast, diver Melvin Berger testified earlier that a piece of scrap paper was shown to him prior to entering the water behind the DeFeo house. According to Berger, it was the only diagram he ever saw.

Therefore, it is safe to say that Berger's recollection about the diagrams being drawn on the police boat was accurate. After all, the divers had been in the cold waters since 8:30 a.m. And the gun, however, was not located until 11:48 a.m.

THE INSANITY PLOY AND ITS FAILINGS

At the hearing, Justice Stark had ruled that the alleged confession that Butch DeFeo had given to Detective Dennis Rafferty during his interrogation was admissible. He also denied Weber a much needed adjournment to prepare a better case. Thus, Butch was left with no other recourse but to participate in the insanity defense.

The only way that the defense had any chance to convince the jury that Butch was insane was through testimony of his closest friends. Many years later, these same friends would recant their testimony, admitting they had committed perjury under the direction of William Weber.

Frank Davidge, who had known Butch since he moved to Amityville in 1965, falsely testified about supposed irrational events that Butch committed, one of which was a hunting trip that took place in November 1972.

Describing the experience, Davidge said, "And [Butch] was looking in my direction, and he had the gun in his hands pointing in my direction . . . I saw the gun pointing directly at me. I stepped back about two feet, and I was behind a tree, and I heard three shots. And one of the shots had gone by me so close that I could see the branches of the tree falling."

Frank Davidge, excited about the incident, claimed in court that Butch did not remember even shooting at him and explained it was an irrational act.

The more irrational the acts that defense witnesses could present to the jury, the more likely Butch would be judged insane. Davidge went on to testify about a supposed event that took place in Butch's room in spring 1973.

Davidge recalled, "As soon as I turned around, he had a gun pointed right at my head . . . And as soon as I turned around, I saw the gun, and he pulled the trigger, and the gun went click."

Adding to the fabrications, Chuck Tewksbury testified about an incident that allegedly happened at Mindy Weiss's house. He said, "We were there for about, I don't know, five minutes, and, I don't know, Ronnie just, I don't know, kind of started throwing people around and stuff."

When asked if the act was rational or irrational, Tewksbury stated it was "irrational."

Completing the picture was Mindy Weiss, Butch's one-time mistress. She also testified about the so-called irrational acts that Butch had committed, including starting fights and insisting that he was paranoid because he thought that even his own friends were out to get him.

The fabricated timeframe that the defense used was that Butch had seen Bobby Kelske first at about 1:00 p.m. and then again at 3:00 p.m. on the afternoon of November 13. Weiss, however, testified that Butch was with her from 1:00 p.m. until 4:00 p.m. that day.

In reality, Butch had not even seen Weiss on the afternoon of November 13, 1974. Lucy Burkin testified that Butch DeFeo had called his home from her office at the Buick dealership at 2:30 p.m. on November 13. This accurate timeframe was substantiated earlier by Vito D'Iorio in his statement to the police.

Regardless, several times during her testimony, Weber requested time to "confer" with Mindy Weiss in a separate area of the courtroom. It was an obvious coaching session.

During his cross-examination of Weiss, Sullivan asked her about the time she had exposed her breasts once at a bar she had worked in. Weber, outraged, asked for a "good faith" hearing on Sullivan's ethics.

Once again Justice Stark ruled in Sullivan's favor, and Weiss was forced to testify about the incident, which served to discredit her. The way Sullivan belittled Weiss made it appear that he had actually enjoyed embarrassing the girl on the stand.

During Roger and Linnea Nonnewitz's testimony, Roger covered Big Ronnie's E.S.P. and fortunetelling abilities, saying, "And I don't exactly know word for word how it started, but as in other occasions, Ronnie Sr. started making statements that had my wife

Chapter Ten

crying and getting hysterical over the things of the world is coming to an end again bit. And this constant thing that he had of telling people's fortunes or looking into the future."

Like so many others had done, Linnea's testimony pointed out that Butch DeFeo never hit his father, even in self-defense, or struck his brothers and sisters. Furthermore, she testified that Butch was not lazy and would help her routinely with the housekeeping work. To counter the prosecution's assertions that Butch DeFeo was not capable of showing real emotion, Linnea said under oath that Butch showed real sympathy when her dog died, telling her, "Lin, I'm sorry."

It was during Linnea Nonnewitz's testimony that Gerard Sullivan lost it. Because Linnea was unresponsive with her answers, Sullivan, flabbergasted, said, "Judge, I can't proceed under these circumstances."

After Justice Stark admonished him for throwing a fit, Sullivan said, "The witness does not want to be questioned, and I don't know how I can put questions to her and get a responsive answer. If I can be shown this, I am willing to learn."

The one item, however, that the Nonnewitzes wanted to testify about was when Detective Rafferty came to their house wanting to know if Butch DeFeo had ever owned a .38-caliber pistol. Linnea said in a later affidavit, "William Weber at the trial did not pursue this issue as it was very important and he only briefly made mention of it."

The psychiatrist retained by the defense, Dr. Daniel Schwartz, testified that Butch, who he claimed was unable to deal with the anger he had for his father in a proper way, was acting under a paranoid delusion at the time of the murders.

However, the prosecution's psychiatrist, Dr. Harold Zolan, saw through Butch's act. Instead of characterizing Butch as being insane, Dr. Zolan labeled Butch DeFeo "an antisocial personality."

To combat Weber's insanity strategy, Gerard Sullivan called Phyllis Procita, Big Ronnie's sister and Butch's aunt, to testify.

Procita stated that Butch had told her many versions of the events of November 13, 1974, including that he had spent time cleaning up the mess and had help from his friends.

Procita said, "Once he said that Bobby Kelske killed them, and I shouldn't trust him and I should keep my children out of Amityville. Another time, he blamed a Mr. Degenaro. He said to me he was a real tough guy. Another time he said that his father was shot in the hall and he had to carry him to bed. I asked him another time if he would cover up for somebody and take the rap himself. And he said, 'Why not? What makes you think I'm not covering up for someone in the family?' His sister Dawn."

Interesting enough, Phyllis Procita brought out that her father, Rocco DeFeo, could not "understand how one person could do this." On that point, Rocco DeFeo and Michael Brigante Sr. agreed. Brigante also testified that he did not believe his grandson had committed the crime alone.

On cross-examination, Weber tried to connect the fabricated shotgun incident, where Butch allegedly had tried to kill his father, with Big Ronnie's religious fervor. Procita, however, explained that the real reason for her brother's finding religion went back to 1970, three years before the entire mythical shotgun incident had occurred.

Procita said, "My brother went on vacation. He went to St. Joseph's Oratory. When he first saw the Oratory, he thought it was a big waste of money; all of this money used in such a splendid building, you know, where it could be used elsewhere. He came home and he read the life of Brother Andre, who started this building, and he was very impressed. And he sent a contribution to the Oratory. They invited him up to the Oratory, and he got great devotion to St. Joseph after that."

Regarding Weber's assertions that Butch was not drafted into the army because he was insane, Procita countered that Michael Brigante Sr. and her brother had paid for her nephew to be kept out.

BUTCH TAKES THE STAND

During the hearing, Michael Brigante Sr. asked permission to kiss Butch. In comical fashion, the prosecution team raced to the rear of the courtroom since they were unsure what Brigante would do to his grandson.

After being granted permission to hug each other, the two men embraced warmly. Brigante asked his grandson to "tell the truth," to which Butch allegedly replied, "Don't worry, grandpa." Later in his book, however, Gerard Sullivan suggested that Butch said, "The truth will get me life."

Forced to feign insanity, Butch DeFeo soon found that his own testimony hurt him more than anything else. In fact, the testimony he gave at the hearing prior to jury selection was much different from what was presented in front of the jury.

At the hearing, most of Butch's testimony had to deal with his plight in the hands of the Suffolk County Police Department. At the trial, though, he began the insanity act he had been practicing.

Regardless, many interesting pieces of testimony came out in both the direct questioning and cross-examination of Butch DeFeo, such as:

1. His poor eyesight, which was verified by his aunt Phyllis.
2. His problem of holding a job, which Sullivan later countered by producing his past employers who said Butch was a good worker.
3. His thievery at his aunt's pharmacy.
4. Dawn's constant fights with Big Ronnie.
5. The fake holdup that Butch had orchestrated prior to the murders.
6. His father's embezzling.
7. And, of course, the beatings he had suffered during his interrogation.

While in the Suffolk County jail, Butch would often talk about hearing voices, sit on the ledge in his cell, and, for no reason, enter into a crazed stupor. It was method-acting at its worst.

At trial, Butch testified that he heard voices all the time. Butch said, "Well, a lot of times I heard somebody calling my name. You know, I looked around, there would be nobody there . . . To be quite honest, I believed it was God. There was nobody else there. That's who I believe it was."

Later, during an interview with parapsychologist Hans Holzer in 1979, Butch admitted it was all an act in order to try to convince the psychiatrist he was insane.

Under direct examination from Weber about the murders, Butch said, "All I know is somebody was standing there with a rifle in their hands, and the hands that the person had were black."

"Ronnie, who was that person," Weber asked.

"I thought it was my sister," Butch replied.

Under cross-examination by Gerard Sullivan about the person with the black hands, Butch added theatrics, saying, "It didn't leave. It disappeared."

Sullivan countered, "That's what you want these people to believe."

Recounting the murders and mixing fact with fiction, Butch testified that he saw the figure of Dawn come from his younger siblings' room after they had been shot. Butch tried to maintain that he had shot only his father and mother and Dawn shot the kids.

He then testified that he went upstairs to confront Dawn. Recalling the struggle with his sister, Butch said, "I remember somehow or someway I got the gun. I remember pushing her down in the bed, and I remember shooting her. That's what I remember."

Later, Sullivan's questioning began to expose Weber's strategy. He asked Butch, "Let me ask you a question, Mr. DeFeo. You remember talking about that, going to a mental institution with James DeVito, with the correction officer in jail?"

But Sullivan wasn't through. He pressed Butch, asking, "And you got all the money waiting for you when you get out?"

Of course, Butch played dumb and said, "No."

Weber, on the other hand, moved for a mistrial, saying, "And this bit about two years was highly out of order by this district attorney, who knows better." The request for a mistrial was denied.

Butch's goal was to convince a jury that he was insane. When asked by Weber if he killed his father, Butch responded, "Did I kill

Chapter Ten

Fallacies revealed.
Pictured above and below are two pieces of evidence that prove the prosecution's theory of robbery was erroneous. Above, police uncover an envelope filled with money in the DeFeo master bedroom. Below, a list of the jewels that were kept in the bank.

```
   ESTATE OF RONALD DE FEO
   RIDER TO SCHEDULE F – OTHER MISCELLANEOUS PROPERTY

 1.  One ladies gold pin 5 baby faces 10 sapphire eyes          125.00
 2.  Two ladies gold bangles ¼" wide $500                       100.00
 3.  One ladies gold charm filigree with chain                   75.00
 4.  One ladies gold bracelet                                    50.00
 5.  One ladies double strand gold necklace                      35.00
 6.  One mans gold ring light green stone and 3 diamond chips   200.00
 7.  One ladies ring large oval opal with 12 diamonds           800.00
 8.  One ladies diamond dinner ring, 4 tiers                  1,000.00
 9.  One ladies starburst diamond ring approx. 25 diamonds      700.00
10.  One ladies ruby and diamond ring                           700.00
11.  One ladies white gold ring, one round diamond            1,000.00
12.  One ladies diamond ring oval shaped                      1,500.00
13.  One ladies pair pierced diamond earrings                 1,200.00
14.  One ladies pin gold and blue with diamond flower           800.00
15.  One ladies gold rope bracelet ¼" wide                      350.00
16.  One ladies gold bracelet with 7 jade stones                400.00
17.  One ladies gold bracelet with 4 charms                     300.00
18.  One ladies gold bracelet 3/4" wide plain gold               35.00
19.  One gold charm                                              25.00
20.  One silver or white gold pierced earring (single earring)   35.00
21.  One single earring pierced drop gold                        50.00
22.  One silver jewelry box 8" x 6"                             150.00
23.  One mans gold ring initial in diamonds "R D"               250.00
24.  One ladies diamond and emerald cocktail ring               800.00
```

245

him? I killed them all, yes, sir. I killed them all in self-defense."

After the admission, the question of guilt or innocence was no longer relevant. Neither was the fact that there were other perpetrators in the crime. From that point on, Butch stood alone.

THE SUMMATIONS

During the trial, Gerard Sullivan and William Weber were often at each others' throats. Sullivan's antics were reminiscent of temper tantrums, while Weber's were a steady barrage of objections and requests for a mistrial.

On one such occasion, Sullivan complained about Weber, saying, "I have a motion. My motion is to instruct this jury to disregard the comments between counsel."

Whereas Justice Stark replied, "They have been instructed practically everyday we have been here to disregard any of these gratuitous comments, either his or yours."

It was a long and arduous trial. Although the trial had begun in October, by the time both sides were ready to give their closing statements, Thanksgiving was fast approaching. Everyone wanted to finish before the holiday.

Weber was first to offer his summation. He said, "The only thing I'd like to point out is that this whole trial, every trial that occurs in a criminal court house, is designed to achieve one end: justice. Justice as we know it, or as we believe it to be . . . Sometimes justice dictates psychiatric treatment, even in the face of six murders, even in the face of what we are dealing with today."

More important, Weber said, "There has been a serious, serious omission in presenting important evidence to you."

Throughout Weber's summation, Sullivan often objected. When Weber began talking about Michael Brigante Sr.'s kissing his grandson, Sullivan said, "I will object to this, judge."

Justice Stark agreed, saying, "Yes, this is in no manner part of the proof in this case."

Weber also reminded the jury about Brigante's attempts to have Richard Wyssling, an attorney, find and represent his grandson.

Regarding Sullivan's claims that Wyssling never represented himself as an attorney, but rather a family friend, Weber said, "And you heard Michael Brigante say, 'Your honor, if I wanted a messenger boy, I could have told any one of the other relatives present. I wouldn't have told an attorney.'"

Weber also reminded the jury, "If Ronnie's rights were violated, all the evidence on this table right here would be suppressed. You wouldn't be allowed to use the gun because the gun was derived in this case as a result of his constitutional violation. You wouldn't be allowed to use anything that was found in the sewer because this evidence was gathered only as a result of a violation of his constitutional rights."

Weber also pointed out the questionable credibility of some of the prosecution's witnesses, including Burt Borkan, a corrupt cop; John Donahue, a little boy who fabricated his testimony under the direction of the prosecution; John Kramer, a jailhouse snitch incarcerated for robbery and rape. In fact, Sullivan would later appear at Kramer's sentencing to request leniency in part of a deal he had made to testify against Butch DeFeo about his insanity ploy.

In his own summation, Sullivan said Butch "had a need to demonstrate his virility, and this was part of his antisocial personality . . . The need to possess money was an integral part of his antisocial personality. He fed upon it. He derived his manhood from spending it, from flashing it, and impressing others with it. And ultimately, Ronald DeFeo, I suggest to you, killed for it."

Incredibly, Sullivan's claims that Butch had killed for "big money" were ludicrous. Not only did the court forbid testimony that would have exonerated Butch of any robbery, but there was no indication that any large amounts of money or jewelry were kept at the DeFeo house at the time of the murders.

Regarding the insanity issue, Sullivan countered that Butch was sane because he knew enough to hide incriminating evidence. Concerning Butch's testimony, Sullivan added, "Did you see one ounce of guilt in Ronald DeFeo in three days and in seven weeks of trial? The selfishness, the consuming selfishness of that defendant on that stand in three days. Doesn't learn from experience. Lie after lie Ronald DeFeo told."

Upon hearing this, Weber immediately objected, saying, "Your honor, I object to the unfair remarks made concerning the defendant's testimony in this courtroom."

Justice Stark replied, "Do you seek a ruling at this time?"

"Yes, I seek a ruling at this time."

"All right, your objection is overruled."

Although it was Weber's last objection, Justice Stark once again sided with the prosecution.

Recapping the trial, *The New York Times* summed it up best on November 23, 1975, saying, "Mr. Weber's argumentative courtroom style visibly irritated Justice Stark throughout the trial, in contrast to the low-key approach taken by Mr. Sullivan, whose presentations occasionally drew a smile from the judge."

On Wednesday, November 19, 1975, Justice Stark spent two hours charging and then sequestering the jury. They had several options, including finding Butch guilty of manslaughter, guilty of first-degree murder, not guilty by reason of insanity, guilty as charged, or simply not guilty.

It was no surprise that on November 21, 1975, Butch DeFeo was found guilty as charged on all six counts of second-degree murder. He was sentenced by Justice Stark on December 4, 1975 to six concurrent life sentences, and would not be eligible for parole until 1999.

From the outset, the DeFeo trial was anything but fair and proper. According to Butch, Sullivan was not only a hypocrite and a liar, but also uninterested in the pursuit of justice. Although transcripts state otherwise, Butch DeFeo insisted, "The assistant district attorney's opening statement to the jury was that I committed the killing with two other people and they will never know who they are because I won't tell them." It is evident, nonetheless, from his statements during the post-hearing conference that Sullivan knew there had been more than one guilty party involved with the DeFeo murders, even though he chose not to pursue the issue.

If another judge had presided over the case and the defense was given adequate time and resources to prepare for trial, then the outcome might have been different because the other perpetrators might have been brought to justice. Furthermore, the mystery of the DeFeo murders would have never endured.

PART FIVE: ALTERNATIVE PATHWAYS TO FREEDOM

CHAPTER ELEVEN
Capitalizing on a Tragedy: The Amityville Horror

IN 1977, A runaway bestseller titled *The Amityville Horror*, written by Jay Anson, took the nation by storm. The promotional copies sent out by the publisher, Prentice Hall, hailed it as "the non-fiction *Exorcist*." The cover carried the subtitle of "A True Story," while the copyright page read:

> The names of several individuals mentioned in this book have been changed to protect their privacy. However, all facts and events, as far as we have been able to verify them, are strictly accurate.

In 1976, author Jay Anson undertook the daunting challenge of chronicling George and Kathleen Lutzes' claims that they and their children felt threatened from strong supernatural forces while living at 112 Ocean Avenue. Apparently, the Lutzes moved into the DeFeo house believing it to be their dream home.

On December 18, 1975, George and Kathleen Lutz with their three children—Daniel, 10, Christopher, seven, and Missy, five—moved into the DeFeo home. Although it had only been 13 months since the DeFeo murders had occurred, George Lutz claimed at a press conference, "The DeFeo slayings weren't something that would bother us."

Because of the murders, one of George Lutz's friends suggested he have the house blessed. A Methodist, Lutz claimed he knew only one Catholic priest, Father Ralph Pecoraro, who worked as an ecclesiastical judge in the Rockville Centre Diocese. Father Pecoraro had apparently helped George with the annulment of his first marriage.

According to George and Kathy Lutz, Father Pecoraro arrived to bless their new home on the same day they moved into it. While the Lutzes unloaded their rented moving van, Father Pecoraro entered the house and began his ritual blessing alone. He made his way upstairs to the second floor and entered the northeast bedroom, which had been Marc and John DeFeos' room.

As he sprinkled holy water around the room and recited a prayer, he heard a loud male voice say, "Get out!" Although the priest supposedly did not tell the Lutzes about the voice, he did warn them about the room, saying, "Don't use it as a bedroom. Don't let anyone sleep in there." The Lutzes followed his advice, turning the room into Kathy's sewing room.

From the very first night they moved in, the Lutzes claim they felt strange sensations. They also claim their personalities began drastically changing. On one occasion, George and Kathy Lutz beat their children with a strap and large wooden spoon. After moving to the house, the children apparently had become brats.

Purportedly, things worsened over the next few weeks. From the stench of bile to the smell of cheap perfume, the Lutzes became increasingly perplexed by the mysterious odors that would emanate from different locations of the house. Black stains appeared on the toilets and could not be lifted even with Clorox. Green slime ran down walls, although there appeared to be no reason or source. Hundreds of flies would appear in the sewing room despite it being the dead of winter.

112 Ocean Avenue located in the affluent Village of Amityville.

During their alleged stay, the Lutzes boasted of supernatural activity, including a demon standing at the top of the third floor (above) and a demonic force supposeably blowing open the front door (below).

Their flight.
The Lutzes claimed that after 28 days they had to flee the DeFeo house out of fear for their lives, even though neighbors said this was absolutely false and absurd.

Artist rendition.
Below is the crime-scene photo that William Weber claimed he showed George and Kathy Lutz prior to their concoction of *The Amityville Horror*.

According to the Lutzes, the phenomena then turned physical. Kathy was victimized by unseen touches, which had sometimes forced her to pass out. On the other hand, George would sit hours by the fireplace because he suffered from constant chills. In addition, he would wake up nightly at 3:15 a.m., reasoning that there was a connection between that hour and the hour of the DeFeos' deaths.

As the month progressed, apparently the situation worsened again for the Lutzes. George awoke one night to witness Kathy transform into a 90-year-old hag. The next night, she began levitating off the bed, forcing George to grab her before she floated away.

Realizing they needed a priest, the Lutzes contacted Father Pecoraro to ask him to return to perform another blessing. Little did they know, but Father Pecoraro had been feeling the aftereffects from the first blessing. Whatever was plaguing the Lutzes was also bothering the priest. Reportedly, the priest was suffering from a high temperature, blisters, and other flu-like symptoms that worsened each time he tried to contact the Lutzes.

After failing to get Father Pecoraro to return, the Lutzes took matters into their own hands. Armed with a crucifix, the Lutzes walked throughout the house reciting the Lord's Prayer. A chorus of voices erupted in response, asking them, "Will you stop?"

But the most incredible part of the couple's story was their claim that their daughter had befriended an invisible, red-eyed pig named Jodie. "Jodie could not be seen by anyone unless it wanted to. At times it was a little bigger than a teddy bear and other times bigger than the house," George explained in October 1979 on the TV show "In Search Of."

One night while coming back from the boathouse, George claimed he saw Jodie standing behind Missy in her room. Yet Kathy's introduction to her daughter's friend was just as disturbing. On a separate evening, Kathy was startled to see two red eyes peering in through the darkness from the window.

The Lutzes also claim that the malevolent forces caused significant property damage to the house, such as the front door being ripped off its hinges, windows being smashed, banisters being torn from their fittings, damage to the garage door, and water damage from hurricane-force winds, which local meteorological stations had no record of.

Even the Lutzes' dog, Harry, a malamute-Labrador mix, supposedly suffered from the strange forces. Although the animal was normally hyper, it had become increasingly lethargic while at the house. One time the dog had almost choked itself because it tried to scale the fence. The Lutzes reasoned the dog was trying to flee the property.

One of the more chilling events was when George awakened to the sound of a marching band in his living room. He claimed he raced downstairs and entered the room, only to find dead silence and the furniture pushed to one side of the room.

After 28 days in the DeFeo home, the Lutzes claimed they could take no more. They grabbed only a few belongings and fled the house, taking shelter at Kathy's mother's home in nearby Babylon.

Jay Anson's *The Amityville Horror* sold more than three million copies and was turned into a major motion picture that grossed more than $80 million dollars. The Lutzes happily went on a nationwide tour to promote the book as their "true story." Nevertheless, questions remained about the validity of the claims made by the Lutzes and Anson.

HOW THE HOAX BEGAN

On January 15, 1975, Butch's lawyer, Jacob Siegfried, motioned the court to be permitted "the right to examine, inspect, copy, photograph, or make and take photostatic copies of the original notes of the arresting officers, together with police reports containing statements of the witnesses . . ."

Siegfried insisted these items were crucial in his affidavit, saying, "The defendant was deprived of his right to a preliminary hearing in the district court by the district attorney's actions in presenting the case directly to the Grand Jury."

Regardless, the court did not believe these items necessary for

Butch's defense, and on March 11, 1975, presiding Judge John Jones denied the request. With little choice remaining, Siegfried later filed a notice of defense of mental disease or defect for his client. Since the defense had been denied an equal opportunity to have the same reports, records and photos that the prosecution had in its possession, there was only one choice left: an insanity plea.

Butch did not want his sanity questioned, and he threatened to strangle Siegfried. With little recourse, and after spending more than $40,000 on attorneys, Michael Brigante Sr. told his grandson, "Sweetheart, your dime is played out." This meant that Butch would have to use a court-appointed attorney.

On July 7, 1975, William Weber, from the firm of Fredrick Mars and Bernard Burton in Patchogue, New York, was assigned by the clerk of the Suffolk County Court to represent Butch in his trial.

On July 29, 1975, Judge Ernest Signorelli, who was at that time presiding over the DeFeo trial, had a conference between Butch, prosecuting attorney Gerard Sullivan, and William Weber. The major concern was that there be no objections to Weber's playing an active role in Judge Signorelli's campaign to be elected to the surrogate court. After everyone agreed Weber's role in Judge Signorelli's campaign did not pose a problem, the matter of an insanity defense came up.

Weber first requested permission to retain two psychiatrists for the defense. Needing a confirmation on a defense, Judge Signorelli pressed Weber, asking, "Well, when would you be able to know whether you're going to interpose a defense of insanity definitely?"

Weber said, "I believe, your honor, at this point we intend to go ahead on that. But I reserve the right to withdraw it after future investigations of this case."

The fact of the matter was Weber was still having problems convincing Butch to plead insanity. So Weber needed an out if Butch became a problem. Furthermore, Weber was hoping Judge Signorelli would grant the defense motion to obtain copies of all the police reports and crime-scene photographs the prosecution had.

On August 1, 1975, Judge Signorelli issued a ruling on Weber's supplemental omnibus motion, granting the defense copies of the reports and photographs in the prosecution's possession. Since Weber did not receive the documents until the end of August, he had little time to use them in preparation for the trial set to begin September 15.

Needing time to prepare a better defense, Weber requested a 60-day adjournment. After Weber was denied his adjournment, the trial began with Judge Thomas Stark presiding.

THE SIDESHOW BEGINS

In an affidavit, Barry Springer stated that William Weber had told him that people approached him to write a book even before Butch's trial had started. Thus, on February 14, 1976, Weber formed a corporation for the book, naming himself as president. He would later have to dissolve and reform it because the Lutzes had been left out.

Geraldine DeFeo further explained, "Because Butch felt insulted that his insanity could be questioned, Weber had to convince him by alternative means. He promised Butch that he'd get out in two to three years, and that he'd be rich from the book's success.

"Butch never became comfortable with the prospect of an insanity defense, but the idea of becoming rich soothed his uneasiness."

Butch said, "Amityville was a hoax that Weber and the Lutzes started. Yes, to make money. It started as my trial was in progress."

Through mutual acquaintances, Weber met George and Kathy Lutz. Kathy, 30, was a divorcée and mother of three children. At the time she met George, she was working as a waitress in a diner. George Lutz, 28, was owner of a third-generation land surveying business his grandfather, William H. Parry, had founded.

In fact, in 1908, George's grandfather had the prestigious job of surveying the train tunnels that eventually connected the East River to Long Island. But in 1972, George's father died, and he was forced to take over the family business. All over Long Island, the construction business was suffering; thus, George's business was also suffering. A further aggravation came from the IRS, which wanted to conduct an audit of the surveying firm.

Although she disagreed with Weber's plans, Geraldine was asked to help convince Butch that he had to act unstable. So, sometime in the fall, she accompanied Weber to a bar in Amityville to meet the Lutzes. It was clear to Geraldine that Weber and the Lutzes had already been planning the hoax for sometime, even possibly as early as Weber's entrance as defense counsel in July.

"The Lutzes claimed they were involved with Transcendental Meditation and witchcraft. Ludicrous as it sounds, Kathy told me she had uneasy vibrations soon after the murders," Geraldine recalled.

The four sat around the table for about 30 minutes. Weber, Geraldine and Kathy drank wine, while George drank a beer. Although Geraldine thought the entire notion was crazy, she sat and listened to the Lutzes.

"George was all business and kept insisting moving into the house to corroborate the existence of a force would help Butch in the upcoming trial. And he would constantly cut Kathy off, who would go off in tangents about witchcraft.

"The Lutzes asked several questions about mannerisms of Butch and his family. The plan was for them to move in and say they were having murderous thoughts and uneasy feelings living in the home. George Lutz also wanted to know about Butch's beard, so that he could make sure to cut it like his.

"I had enough when Kathy began rubbing her head, insisting she was getting psychic impressions at that moment. At that point, I got up and told them that this was the worst bullshit I had ever heard and that they could count me out."

Weber and the Lutzes, claimed Geraldine, proceeded forward with the plan. The next step involved the actual purchase of the home. Because they could not raise suspicions, the Lutzes had to contact Conklin Realty, the agency handling the sale of the DeFeo property, on their own. Real estate agent Edith Evans was unsuspecting of the Lutzes' real intent.

In fact, after her death in December 2000, Evans' husband commented in *The Amityville Record* on the Lutz hoax. He said his

Chapter Eleven

wife thought that the Lutzes "had made up a good story."

Despite the Lutzes' claims that they were looking for a house in the $30,000 to $50,000 range, once they saw the $90,000 DeFeo house, they immediately wanted it. Oddly enough, the property's past made no difference.

"At this point, things were not going as expected. Weber did not get the adjournment he wanted, and the Lutzes could not get the house when they expected because of problems with the DeFeo estate," Geraldine explained.

On December 4, 1975, Butch returned to court to receive his sentence. He had been found guilty on all six counts of murder on November 21, 1975. Justice Stark issued the strictest sentence he could impose: 25 years to life. Butch replied, "I am going to appeal this sentence and conviction. Without disrespect, judge, I believe I'll be back within one year."

Weber decided to handle the appeal. Obviously, he planned on using the Lutzes and their corroboration of the nonexistent malevolent forces residing in the DeFeo home. In fact, one of the first trips the Lutzes made after leaving the DeFeo home was to Gerard Sullivan's office. There, they requested blueprints of the house; they also mentioned sudden heat loss, loss of electrical power, and vibrations throughout the house.

In late January 1976, Weber and the Lutzes began a series of meetings at Kathy's mother's house in Babylon. During these meetings, Weber brought crime writer, Paul Hoffman, who was introduced to him by Herman Race, the Brigantes's investigator. Hoffman had previously written books such as *Lions in the Street, Tiger in the Court, What the Hell Is Justice?* and *To Drop a Dime.*

On February 14, 1976, *Newsday* published an article headlined, "DeFeo Home Abandoned; Buyer Calls It Haunted." Next to the article was a photo of the DeFeo house's screen door, battered and torn. The article was just the beginning of an ensuing publicity campaign.

Several Long Island newspapers picked up the story and ran articles over the next few weeks. In these articles, it was speculated that these mysterious energies were possibly influencing Butch at the time he killed his family.

On February 16, 1976, Weber and the Lutzes held a joint press conference. At the conference, George Lutz said, "No objects flew around; there was no wailing. But we moved out because of concern for our personal safety as a family. There is a very strong force in there."

Weber added, "Facts supplied by the Lutzes and physical evidence brought to our attention put some of the evidence in our favor."

Days later, during an interview with reporter Steve Bauman from Channel 5 in New York City, Weber explained that the force the Lutzes spoke of may be of natural origin and felt it might be the evidence he needed to win his client a new trial. Weber also added that he was aware that "certain houses could be built or constructed in a certain manner, so as to create some sort of electrical currents through some rooms, based on the physical structure of the house."

It was a clever ploy to promote the hoax and gain public sympathies for Butch on his upcoming appeal.

MY INVESTIGATION BEGINS

When I was put in contact with George Lutz in 1999, I was very excited to meet the man I had read so much about. Since we both lived in Las Vegas, we met at a local Starbucks coffee shop. Lutz, who still sported his trademark beard and haircut, brought with him a number of black-and-white photographs that he believed proved his story was true. At that time, since I had no reason to doubt him, I trusted what he told me.

More than a year later, however, I would learn that George Lutz was not the credible individual I originally credited him with being. In recent years, even his own ex-stepsons have publicly criticized him about the way he handled their family's story, not to mention his poor treatment of their mother. But what really began to make me doubt George's credibility was his own words.

For example, at the press conference held on February 16, 1976, George Lutz was asked by a reporter to describe what hap-

Chapter Eleven

pened. In addition to explaining there had been no objects thrown around or wailing noises heard, Lutz said, "What didn't happen were all the usual things associated with a haunted house."

Yet in a tape-recorded interview with me in March 2000, George recalled the last night he was in the house. Contrary to what he previously had said at the press conference, George Lutz stated, on tape, that he had heard creaks, groans, voices and music during their exit. He also claimed that the temperature was fluctuating constantly between hot and cold. According to George, even the lights were flickering as the forces in the house were building in intensity. Contradicting himself once more, George claimed, in the interview, that the event was just like the stuff seen in haunted-house movies.

Incredibly, the simple negative feeling George had described in his first press conference had now become the total opposite of what he originally insisted took place. Besides, the black-and-white photos George had, which were taken almost two months after they had left the house, showed a neat and well-ordered home. There was no slime on the walls, blood on the stairs, or broken windows as the book and movie portrayed. And they did not show a hurried exit as the Lutzes had described.

I was growing more and more suspicious as July 2000 approached, especially when George informed me that setting the record straight was not as important as making money off fictional sequels. Furthermore, he wanted to take advantage of the resurrected Amityville hype by collecting movie posters from the various Amityville films. His plan was to autograph them and then have me sell them at various online auctions and poster shops for $2,000. Of course, I refused. By that time, I undoubtedly had lost all confidence in him.

Coincidentally, in June 2000, I was contacted by Geraldine DeFeo, who originally thought I was another charlatan interested only in making a buck. She, nonetheless, showed me a much different side to the Lutz story. The rest, as they say, is history.

After I ended my friendship with George Lutz, who, by the way, claims I am only interested in money and fame, I received a threatening letter from his Las Vegas attorney. The letter basically said that if George Lutz ever found out that I had infringed on his copyright or trademark, then "he will own me." But I suppose I am in good company since George Lutz has said similar things about other legitimate researchers that have debunked his absurd claims.

At the same time I broke my friendship and partnership with George Lutz, I also broke off my ties to the History Channel documentary on the Amityville case. In my opinion, the producers were interested only in producing a scary, sensational show, and not the unequivocal truth. An *Amityville Record* article, dated November 1, 2000, summed up my feelings best. Reporter Carolyn James wrote, "Osuna said the truth is a side the writers of books and producers of documentaries do not want the public to know because it does not meet 'sensational criteria.'"

Now that I was an independent researcher again, I vowed to remain objective. I had made the unintentional mistake of allowing my friendship with George Lutz to cloud my thinking.

Nevertheless, one of the first things I did was request court records of the *Lutz vs. Weber* civil case, also known as the *Lutz vs. Hoffman* lawsuit. I was sure that the case would contain many unknown facts about the hoax and the Lutzes' relationship with William Weber.

Although I got part of the case files in February 2001, the remainder of the case was not unsealed until May 31, 2001. Much of the credit for convincing Judge Jack Weinstein to unseal it needs to go to Geraldine DeFeo, whose letters to the Judge Weinstein provided very convincing arguments.

The *Lutz vs. Weber* case proved invaluable in determining the origins of the hoax. And even though I felt George Lutz contributed to a hoax, I wanted him to have an opportunity to address several troubling issues, such as what his finances were like prior to buying the house at 112 Ocean Avenue.

So on August 2, 2001, I sent a letter to George, via his attorney. In my letter, I asked George to "consider being forthcoming and honest with his answers to the questions I have submitted." Apart from a phone call I received from George's attorney acknowledging the letter, my questions went unanswered. However, this was not the first time that George Lutz refused to address several inconsistencies in his story.

Doug Spero, a former WNBC reporter, said, "If a person is truly innocent, or truly believe they are, they make themselves available through their lawyers or by themselves." Spero, who produced a television segment on the Amityville hoax in the late 1970s, had offered George and Kathy Lutz a chance to comment on the discrepancies of their story. He, too, found them "unavailable."

LUTZ VS. WEBER

In the beginning of March 1976, Weber sent a book contract to the Lutzes, which covered a proposed company, called the Hoffman, Weber, Burton and Mars Corporation. Like Weber, Mars and Burton, Kathy and George were to receive, each, 12 percent of the shares of HWBM. Since Paul Hoffman was the writer, he would receive the largest share, 40 percent.

In the contract, the Lutzes also were supposed to "warrant that the experiences they had related and will relate . . . are true." Furthermore, the Lutzes' equity in the company depended upon their "willingness to cooperate with the media."

The Lutzes terminated their proposed venture with Weber because they felt he wanted to tie them up with an unfavorable contract. Instead, the Lutzes chose to go with author Jay Anson. The contract they eventually signed with Anson offered a more lucrative split of 50 percent. Nevertheless, this did not stop Hoffman from selling two articles about the Lutzes' experiences.

The first article appeared in an issue of *New York Sunday News* on July 18, 1976, and was titled "Life in a Haunted House." The second was titled "Our Dream House Was Haunted" and appeared in the April 1977 edition of *Good Housekeeping*. Both articles were nearly identical and were based on the experiences that the Lutzes, Weber and Hoffman brainstormed in January 1976.

In May 1977, George and Kathy Lutz filed suit against Paul Hoffman, William Weber, Bernard Burton, Fredrick Mars, *Good Housekeeping, New York Sunday News* and the Hearst Corporation.

In the suit, the Lutzes alleged invasion of privacy, misappropriation of name for trade purposes, and negligent infliction of mental distress. They sought relief in the form of $4.5 million.

In turn, Hoffman, Weber and Burton each placed a counterclaim against the Lutzes for two million dollars, citing they had perpetrated a fraud and breached a contract.

In the early days of the case, Judge Jacob Mishler presided over it. Judge Mishler dismissed the claims against *Good Housekeeping*, *New York Sunday News* and the Hearst Corporation because there were no invasion of privacy issues and because the plaintiffs had failed to state a claim upon which relief could be granted to them. Judge Mishler, however, eventually handed the case over to Judge Weinstein. It is said that Judge Mishler, who had seniority, did not want to preside over such a ridiculous lawsuit.

Regardless, the plaintiffs were faced with a much bigger problem. Citing ethical reasons, the Lutzes' New York counsel also resigned from the case. Nevertheless, the Lutzes showed up in Brooklyn with William Daley, their California attorney, ready to make their case.

Linnea Nonnewitz said, "I faced George Lutz in court, in Brooklyn. He had bodyguards. Why? I'll face him any day with the truth."

It was rumored that either the Brigantes or Butch DeFeo would seek retribution for the pack of lies that George and Kathy Lutz had told. Therefore, George may have felt it was prudent to hire a set of bodyguards.

When the actual trial began, Judge Jack Weinstein, known to be a "no-nonsense" judge, presided over the case in his Brooklyn U.S. District Court. On September 10, 1979, Judge Weinstein dismissed the rest of the Lutzes' suit and allowed the defendants' counterclaim to continue. He said, "Based on what I have heard, it appears to me that to a large extent the book is a work of fiction, relying in a large part upon the suggestions of Mr. Weber."

Judge Weinstein also pointed out that he saw serious ethical questions regarding Weber and Burton's conduct. Therefore, he proposed to refer the entire matter to the New York State Bar

Association. Judge Weinstein said, "There is a very serious ethical question when lawyers become literary agents."

The next day, the counterclaim was settled, and the entire case was dismissed. According to the case docket sheet, "The court made no findings of fact or law." Weber and Burton had narrowly avoided facing an ethics charge before the state bar association.

THE PLAINTIFF'S CASE

The memoranda, motions, affidavits and interrogatories, which are formal questions submitted under oath, found in the *Lutz vs. Weber* case file were invaluable in determining what really happened during the first three months of 1976. These documents also pointed out the discrepancies in the Lutzes' story.

In a motion for a protective order to prevent discovery, the Lutzes' attorney stated that "the plaintiffs have four young children ranging in age nine months to 12 years, whom they wish to protect from harassment, annoyance and embarrassment."

Yet the Lutzes were not overly concerned with Jay Anson's using the children's names in his book. Moreover, in the July 24, 1979 issue of *The Star*, the entire family, minus the infant, posed for a publicity photograph. In reality, George and Kathy did not care enough to protect their children's identities.

A fact that was stated in the plaintiff's trial brief that neither side denied was that "George and Kathleen Lutz met with Mr. Weber attempting to be of assistance in a possible appeal or re-trial for Ronald DeFeo Jr."

Additionally, the brief stated that the articles Hoffman wrote jeopardized the publishing of *The Amityville Horror*. The suit brought by the Lutzes contended that their "right of privacy was destroyed and plaintiffs were humiliated and annoyed and exposed to public contempt and ridicule."

In George and Kathy Lutzes' interrogatories, dated October 27, 1978, they stated that the press conference they attended at Weber's office on February 16, 1976, was "called by William Weber without [their] permission and with coercion on his part in having us attend."

In a second interrogatory dated December 8, 1978, George went into more detail about how Weber coerced them into attending the press conference. He stated, "We received a call from William Weber in the late afternoon on the day of the press conference, and were told by William Weber that the press was aware of where we were staying, as well as where the children were going to school, and that we had better attend the meeting at his office; otherwise they would go to our relatives, where we were staying, and go to the school the children were attending."

When Judge Weinstein dismissed the Lutzes' suit, he stated that there was no privacy issue and that the Lutzes voluntarily, and without coercion, attended the press conference. Judge Weinstein also said, "The Lutzes deliberately made themselves public figures during this entire period."

Judge Weinstein's beliefs were substantiated by *Exhibit A* of the Lutzes' interrogatories. *Exhibit A* listed all the public interviews the Lutzes attended from September 13, 1977 to September 22, 1978. In just over a year, the Lutzes had made themselves available for more than 30 interviews to promote *The Amityville Horror*.

Regarding the issue of helping Weber with getting Butch a new trial, Judge Weinstein said, "I don't believe Mr. Lutz is a credible witness on that issue."

THE DEFENDANT'S CASE

Because of attorney-client privilege, William Weber first had to get Butch's permission to reveal certain facts in publications. In a letter dated February 27, 1976, Butch assigned all of his rights in connection with the events of November 1974 to Weber. By doing so, Butch stood to gain:

1. Five percent of the first one million dollars grossed.
2. Four percent of the second million grossed.
3. Three percent of the revenues thereafter received.

Chapter Eleven

The information that Weber imparted to the Lutzes in their meetings later appeared in *The Amityville Horror*. In fact, in his deposition, George Lutz stated that he did not consider writing a book until it was suggested by Weber and Burton. Nevertheless, that did not stop the Lutzes from pursuing other avenues.

In Kathy Lutz's interrogatories dated October 27, 1978, she was asked the date and time she and George met author Jay Anson for the first time. She answered, "Approximately 8:00 p.m., March 4, 1976." At the time, Anson was living with his sister at her home in Roslyn, New York.

In contrast, during Anson's deposition, he stated that he met with the Lutzes around March 1, 1976, and possibly as early as February 18, 1976. Anson also testified that he was told how to contact the Lutzes by Tam Mossman at the end of February. Apparently, Al Carter, George Lutz's friend, contacted Tam Mossman, a senior editor at Prentice Hall, to see if there would be interest in pursuing a book. So what the defense argued was that "as early as February 15, 1976, the plaintiffs were actively, and unbeknownst to the defendants, pursuing their own project."

During his 2000 interview with the History Channel, George Lutz stated that after he and his family had purportedly fled the house, they only wanted to "get it fixed and move back in." Yet the facts indicated otherwise. The so-called psychics and paranormal investigators the Lutzes chose to "investigate" the house were not contacted until the end of February 1976. And the "official" investigation did not take place until March 6, 1976. But, by that time, George and Kathy Lutz already were engaged in talks with Jay Anson about a book deal.

The defense's memorandum further argued that the Lutzes' "desire to assist in the DeFeo defense and later to join with the defendants in writing the planned book were knowingly false."

Regarding the intent to deceive, the attorneys for the defendants argued that the Lutzes did not turn over all the audio tapes made of the meetings with Weber because they were incriminating. However, one tape "bypassed the plaintiffs' scrutiny."

On February 21, 1976, George and Kathy Lutz confided with

Laura Didio, a news assistant working for Channel 5 News in New York City, on tape, that they were planning to write a book and that Weber had imparted "substantial" information regarding the DeFeo murders, not to mention other pertinent information.

The defendants were successful in arguing that contrary to George and Kathy Lutzes' claims that they had no thought of writing a book until February 28, 1976, the couple was already in the planning stages prior to that date. It is evident from the case of the counterclaim that George and Kathy Lutz did, in fact, misrepresent their intentions and obtain confidential information from Weber about his client and the DeFeo murders that eventually wound up in *The Amityville Horror*.

Eventually, the Lutzes settled the counterclaim for an unspecified amount. According to a September 4, 1980 letter from William Weber to Butch, the Lutzes had yet to pay all the monies owed. An excerpt read:

> Incidentally, even though I sent you your share of the money from the Lutzes, the Lutzes have not fulfilled their agreement and have still not paid the balance of monies due.

Regardless, there is every indication that the Lutzes' gamble with the hoax proved to be a financial success. According to *Newsday*, as of September 12, 1979, the Lutzes made about $200,000 from book and movie royalties. In fact, as early as October 5, 1978, the Lutzes were able to buy a $180,000 house with a down payment of $13,528. In contrast, the DeFeo home had cost them only $80,000, a sizeable amount in 1975.

It was amazing to learn that in just under three years the Lutzes had not only become household names, but they also had been able to recover from the financial hardships they claimed they had previously experienced.

Chapter Eleven

FATHER RALPH PECORARO

The facts presented in the *Lutz vs. Weber* lawsuit showed *The Amityville Horror* to be a hoax. Moreover, facts uncovered in the suit told a very different story about Father Ralph Pecoraro than the one presented by the Lutzes and Anson.

There are discrepancies between what was written in Anson's book about Father Pecoraro and what George Lutz described in the civil case against Weber. Anson's book, which both George and Kathy Lutz publicly supported, said that Father Pecoraro, a.k.a. Father Mancusco, had met George Lutz two years earlier and that "he had helped Kathy and George in the days before they were married."

Question #43 of George Lutz's interrogatories asked, "State whether or not you know the Reverend Ralph Pecoraro. If so, state the date, time and place you first met him."

Over objections, George Lutz answered, "On or about July 14, 1975, 1:00 p.m., 258 Sunrise Highway, Rockville Centre, New York."

Kathy's response to the same question was, "On or about July 30, 1975; spoke to him on the telephone."

After reading the Lutzes' answers, it becomes evident that Father Pecoraro did not know the Lutzes for any appreciable amount of time. It should also be noted that the Lutzes were married on July 4, 1975, so Father Pecoraro could not have offered guidance to the Lutzes before they were married.

Moreover, Father Pecoraro's relationship to the case was described in an affidavit from William Daley, the Lutzes' attorney. It read, "Father Ralph J. Pecoraro has indicated that his only contact relating to this case was a telephone call from the Lutzes regarding their psychic experiences."

During the trial, Father Pecoraro testified over the phone and denied any of the so-called supernatural afflictions that Anson claimed the priest had suffered in his book. He also told Judge Weinstein that he was not sure if there were any supernatural occurrences at the house. According to *Newsday*, Father Pecoraro stated that when he went to bless the house that he did, in fact, hear a voice say, "Get out!"

But just what exactly did Father Pecoraro hear? And just how virtuous was this priest?

Angered over the magnitude of the hoax, in the early 1980s, Geraldine DeFeo sought out Father Pecoraro. Geraldine recalled, "The first time I talked to him, I must have called him every name in the book. I considered it a sin for a priest to do what he did. All he could tell me was to calm down and that he would pray for me.

"I then tracked him down to a bar in Asbury Park, New Jersey, to confront him about the ordeal the Lutzes were putting the DeFeos through. He finally admitted to me that the voice he heard say 'get out' was, in fact, George Lutz, on a tape recorder."

One final inconsistency with Father Pecoraro can be found in his 1979 interview on the TV show "In Search Of." First and foremost, his willingness to go on camera contradicted his statements to Judge Weinstein that he wanted to avoid harassment from the media. He also insisted there was "something there," referring to a supernatural force in the DeFeo house. This directly contradicted his testimony to Judge Weinstein, for which he later provided a written affirmation.

It seemed that Father Pecoraro himself was set to profit from the first book and movie. Not only did he allegedly receive several thousands of dollars from the publisher for relocation expenses, but the Lutzes also bought him a new car. Since Father Pecoraro is now deceased, it remains unclear if he was a willing participant in the Lutz hoax or an unsuspecting party to it. Therefore, it seems likely that despite his reluctant and often contradictory claims, Father Pecoraro never even ventured to 112 Ocean Avenue, but rather was pressured into saying he heard a voice while performing a blessing. Even William Daley, the Lutzes' attorney, had originally told the court in an affidavit that Father Pecoraro's only connection to the case was a phone call from the Lutzes.

Father Pecoraro was eventually sent to an entirely different diocese, where he purportedly was forbidden to practice certain

DIOCESE OF ROCKVILLE CENTRE

Office of the Vicar General

May 15, 2002

Mr. Ric Osuna

Dear Mr. Osuna:

Bishop Murphy has asked me to respond to your letter of March 22, 2002.

At the time in question Father Ralph Pecoraro worked at the Tribunal of the Diocese of Rockville Centre. Father Pecoraro was involved as a counselor of the Lutz's during, as you call it, "the Amityville Horror Story/Hoax." Because of his concern over the publicity attached to the story he petitioned and was granted a leave of absence for personal reasons on May 1, 1978. At that time he no longer worked for the Diocese. He went to the Diocese of Oakland and worked there, however, he eventually left there and dropped out of sight. He surfaced on occasion but made no attempt to return and serve within this Diocese even though we encouraged him to do so. Eventually, his whereabouts became unknown to us until hearing of his death in 1987.

The Diocese maintains that the story was a false report. In November of 1977 Diocesan attorneys prepared a substantial list, to be submitted to the publisher, of numerous inaccuracies, factually incorrect references and untrue statements regarding events, persons, and occurrences that never happened.

Enclosed is an article that ran in *L.I. Newsday* on September 12, 1979. I believe it correctly summarizes this situation.

Sincerely yours,

Reverend Robert O. Morrissey, J.C.D.
Ass't. to the Vicar General

Letter from Rockville Diocese

After several repeated requests, the Diocese of Rockville Centre finally broke its years of silence and commented on the Amityville case to author Ric Osuna. In a May 15, 2002 letter to Osuna in response to his questions regarding the hoax, the assistant to the Vicar General wrote, "The Diocese maintains that the story was a false report..."

Pictured above is the Lutzes' Deerpark home (above), where they resided prior to moving to Amityville. For some village residents, these unimpressive beginnings proved the Lutzes could never afford to buy the DeFeo home on their own.

According to a few "psychics," the DeFeo pool (left) was where the Native Americans once housed their insane.

Catholic rites. But this claim cannot be substantiated. Either way, the Diocese of Rockville Centre denied that any psychic events took place or affected clerical officials as reported in *The Amityville Horror*.

After several repeated requests, the Diocese of Rockville Centre finally broke its years of silence and commented on the Amityville case. In a May 15, 2002 letter to me in response to my questions regarding the hoax, the assistant to the Vicar General wrote, "The Diocese maintains that the story was a false report. In November of 1977, Diocesan attorneys prepared a substantial list, to be submitted to the publisher [of *The Amityville Horror*], of numerous inaccuracies, factually incorrect references and untrue statements regarding events, persons and occurrences that never happened."

ED AND LORRAINE WARREN

Toward the end of February 1976, the Lutz story was making headlines around New York. In response, Laura Didio called Ed and Lorraine Warren to see if they would investigate the DeFeo house. The Warrens were self-proclaimed demonologists from the New England area who have since gone on to become quite famous. However, their official Web site states that the Amityville case was, by far, their most famous case.

After their departure from the DeFeo house, the Lutzes had befriended news assistant Laura Didio and had given her an exclusive on their story and permission to access 112 Ocean Avenue with the Warrens. Of course, cameras would be in tow, filming the entire episode. All of this activity came from a couple who claimed they wanted no media attention.

At the end of February, the Warrens accompanied Laura Didio and her cameraman. Although the Warrens planned a seance on another night, this cursory tour offered the public its first chance to see inside the so-called "house of horrors."

To the casual observer, it appeared that the Lutzes had just walked out and left behind a house full of possessions. But it seemed a bit too perfect. For example, the laundry room contained laundry in the process of being folded, but all of the beds upstairs were made up neatly. Even the children's toys were put away. This was odd since *The Amityville Horror* had the Lutzes fleeing at 7:00 a.m. on January 14, 1976, after a restless night.

The kitchen was another story. In preparation for watering, plants had been placed in the sink, while a nearby banana sat turning black on the counter. Yet the master bathroom was quite spotless with a single toothbrush in its receptacle with a few sparse toiletries. Underneath the sink sat an empty trashcan with a brand new liner.

Remarkably, there also seemed to be no photographs of the Lutz family hanging on the walls, although paintings hung in almost every room of the house. Even the master bedroom, where one would expect a mother to have photographs of her children, was void of any.

Downstairs in the sunroom, there were bottles of liquor in the bar that had yet to be opened. In the living room, newspapers and magazines, conveniently dated mid-January 1976, were scattered everywhere. Sitting on the coffee table next to the newspapers, however, was a book that confirmed Geraldine DeFeo's allegation that the Lutzes boasted they were into witchcraft when she met them before they moved into the house. The book was Ronald Seth's *In the Name of the Devil*, which revealed the ancient spells, incantations and methods of supposed witches and sorcerers persecuted in Scotland between the 15th and 18th centuries.

Incredibly, there were striking similarities between the Lutzes' claims, which were later chronicled in Anson's book, and Ronald Seth's *In the Name of the Devil*.

For example, page 104 of Seth's book read, "At nights, they were prevented from sleeping by 'something' coming and pulling their bedcovers and nightclothes off them, 'leaving their bodies naked.' Page 89, Chapter 13, of Anson's book, read, "The blankets on the bed had been virtually torn from their bodies, leaving George and Kathy shivering."

Even more incredible was the similarity of an attack the Lutzes faced while lying in bed. Page 113 of Seth's book read, "Several

Chapter Eleven

times, hath he beat the children in their beds, and the claps of his hoof upon their buttocks would have been heard, but without any trouble to them." Page 189, Chapter 24, of Anson's book read, "Then George let out a horrible, silent scream. Somebody was on the bed with him! He felt himself being stepped on . . . They're hooves. It's an animal!"

"The Lutzes staged the entire thing and planted all the furniture. Besides, what mother in her right mind would place in their children's room a bed that someone else's daughter was murdered in?" Geraldine said, referring to Dawn DeFeo's bed in Missy Lutz's room.

On March 6, 1976, Ed and Lorraine Warren returned with Marvin Scott, a reporter for Channel 5 News, to conduct a séance in the house. More than a dozen people showed up, including Dr. Karlis Osis and Dr. Alex Tanous, from the American Society for Psychical Research in Manhattan, and Gerald Solfin, a senior research associate from the Psychical Research Foundation in Durham, North Carolina.

Lorraine Warren, who claimed to be clairvoyant, insisted she encountered Butch's spirit. "The encounter was so awful and he was so sinister, that she felt there was absolutely nothing she could do to help or eject his spirit from the house," claimed the Warrens' Web site.

Nothing remotely supernatural transpired during the two seances held that night. But the so-called psychics the Warrens had brought put on a wonderful performance for the cameras. Accompanying their moans and groans, these individuals described an evil black shadow that "comes at you and makes your heart speed up."

During the night of the séance, it has been alleged that the Warrens' photographer captured an image of a ghost peaking out from one of the bedrooms. For believers, this was tangible proof of phenomena in the DeFeo house.

Believing otherwise, Amityville researcher Blaine Duncan conducted an in-depth analysis that determined the "ghost" had human characteristics. Duncan explained, "The flash of the camera caused shadows to lay across the subject's shirt, which seemed suspiciously similar to that of one of the investigators accompanying the Warrens during the night of their televised séance. Not only was the tangible shirt similar, but the facial features and hairline of both the mysterious 'ghost' and the investigator were practically identical."

In a recent interview with The History Channel, the Warrens stated they never felt a need to authenticate the photo. "I was the [DeFeos'] housekeeper for seven years . . . I never saw a ghost in that house, not once, as God is my witness," Linnea Nonnewitz said.

However, neither the Warrens nor Channel 5's cameramen captured any images of black toilet bowls, dead flies, green slime, a damaged garage door, a torn banister or any other proof that would substantiate the Lutzes' claims.

During televised interviews in 1979, Kathy Lutz claimed that the same paranormal organizations had seen the physical evidence mentioned in Anson's book, but that they did not want to damage the interior of the house by taking samples, which turned out to be a blatant lie. Kathy also "conveniently" stated that the researchers could not release their findings for five to seven years, a claim both organizations also later denied.

In fact, both the American Psychical Foundation and Psychical Research Foundation said there was nothing paranormal in the house. They further added that they would have used scientific methods to measure any phenomena had any been present and not the psychic methods of the Warrens.

In a January 24, 1976 interview with George Kekoris, a representative of the Psychical Research Foundation, the Lutzes informed the researcher that they, in fact, left the house at 7:00 a.m., just as Jay Anson had written. Today, however, the Lutzes now insist they left the house in the late afternoon. More important, the Lutzes informed Kekoris that they had first viewed 112 Ocean Avenue when it was only nine months vacant. In other words, the Lutzes would have found the house in August 1975, shortly after William Weber had been assigned the DeFeo case.

Nevertheless, the Lutzes got the media attention they sought. After all, what better way to promote an upcoming book than to

Chapter Eleven

have a recorded seance broadcasted on TV?

The Warrens' campaign of misinformation did not stop the night of the seance. They have toured the world speaking of the so-called events that they claim took place in the Amityville house. They also have sold audio tapes about the Amityville case that contain erroneous information. It seems that when they made the tape, the Warrens were under the presumption that the house may have burned down, even though it had not.

The Warrens also have stated that Butch practiced black magic. Angered over the Warrens' allegations, Geraldine said, "Butch was a Catholic and not the monster the Warrens make him out to be."

Ed and Lorraine Warren have promoted a less than accurate history of the Amityville property. They claimed that the land was used by the Shinnecock Indians as an insane asylum to place their sick and dying. All of this came from a couple whose organization's mission statement supported a dissemination of accurate information.

Contrary to the Warrens' claims, the Shinnecocks resided farther east, approximately 50 miles from Amityville. The tribe that would have been most dominant in that part of Long Island were known as the Massapequan Indians. Additionally, neither the local Native American population nor the local historical societies have any records of the land being used as an insane asylum or burial ground.

And the local Native American population was outraged at such an inaccurate portrayal of their culture. They claim they would have never left their sick and dying outside, exposed to the elements. Rather, they would have nursed them in a caring fashion.

The closest bones ever discovered were unearthed a quarter of a mile away from the DeFeo house in a shell mound in 1920. Yet not even the historical society is clear where the bones now reside or whether they were Native American, let alone human.

Further proof that there was no burial ground came from records dating back to 1913. In May 1913, William A. Eardeley was commissioned by New York state to record the burial grounds in and around Amityville because many cemeteries were to be relocated. Eardeley made an extensive list of well-maintained and neglected cemeteries. In the end, Eardeley found no cemetery on or around 112 Ocean Avenue. Moreover, if there were bodies on the property, then they undoubtedly would have been unearthed when the DeFeos installed their swimming pool.

During the promotion of the movie *Book of Shadows: Blair Witch 2*, the Warrens participated in a Web telecast discussing their role in Amityville. In her interview, Lorraine described going into the master bedroom and feeling awful. She then went on to describe that she realized, through her psychic impressions, that the bed she was sitting on was where Mr. and Mrs. DeFeo had been shot.

Contrary to Lorraine's psychic thoughts, Mr. and Mrs. DeFeos' bed was removed from the house before the Lutzes arrived. "The bed was not there after the family died," insisted Linnea Nonnewitz. Furthermore, in March 2000, George Lutz admitted to me that he and Kathy had brought their own bed with them.

Continuing the deception, Ed Warren insisted Butch initially told police that during the murders "a dark black shadow was alongside him." In reality, as part of the insanity ploy, Butch testified at his trial that a figure resembling his sister, wearing black gloves, handed him the gun. Besides, it was not until his trial that the insanity defense came up, and Butch began claiming he heard voices.

Transcripts from Butch's trial, however, indicated he was still having trouble with accepting the insanity ploy.

Under cross-examination from prosecutor Gerard Sullivan, Butch was asked, "You told us earlier today that, Mr. DeFeo that you felt that God talked to you. Do you recall that?"

"Yes, sir, I do," Butch responded.

"On the night that you killed your family, did God tell you to do that?"

"No, sir, I didn't hear no voices the night this happened," Butch testified.

The Warrens, nevertheless, insisted that during the murders the DeFeos were in a state of phantomania, which supernaturally paralyzed them.

Herman Race, the retired New York City detective that the

Brigantes hired, however, stated to the court that in his professional experience there were several perpetrators involved in the crime, and that he had good reason to believe all the bodies found in the beds were not shot in their beds. This testimony effectively destroyed the Warrens' claims that the DeFeos were supernaturally restrained.

"There is no way that my father could have done this all by himself," Shea Marie DeFeo, Butch's daughter, said.

The last bit of misinformation the Warrens have willingly spread throughout the years has to do with a supposed exorcism of the house. Legend has it that Ronald DeFeo Sr. brought back with him an exorcist from St. Joseph's Oratory in Montreal, Canada. Not only does St. Joseph's have no record of such an event, but the DeFeos' surviving friends and family insist the event never happened. According to the Warrens, those who doubt the validity of their claims are skeptics and nonbelievers in the supernatural.

One source of skepticism is The New England Skeptical Society. In 1997, Perry DeAngelis and Steven Novella, two researchers from the society, published an article in *The Connecticut Skeptic* about their investigation of Ed and Lorraine Warren. The article, titled "Hunting the Ghost Hunters," scrutinized the Warrens' investigation techniques and their claims.

The authors had a professional video company run a detailed analysis on one of the Warrens' videotapes that was supposed to be evidence of a man dematerializing. "On the tape, a young man walks into the room, scratches his head, and 'poof!' disappears," the article explained.

The video analysis, however, indicated the camcorder shooting the video had employed a simple "wipe" effect, whether accidentally or deliberately, by stopping on the final frame.

In its conclusions, the article found that when the Warrens were "confronted with the lack of scientific quality to their methods and evidence, they typically retreat . . . they want the respectability of science without the tedious work, careful thought, and high standards of evidence that it demands."

But some of the most damming evidence against the credibility of these "psychic" investigators arose from the experience of popular horror writer Ray Garton, author of *In a Dark Place: The Story of a True Haunting*.

In a Dark Place, published in 1992 by Villard Books, told the story of the Snedeker family and their alleged "demonic siege." Feeling their son was possessed and their house was plagued by evil forces, the Snedekers contacted Ed and Lorraine Warren for help.

Ray Garton, however, questioned the truthfulness of the Snedekers' claims after discovering major inconsistencies with their story during his research. Needing advice, Garton approached Ed Warren, whom he originally was eager to work with since he had followed this couple's exploits as a child.

"When the details of the Snedekers' stories still didn't match up," Ray Garton said, "I became concerned and called Ed Warren. I didn't even have to tell him which details weren't meshing, I simply pointed out to him that the stories weren't matching."

"Ed laughed and told me not to worry about it. He said the Snedekers were 'crazy.' Then he said, 'All the people who come to us are crazy. Why do you think they come to us?' I was, quite literally, speechless. Without even asking for details, Ed had a solution. He reminded me that I wrote scary stories and told me to 'make it up and make it scary.'"

Bound by a publishing contract, Garton disagreed with the book's nonfiction label and felt the Warrens were frauds, who simply took advantage of troubled families.

Garton explained, "The families who come to the Warrens are, to say the least, dysfunctional. I think they tend to be people who are in need of serious help, *not* in need of the services of ghostbusters. Ed Warren's contempt for them is despicable. If he were to approach them with any sensitivity whatsoever, he would see that their biggest problems are not supernatural, but are very real. The Warrens enable these families to sublimate those problems by nurturing their dark fantasies."

It certainly can be argued that the Warrens, at times, promote an inaccurate history of the cases they are involved with. Another such case dealt with the history of Dudleytown, which is part of the

New England town of Cornwall.

According to Dudleytown researcher Reverend Gary P. Dudley, in their 1989 book *Ghost Hunters,* Ed and Lorraine Warren "totally ignored any semblance of research. They not only seemed to ignore the facts that were easy enough to obtain if they had wanted, they also ignored all the other stories that had gone on before them. The Warrens apparently found something that nobody had ever heard of before."

Reverend Gary P. Dudley, history teacher, genealogist and author of *The Legend of Dudleytown,* insisted the embellishments and inaccurate "facts" reported by the Warrens about the notorious Dudleytown rivaled the discrepancies found in their "investigation" of the Amityville case.

THE HISTORY OF 112 OCEAN AVENUE

In a recent interview with The History Channel, Kathy Lutz claimed that a tragedy befell every family that lived in the DeFeo home. Moreover, *The Amityville Horror* suggests that the property is cursed because it had once belonged to John Ketcham, a suspected witch who had fled Salem, Massachusetts before taking up residence in Amityville.

During an August 9, 1979 press conference, Jim Cromarty, then-owner of the Amityville house, said, "I was born in Amityville. I knew every family that grew up in this house. And that is another crock. They [the Lutzes] say that every family that was brought up in this house had bad things happen to them. It happens to be a fact that only one family had a tragedy happen to them in this house. Every other family had nothing but good things come out of the house."

In the late 1600s, Amityville was part of Huntington Township. A check of the historical society located in Huntington, a town approximately 13 miles from Amityville, revealed that there were several John Ketchams in the area. Because records of this time period are sketchy at best, there was no clear proof that Ketcham ever resided on the property. The most definitive proof against any John

Ketcham's being a witch came from the Ketcham family's own extensive research into their genealogy. After careful investigation, they have been able to determine there never was a witch named John Ketcham.

According to deeds and information compiled by the Amityville Historical Society, the Ocean Avenue property had once been farmland belonging to the Irelands, one of Amityville's most prominent and influential families. On January 14, 1924, Annie Ireland sold the property to John and Catherine Moynahan. The following year, Amityville builder Jesse Perdy constructed the large Dutch Colonial that still stands there today. While their new home was being built, the Moynahans relocated to the old house down the street. When the house was finished, the family of six moved back in and once again enjoyed life by the Amityville Creek.

When John and Catherine Moynahan died, their daughter, Eileen Fitzgerald, moved in with her own family. She lived there until October 17, 1960, when John and Mary Riley bought the house. Because of marital problems, the Rileys divorced and sold the house to the DeFeos on June 28, 1965.

The DeFeos lived in the house for more than nine years until on November 13, 1974, the years of abuse and turmoil from Big Ronnie came to a head. After the DeFeos, the Lutzes moved into the property and then moved out in 28 days. Their stay was so short that they did not even make a payment on the $60,000 mortgage they had on the house. On August 30, 1976, the Lutzes returned the house to Columbia Savings and Loan.

On March 18, 1977, Jim and Barbara Cromarty purchased the home from the bank. Although plagued by hordes of tourists searching for Jodie the pig and other supernatural phenomena, the Cromartys managed to live there happily for a decade. Nonetheless, they found it necessary to change the address to confuse the curious. It proved ineffective, so the Cromartys even added a fake middle window in between the third-floor, quarter-moon windows. It too failed to fool those determined to find the property.

During a press conference to refute the Lutzes' allegations, the Cromartys issued a two-page statement. An excerpt read:

Chapter Eleven

> The quiet village of Amityville, Long Island, has been made infamous by a hoax. It will possibly never be the same. It is Long Island's equivalent to Watergate. None of us would be here today if a responsible publisher and author had not given credibility to two liars, and allowed them the privilege of putting the word *true* on a book in which in all actuality is a novel . . . the credibility of the hoax stems from using a charlatan Catholic priest, who has been banned from performing his religious duties by the Diocese of Rockville Centre, the equivalent of disbarment of a lawyer . . . this charlatan priest has been involved with a complicity to a lie and, therefore, deserves no credibility, and should be dealt with accordingly.

The Cromartys sued the Lutzes, Jay Anson and the publishers of *The Amityville Horror*. Their multi-million dollar suit argued that not only was the book an invasion of privacy, but that "false misrepresentations were made willfully and solely for commercial exploitation." Eventually, the parties arrived at an undisclosed settlement.

On August 17, 1987, Peter and Jeanne O'Neil purchased the house from the Cromartys. During their stay, they changed the famed eye-windows to square ones and filled in the DeFeo pool. Since the yearly property taxes are in excess of $8,000, neighbors state that the O'Neils moved to save money for their children's college tuition.

On June 10, 1997, Brian Wilson purchased the house for approximately $310,000. Since 1997, Wilson has renovated the property. Among the many improvements, he has strengthened the foundation of the sinking boathouse and added a sunroom to the back of the house.

Since the renovation was anything but cheap, it is quite preposterous to think that a malevolent force resides there. Over the years, none of the families, except the Lutzes, has ever reported anything out of the ordinary in the house, and none of the families, except the Lutzes, has ever capitalized on the house's notoriety. The only thing the current house owners want is for the hoax to end and the tourists to leave them alone.

EXPOSING THE INCONSISTENCIES

In the September 17, 1979 issue of *People* magazine, William Weber admitted that the Lutzes and he created the stories over many bottles of wine. He further added that "George was a con artist."

In August 1979, William Weber participated in a radio interview with radio host Joel Martin in "Spectrum with Joel Martin." Among the many things that were discussed, including Weber's involvement with the hoax and George's futile search to get information from friends of Butch DeFeo prior to moving into the house, Weber discussed the "High Hopes" sign.

Weber said, "The Lutzes say that when they were shown the house by the real estate lady for the first time, there was a large sign in front of the house that said 'High Hopes.'

"They never saw a sign. They never knew the house was called 'High Hopes.' The reason why they found out is because I showed them a crime-scene photograph of an artist's sketch of the house. The sketch was hanging on the wall in the DeFeo residence, and in that sketch there was a sign called 'High Hopes.'"

Weber went on to allege that the Lutzes claimed they had seen the sign because it added a horrifying foundation to their story.

Weber's claims can be substantiated by the black-and-white photos of the Lutz house that were taken in early March 1976. They clearly show the sign missing. Regardless, in April 2000, during her interview for the History Channel documentary, Kathy Lutz once again described seeing the "High Hopes" sign before touring the house with the real estate agent.

Host Joel Martin also asked Weber if he thought the Lutzes had known the DeFeos. Weber replied, "It's funny because there's a story about that from one of the local Amityville boys in *Newsday* that the

Lutz boat had been tied up at the DeFeo's boathouse. I was never able to substantiate that, but the boy was reliable."

On May 26, 1988, Steven Dunleavy from Fox Television interviewed William Weber again. On national television, Weber admitted that the mythical Jodie the pig was inspired by the cat next door. Curiosity got the better part of the cat as it would often peek into the 112 Ocean Avenue.

Many of the so-called truths and facts stated in Jay Anson's *The Amityville Horror* were anything but that. Among them:

1. In Chapter One, when the Lutzes see the DeFeo home for the first time, they noticed that the neighbors on either side had their window shades drawn only on the sides that faced 112 Ocean Avenue. Not only did the neighbors deny having shades on the ground floor of their homes, but they also pointed out that often the Lutzes would come and go only to make it appear they lived there. Former next-door neighbor Diane Ireland also recalled to me a bizarre incident involving the Lutz children. In an attempt to welcome the Lutzes to the neighborhood, Mrs. Ireland offered the Lutz children, who were playing outside, some homemade donuts. She recalled that the instant she approached the children, Kathy Lutz came running out of the house screaming orders for her children to get back inside.

2. In Chapter Three, Anson wrote about the Lutzes' Transcendental Meditation practice. Incredibly, George Lutz told reporters during the February 16, 1976 press conference at Weber's office that they were always skeptical of the supernatural. Yet the couple admittedly practiced Transcendental Meditation, which is supposed to give the practitioner a higher

state of consciousness. Therefore, how could the Lutzes say they practiced TM, but also say they were closed-minded to the existence of the supernatural?

3. In Chapter Seven, Kathy Lutz woke up from a nightmare about the murder of Louise DeFeo, screaming, "She was shot in the head!" In reality, none of Louise DeFeo's wounds were located on her head. Furthermore, Weber admitted in a July 27, 1979 Associated Press interview that while discussing their business venture, Kathy concocted the nightmare idea about Louise DeFeo.

4. In Chapter 12, George and Kathy were terrified to see a demon with horns materialize on the inside wall of their fireplace. In federal court before Judge Weinstein, however, George admitted that it was just something very ugly.

5. In Chapter 15, Anson claimed that Sergeant Pat Cammaroto of the Amityville Village Police was called by George Lutz. According to Anson, the cop witnessed the damaged garage and hoof prints in the snow that were left by Jodie the pig. Sergeant Cammaroto sued Anson, insisting that he never even met the Lutzes, let alone had come out to the property to investigate their claims. Eventually, the publisher changed the name Cammaroto to Zammataro in later printings.

6. In Chapter 22, during their fight with the supernatural forces, George Lutz was compelled to nail pine boards over certain bedroom doors to trap the force inside. Yet the doors to the rooms opened inward, not outward as Anson assumed. Therefore, the boards were rendered useless.

7. In Chapter 24, green slime oozed from an empty lock hole in the third-floor bedroom that had belonged to Dawn DeFeo. Unbeknownst to Anson, there was neither a lock in the door nor a lock hole for ooze to escape.

8. In the Afterword, Anson wrote how the chilling cold George had noted feeling at 112 Ocean Avenue was quite common in haunted houses. But since the DeFeo house is located on the banks of the Amityville Creek, there is nothing supernatural about a cold chill rolling off the water. If the Lutzes had stayed until summer, then they would have discovered that it was also a very warm house because it was built in 1925 and had very little insulation in the walls.

In the March 1979 issue of *Writer's Digest*, Anson addressed the inconsistencies by saying, "Yeah, I know the psychical research people say I have made mistakes. They say that on such and such a day when I said it rained, it didn't rain. So what? I am a perfectly normal human being, and sometimes I make mistakes."

Yet in the book contract between Anson and the Lutzes, the Lutzes indicated they had checked and corrected the pre-publication galley proofs. In turn, Anson had agreed he incorporated the changes the Lutzes made. In court documents, for a later civil lawsuit against producer Dino De Laurentiis, George Lutz proclaimed Anson's book an "accurate statement."

When George Lutz was asked by Pete Stevenson of *The Morning Call*, a newspaper in Allentown, Pennsylvania, why they wanted a book written, Lutz responded, "One of the primary reasons was to set the record straight because of what was put in the media."

When a book carries the subtitle "A True Story," the public expects that the events described in the book are true and accurate. In 1995, authors Dr. Stephen Kaplan and Roxanne Salch Kaplan wrote *The Amityville Horror Conspiracy* to expose many of the inconsistencies in Anson's book as being a "consumer rip-off."

In fact, Dr. Kaplan was the first paranormal investigator called by George Lutz. On February 16, 1976, Dr. Kaplan received a phone call from George Lutz, who wanted him to investigate the DeFeo house. Dr. Kaplan agreed, but warned him that he would make public the details of his investigation and expose any hoax. After a couple of days, George cancelled the investigation Dr. Kaplan had planned, claiming he wanted to avoid any publicity. Dr. Kaplan and his wife contended the Lutzes backed out because they did not want to take a chance at being exposed.

With regard to their initial suspicions of George Lee Lutz, the Kaplans wrote, "In a discussion about Witchcraft, Lee mentions Ray Buckland, a prominent witch in the area who ran the Witchcraft Museum in Bayshore before moving to New England . . . That would mean that George had discussed 'the craft,' as it is called, with one of the most knowledgeable witches in the country long before he bought the house."

Wanting to confirm or refute the Kaplans' suspicions, I contacted Ray Buckland to see if he ever remembered meeting the Lutzes. When questioned, he had this to say, "I think it must have been the Lutzes, though, as I've said, I am bad with names."

With regard to 112 Ocean Avenue, Buckland recalled, "I went with another psychic, but neither of us picked up anything! We were therefore greatly surprised shortly after when all the stories started appearing."

Neither fear of publicity nor the inaccuracies contained in Anson's book prevented the Lutzes from touring around the world to promote it as their true story. Nonetheless, many of the inconsistent statements made during the televised interviews would come back to haunt the couple.

In a 1979 "Good Morning America" interview, Kathy Lutz was asked if the things described in Anson's book happened to her family quite often. Shaking her head, Kathy replied, "No, not to us."

On the TV show "In Search Of," hosted by Leonard Nimoy, George Lutz confidently stated, "We are glad it is over; for us it is over."

Yet after the hype of the first book died down, the terror conveniently returned. Subsequently, George and Kathy Lutz went on to participate in other books and movies that also purport to be true stories. Regrettably, they would no longer have the writing prowess of Jay Anson. On March 12, 1980, Anson died at the Stanford Medical Center of a heart attack. He was only 58.

In 1982, author John G. Jones picked up where Anson had left off and wrote *The Amityville Horror 2*. In 1985, he continued the Lutz saga with *Amityville: The Final Chapter*. Not only did both books carry the nonfiction label, but they also listed George and Kathy's names as joint copyright holders. Jones wrote in his foreword that "Amityville 2 has been written in close constant cooperation with George Lutz and his family."

Yet on May 27, 2002, George Lutz backpedaled by admitting on public radio that these books "were originally supposed to be published as fiction based on fact. They were not supposed to be published as nonfiction. I am not sure how some of those did end up being published as nonfiction."

The books claimed that "the force" in the Amityville house had escaped and was following them. Evidently, things got so bad that George and Kathy had to undergo an exorcism. As expected, the ritual failed, so there was a need of a third book.

In the finale of the third book, the walls to the Lutzes' Arizona home vanished, revealing the depths of hell. Out of the depths of hell, the creature from Amityville arose. Jones described the creature as being nine feet tall with flames for eyes and teeth that dripped bile.

Almost like in a Rambo movie, the creature was finally defeated after George Lutz sprinkled it with holy water and then strangled it to death. At the end of the book, Jones insisted that the horror was over. Nevertheless, in 1988, *Amityville: The Evil Escapes* was published. This time around, thankfully, the publisher labeled the book fiction.

Jay Anson's bestseller may have been based on a hoax, but his storytelling capability captivated the reader, a trait the Jones books lacked. Furthermore, sequel "Amityville" movies have suffered from low budgets, bad acting, and silly plots, which have effectively killed the viability of the franchise.

But for the "true" believers, the polygraph tested administered to George and Kathy Lutz on June 19, 1979 was proof enough that they were telling the truth. But it should be pointed out that the Lutzes were asked only five questions each regarding their so-called paranormal encounter.

Since polygraph tests are not considered credible enough to be admissible in court, the exams proved nothing more than a publicity stunt for the then-upcoming Amityville horror film adaptation of Jay Anson's novel.

Feeling the Lutzes' polygraph exams were anything but credible, California attorney Roger D. Stacy decided to propose to George Lutz a new set of tests. This time, however, George would be asked a series of questions regarding Bill Weber, the DeFeo family, Stephen Kaplan and his motivations for having the books written. In addition, he would be screened for any drugs or medications that could hinder or alter the accuracy of the test. Stacy said, "He was very adamant that he was not about to do the new polygraph under any circumstances even when I practically 'brought it to his door.'"

It should also be mentioned that the Lutzes did not submit to the original exams until three years after they had purportedly experienced any phenomena. Barbara Cromarty commented on this in the July 24, 1979 issue of *The Star*. She pointed out how the Lutzes had three years to get their story down pat.

But possibly the most convincing evidence that George and Kathy Lutz had no intention of living at 112 Ocean Avenue for very long can be ascertained from reviewing their finances. During my interview with George, he stated that his business had been so bad that he was forced to close one of his two land-surveying offices. This was understandable since Long Island faced a slumping construction industry in 1975.

On December 31, 1974, the fourth installment of $1,250 was due on the Deer Park home George Lutz had purchased, interest free, from Elizabeth Lutz, on January 15, 1974, for $4,500. Yet less than a year later, the newly married George Lutz, who suddenly became responsible for his second wife's three children and whose business was suffering and undergoing an IRS audit, was somehow able to afford an $80,000 home with an exorbitant amount of property taxes.

Since the Lutzes had been able to come up with a down payment of 25 percent of the house's asking price, the bank approved them. But according to former realtor Edith Evans, the Lutzes never even made a mortgage payment prior to their departure. Today, Butch and surviving friends and relatives of the DeFeos theorize that the Lutzes may have acquired some of the down payment from William Weber. But this remains unverified.

THE EXPLOITATION CONTINUES

On February 1, 1977, William Weber sent Butch a letter about their stalled book project. Apparently, Paul Hoffman was supposed to have a completed manuscript finished by December 31, 1976. Since the Lutzes' book was already in development, Hoffman was having a hard time convincing publishers that there was a market for a second book. For that reason, Weber wrote Butch to inform him that Hans Holzer, a parapsychologist, was also interested in writing his story.

Weber wrote, "Professor Hans Holzer is also interested in writing the story and that since he (Hoffman) has not written the manuscript, I am going ahead to negotiate with Professor Holzer."

On January 13, 1977, Hans Holzer entered 112 Ocean Avenue with William Weber, Bernard Burton, Laura Didio, and medium Ethel Johnson Meyers. Meyers claimed that Indians resided on the property to protect an old burial ground, insisting that whoever lived in the DeFeo house was going to be the victim of the Indians' fierce anger.

Holzer further theorized in his book, *Murder in Amityville*, that the spirit of a dead Indian chief possessed Ronald DeFeo Jr. and caused him to kill his family. Like the Warrens, Holzer claimed that the DeFeos had an exorcism performed for the house.

In his conclusion, Holzer wrote, "In conversations with family friends, relatives and neighbors, it seems the DeFeos were convinced that there were forces beyond their control in the house."

Geraldine replied, "Holzer is a fraud. The Brigantes, the DeFeos, and I would not cooperate with Holzer's hoax. There was never anything supernatural in the house. The only time there was ever something wrong in that house was the minute Mr. DeFeo arrived home from work."

Despite evidence pointing to the contrary, Holzer claimed the DeFeo house stood on an Indian burial ground. He also stated that in the 1700s some of the residents of the land practiced witchcraft. Once again, the facts proved otherwise. In fact, Holzer even got the dates mixed up. On Page 32, Holzer mistakenly stated the date the police discovered the DeFeo bodies was the morning of November 14, 1974, and not the evening of the 13th.

In all fairness, just as much blame should be placed on Butch for further sensationalizing the murders. Among other things, Butch lied when he said he heard screams throughout the house and had often felt an alien personality in him. But the one thing he never denied to Holzer was having a wife and children.

Why would Butch willingly tell lies about his life and the events that transpired on November 13, 1974? Geraldine answered, "To gain notoriety, money and assistance with his appeal."

Over Butch's objections, Holzer repeatedly insisted that he had sexual intercourse with his sister Dawn. On page 38 of *Murder in Amityville*, Holzer wrote, "He [Butch] freely admitted that there had been a relationship between himself and his sister Dawn, despite their being brother and sister."

But because of the success of the Lutz hoax and Jay Anson's book, the public was craving anything "Amityville." In another letter to Butch, Weber discussed a proposed documentary that Hans Holzer was creating based on his book. An excerpt from Weber's letter dated June 25, 1979, read:

> An independent television producer is paying $10,000 to Holzer for a television article about you and your trial. Mr. Holzer has agreed to pay

Chapter Eleven

you $2,000 and Bernard Burton and myself $2,000 each for participating in this venture with him.

An example of the dilemma Weber faced regarding offering Butch money can be found in an excerpt from his November 15, 1979 letter to Butch. It read:

I had hoped by this time to receive money from Hans Holzer; however, he called today to say I would be receiving $15,000 on Wednesday, November 21. If I do, I'll be up to see you on Friday, November 23. We have a serious problem to face involving the N.Y.S. Crime Victims Act, which says no one can profit from his criminal act. It is serious, but I know we can work out this problem in the best way for you.

Despite the problems, by April 10, 1980, there was already talk of *Murder in Amityville* becoming a movie. In a letter to Jack Glazer, Butch's new attorney, Weber reinforced his business partnership with Butch and speculated on the movie's potential by writing:

. . . since I have been negotiating on his [Butch's] behalf for more than four years and since there is one literary project with a possible movie connected with it already in effect, we will both have to live up to that agreement. I am referring to the book entitled *Murder in Amityville*. I anticipate receiving as much as $200,000, and Mr. DeFeo will receive his share pursuant to our original agreement.

In 1982, *Amityville 2: The Possession* was released in theaters around the United States. The movie was loosely based on Holzer's book, *Murder in Amityville*. Instead of the DeFeos, the family portrayed in the film was called the Montellis.

Regardless, Geraldine complained, saying, "Everyone knew the family was supposed to be the DeFeos. The son in the movie was possessed, and now I had to explain to my daughter that her father really wasn't a demon."

Inspired by Holzer's allegations that Butch and Dawn had sex, the movie's producers included a scene where the older brother and sister sleep together. For traditional Italian families like the DeFeos and Brigantes, nothing could have been a greater insult.

It should be pointed out that Holzer's contract with American International Productions, the studio producing the movie, had him agree to things that seemed to be highly suspect. As the owner of the book *Murder in Amityville*, Holzer stood to make 2-1/2 percent of the gross receipts and $150,000 on the movie. More important, Part B of the sixth clause made it clear that Holzer could never make any public statements inconsistent with the theory of demonic possession of Ronald DeFeo.

After *Murder in Amityville*, Holzer went on to write two fictional Amityville books titled, *The Secret of Amityville* and *The Curse of Amityville*, which was turned into a movie in 1990. The budget for *The Amityville Curse* was so low that the house used did not even resemble a Dutch Colonial home, let alone the DeFeo house.

On Friday, October 26, 2001, I had the opportunity to ask Hans Holzer specific questions about his theories and books during a tape-recorded phone interview with him. One of the first questions I asked was about Geraldine DeFeo. Not only did Holzer recall meeting Geraldine, but he also told me that he knew that she and Butch had been married prior to the DeFeo murders.

Holzer, nonetheless, disregarded William Weber's claims that it was all a hoax, unsure why Butch's former attorney would say such a thing. Today, Holzer remains unchanged about his theory that Butch was the seventh victim, and that he alone killed his entire family because he was possessed by the spirit of an Indian chief.

In the closing portion of my interview, I asked Hans Holzer about the purported incestuous relationship between Butch and Dawn that he alluded as being true in his book, *Murder in Amityville*. His reply was astounding. He admitted to me that he did not believe it had actually happened.

In early 1980, while Hans Holzer's book was still on the bestseller list, William Weber was approached by another filmmaker who wanted the real DeFeo story to come out. Also involved with the project was Herman Race and Dr. Daniel Schwarz, the psychiatrist who testified on behalf of Butch at his trial. After being offered $50,000 and one percent of the "first dollar" share of all revenues, Butch signed the rights of his story over to Herman Race and Dr. Schwartz with the stipulation that:

> . . . the motion picture or teleplay will be based upon my true story and the true facts, which occurred in November 1974 and will not deal in any manner with the theory of possession or demonism as contained in the book *Murder in Amityville*.

Although the project never became a reality, the above clause in the signed agreement was further proof that the possession and demonism theories were nothing but a charade.

What were the real motives of William Weber? Was he trying to do all he could for his client, or was he simply using Butch to line his pockets? A clearer understanding of Weber can be ascertained from reviewing a 1977 audio tape made for Butch by Michael Brigante Sr. and Linnea Nonnewitz.

On the audio tape, Brigante said, "Sweetheart, let Hesterberg and Kelly find you an appeals lawyer; they got a reason for it. Do what grandpa tells you." Indubitably, Brigante wanted the family lawyers to find someone other than Weber to handle Butch's upcoming appeal.

On the tape, Linnea reinforced the family's suspicions of Weber when she said, "I told you that time will tell about Weber. And time is telling. He is more worried about himself."

DEFEO VS. WEBER

On February 27, 1988, Butch filed a lawsuit against William

Weber in the federal court in New York. The complaint declared that Weber conspired against him by exploiting his story, and that Weber "aligned fabricated defenses."

Butch further declared that Weber's interest "was to profit from my case by having me sign written contracts for the purpose of writing a true story in book form, and thereafter produce a movie, and to write a false story, which he started before trial."

Included as amended parties to the complaint were the Lutzes, Holzer, Anson's estate, Jones, and several book publishers. Butch declared that he was denied due process because of the notoriety the hoax created. He made it a point to stress that the possession stories, insanity defense, and allegations of incest with his sister were false, and that the books and movies, purportedly true, actually "defrauded the public at large."

Butch further alleged that the surrogate court had deprived him of monies from his parents' estates. Of course, Butch made it a point to bring up that Weber had worked on the campaign of Judge Signorelli, who was presiding over the DeFeo estate, and who originally presided over Butch's criminal trial.

It was Butch's opinion that "the federal court was the only judicial system that can, in fact, remedy the wrongs done in such a bizarre and extraordinary situation."

Despite his insistence, on July 10, 1990, Judge Leonard D. Wexler dismissed the case, citing a "failure to allege any federally recognized claim." Nevertheless, Butch got partly what he wanted: to refute publicly many of the lies told about him.

Still, Weber's own legal secretary wrote a book about him, criticizing his ethics. In 1994, Betty Carrington, a.k.a. Betty O'Grady, self-published her book, titled *Judicial Carousel*. Although only four chapters are devoted to her time with Weber, Carrington offered a candid account of her boss.

During her tenure, Carrington had the opportunity to assist Weber in Butch's appeal. Regarding the alleged incest between Butch and Dawn, Carrington wrote that Butch "emphatically denied this accusation in many of his letters to Bill."

Furthermore, Carrington referred to Weber as having an "enormous ego," and she stated that the DeFeo case "made him a star." After being disappointed once too often, she eventually departed from Weber's firm, contemplating leaving the legal profession altogether.

* * *

In conclusion, Butch was definitely to blame for allowing the commercialization of his family's deaths, although equal responsibility lay with William Weber, who at times acted more like a literary agent than a defense attorney. Although many of the arguments Weber made in the DeFeo trial and appeal were brilliant, they do not exonerate him for his part in instigating a hoax about the DeFeo home. Although Butch and Weber had little choice other than to pursue an insanity defense, they lost sight of the objective: to get Butch out of prison.

The exploitation, nonetheless, continued with the recent History Channel documentary on *The Amityville Horror*, which aired for the Halloween 2000 season. The documentary may have been grossly inaccurate, but it did provide the original architects of the hoax a chance to speak out. It is not surprising that Holzer, the Warrens and the Lutzes continued to profess the story to be true, while Weber and Roxanne Kaplan insisted that it was all a hoax. The only cast member missing was Butch, who wanted $2,000 to appear on the show. Although all of the crucial participants got paid for their interviews, the History Channel refused to pay Butch the $2,000 he wanted, reasoning he could not profit from his crimes.

In a letter to the producers of the documentary, Butch insisted, "My attorney at my trial, William Weber, and the Lutzes, who I sold my home to, put the hoax together." Yet this statement made no difference. The documentary persisted in contending Butch had to be either insane or possessed at the time of the murders. Because of budget problems, no DeFeo family member was ever interviewed, although they repeatedly protested the content of the show.

In her letter to the producers, Geraldine wrote, "I respectfully request that you portray the members of the DeFeo family with the dignity and respect they deserve." Her request went unnoticed.

Eventually, through his attorney, George Lutz proclaimed that he never met Geraldine DeFeo and that his story was true. In 2002, prior to this book being completed, Weber also refused comment, even though he has publicly called the haunting stories false. In the September 17, 1979 issue of *People* magazine, Weber charged, "I know this book [*The Amityville Horror*] is a hoax. We created this horror story over many bottles of wine."

But the question that remains is why wasn't more done in the early days to combat the hoax? Aside from Butch's belief that he would have become rich and been released from prison in a few short years, his surviving relatives had too much to lose by becoming outspoken critics of the stories. By speaking out, the Brigantes and the DeFeos would have risked exposing the skeletons in their own closets, such as their reputed connections to organized crime.

The hoax also offered the perfect cover for the Suffolk County justice system. In Holzer's TV documentary based on his book, William Weber hinted at his legal strategy for Butch's appeal, saying, "Personally, if you are asking me about possession, I have to reserve that. But in the future is evidence going to be submitted to a court to help Ronnie DeFeo? Is possession part of that? The answer still remains to be seen, but I think we are swaying toward the affirmative in that regard."

Because the public was misled into believing that Butch DeFeo was possessed and his house was haunted, logic fell by the wayside. After all, the 1970s saw such supernatural hits as *The Exorcist* and *The Omen* grace the big screen. So it is not surprising that *The Amityville Horror* was considered by the general public as a plausible scenario for the DeFeo murders.

In the end, nothing can change the fact that the Amityville saga was one of the most successful hoaxes ever conceived. Geraldine DeFeo, who now regrets her years of silence, summed it up best: "Evil never inhabited the DeFeo home. The only evil that exists in the case stems from the exploitation of the memory of six human beings and the tragedy that befell them."

CHAPTER TWELVE
In the Pursuit of Justice

O N DECEMBER 4, 1975, Judge Thomas Stark handed down the strictest sentence he could impose on Butch: 25-years to life. On that same day, William Weber filed a notice of appeal for Butch. It was a given that Weber would remain with Butch during the appeal and, of course, for the subsequent book he had planned.

Realizing Weber was interested more in lining his own pockets than with preparing for the difficult legal hurdles ahead, Michael Brigante Sr. pleaded with his grandson to let his own attorney, Alexander Hesterberg, find him a more qualified appeals lawyer. Luckily for Weber, Butch seemed just as preoccupied with the intended commercialization of his family's house and their murders.

"Butch believed that Weber's proposed book with the Lutzes would not only make him rich," Geraldine DeFeo explained, "but also win his appeal on the grounds of insanity."

Although the original plan called for Weber and the Lutzes' book to defer his legal costs, Butch had to find an alternate method when the Lutzes broke their agreement with Weber. The only recourse left for Butch was to obtain money from his parents' estate. In order for Butch to obtain the $20,000 Weber wanted, he had to agree to relinquish any future rights to the estate, barring, of course, the appeal was successful and Butch was found not guilty by reason of insanity.

Since the court had proven on several occasions its reluctance to diverge from the prosecution's decision that Butch should be the only guilty party prosecuted, Weber still felt the insanity defense was Butch's best choice. According to Butch, Weber also felt the insanity defense would help spark interest in the proposed book.

Weber's appeal brief was approximately 200 pages and challenged Butch's sanity, the initial police interrogation, and the harsh sentence handed down by Justice Stark.

Weber was allotted 30 minutes to argue the appeal in front of the appellate division of New York's Supreme Court. The chief points of the appeal included:

1. The actions by the Suffolk County Police in obtaining written and oral statements from the defendant under the circumstances of this case violated the defendant's constitutional rights and constituted fundamental unfairness.

2. The court improperly charged the jury on the issue of mental disease or defect.

3. The people failed to prove the defendant's sanity beyond a reasonable doubt.

4. The trial court abused its discretion by refusing to grant defense counsel reasonable adjournment in order to prepare for trial.

5. The trial court committed several errors the cumulative effect of which denied the defendant a fair trial.

Chapter Twelve

Weber's foremost argument was that Butch's constitutional rights had been violated when the police had refused Richard Wyssling, an attorney, access to Butch during the police interrogation. Butch, furthermore, had wanted to remain silent until he could contact his own attorney, Richard Hartman. Weber insisted the police had not respected Butch's rights and, therefore, the oral confession and material evidence brought against him at his trial should have been ruled inadmissible in court.

Weber argued, "The fact that the defendant did not make totally inculpatory oral statements until more than seven hours had elapsed after the Miranda rights were given to him strongly suggested the defendant did not knowingly and intelligently waive his rights."

Weber acknowledged in his brief that Detective Dennis Rafferty's testimony appeared to corroborate the fact that Butch was evasive and did not want to cooperate during the interrogation.

Weber established this fact when he asked Detective Rafferty at Butch's trial, "Did you feel at that time that he was in complete control of his mental facilities at the time he committed the act?"

Under oath, the detective responded, "Yes, the way he was dodging around the questions, I thought he was in pretty good control of himself."

This "dodging," according to Weber, provided enough indication that Butch's rights were violated since he was not allowed access to his family or his lawyer during the 21-hour interrogation. It was only after Butch confessed that his lawyer and his wife were allowed to see him.

Weber also attacked Justice Stark in the appeal, citing he had inappropriately instructed the jury about Butch's insanity. Weber stated, "The language, as charged, is confusing at best, and certainly does not convey the substance of the rule . . . Justice Stark's distinction between 'intellectual understanding and appreciation' and 'mere surface knowledge' is wrong as a matter of law and does not adequately explain the substance of the statutory language to the jury."

Justice Stark's instructions to the jury, according to Weber, were inadequate to distinguish between Butch's knowing that murdering his family was wrong and having a deeper appreciation that such an act should have never even been considered. By Weber's contention, the success of an insanity verdict hinged on the jury's ability to understand that Butch could not do this.

"The jurors, therefore, as in *Buthy*, erroneously were led to believe that 'know' and 'appreciate' were synonymous and together stated a single criterion of legal sanity," Weber held.

Weber further alleged that Justice Stark, while marshalling evidence for the prosecution, had inappropriately taken the testimony of Dr. Daniel Schwartz, the psychiatrist retained by the defense, out of context. This made it appear to the jury that Dr. Schwartz had contributed to the evidence against Butch, proving he was sane.

"Due to the years of abuse he suffered from his father," the defense alleged, "Butch would have used excessive violence during the murders if he had been sane." Thus, Weber reasoned that Butch showed every indication that he was insane because he was able to restrain himself and use only enough violence to complete the act.

Another valid argument against the court dealt with Justice Stark's not allowing Weber an adjournment to prepare for Butch's trial better.

"Without notice to or knowledge of, or consent by DeFeo's assigned counsel, Assistant District Attorney John Buonora submitted an affidavit to Mr. Justice Arthur M. Cromarty wherein he stated this case was ready for trial," Weber informed the appellate court. "At no time, on the record or otherwise, did defense counsel state to the court or the District Attorney's office that defendant was ready for trial."

Weber was outraged that the prosecution was allowed a one-week adjournment on September 15, 1975, the original date of the suppression hearing, but the defense was not "given adequate opportunity to prepare his client's defense in light of the magnitude of the crimes charged." It was obvious that Weber was neither prepared nor expecting the trial immediately to follow the suppression hearing.

Judge Signorelli was pressured to remove himself from the case, especially after he granted the defense's supplemental omnibus motion. This supplemental motion granted the defense an equal opportunity to possess crime-scene photographs, reports, and other relevant information that the prosecution had planned on using.

Regardless, Weber did not receive this documentation until the end of August, so he needed more time to incorporate them adequately into Butch's defense. It was not an unreasonable request, given the nature and complexity of the case, especially after Herman Race revealed his findings in the post-hearing conference.

Weber may have felt that the lack of adjournment constituted an unfair advantage for the prosecution, but he insisted in his appeal that Justice Stark proved prejudicial in allowing testimony against Butch regarding his past drug use and crimes. Weber argued this further tainted the jury's image of Butch.

In addition, the admittance during trial of several crime-scene photos was nothing more than a prosecution trick to win the jury over, as Weber demonstrated in his brief when he wrote, "The prejudicial nature of the photographs is obvious upon the viewing of them. It would have to take a super-human emotional detachment on the part of the jurors not to be repelled by such photographs, and not to desire retribution against one accused of this horrible crime."

Assistant District Attorney Mark D. Cohen appeared in front of the appellate court to refute Weber's charges and state the District Attorney's case against Butch. He motioned for the higher court to uphold the original conviction. In his brief, Cohen argued:

1. That Ronald DeFeo knowingly and voluntarily waived his Miranda rights.

2. That prosecutor Gerard Sullivan was able to prove beyond a reasonable doubt that Butch DeFeo was sane and did not suffer from any mental defect at the time of the DeFeo murders.

3. Justice Stark properly ruled on both the admissibility of Butch's past convictions and drug history, and the

allowance of police photos into evidence.

4. That an adjournment was unnecessary.

In addition to the main arguments listed above, Cohen addressed Butch's claims concerning police brutality. But the material Cohen presented opposing Butch's allegations seemed to contradict the prosecution's assertions that Butch was not victimized by the police.

On page 13 of his brief, Cohen reiterated what the Suffolk County police detectives testified under oath. He wrote, "The defendant was not threatened or physically abused in any way during this episode nor were any cuts or bruises observed."

Likewise, page 18 read, "Except for the needle mark on the defendant's arm where he had shot heroin on November 13th, the police noticed no bruises or cuts on the defendant nor did the defendant complain of any injuries."

However, the next page contained a critical flaw with the police's version of events. Cohen mentioned that, "On November 18, 1974, the defendant was given a physical examination by the medical staff of the Suffolk County Jail. The examination revealed subsiding bruises on the abdomen and left leg and healing abrasions on the spinal area, which were said to be between four and seven days old."

Could it be possible for the veteran detectives on the homicide squad to overlook the prominent bruising on Butch? Obviously, not. By simply comparing Cohen's statements of facts, it again can be determined that the police had beaten Butch, an apparent practice in police interrogations in Suffolk County during that time. Additional proof of the conspiracy comes from a daily report made on November 14, 1974.

Prior to being given a holding cell, Butch was stripped and searched on November 14, 1974. At 2200 hours on the 14th, a police officer with shield #2553 wrote, "Prisoner stripped searched, placed in cell; no sign of injury." The entry is further proof that the Suffolk County Police Department intentionally chose not to document the injuries Butch DeFeo had sustained during his interrogation, believing, like in other cases, they would go unnoticed.

On March 27, 1978, the appellate division reached a decision. Despite all of Weber's arguments, an incredibly well-written appeal brief and his tenacious attitude, the higher court affirmed the original judgment. And on May 23, 1978, the Court of Appeals also denied leave for appeal.

Although the insanity issue was the only viable strategy for Weber during Butch's trial, it was clear that Butch was not insane but only feigning it for his defense. Weber, nevertheless, did an extraordinary job of pointing out the injustices that occurred to Butch during his interrogation and of Justice Stark's prejudicial attitude toward Butch to the appellate court.

After the copious amounts of work that Weber put into the appeal, and the complex issues raised and arguments made, it was a disappointment to see the higher court's lack of interest in insuring justice had been served.

"Weber was angered by this," Geraldine said, "because he had worked months on the appeal, and it seemed as if the courts were simply sweeping the case aside."

After the original verdict was affirmed and the higher courts showed little interest in righting the wrongs in Butch's case, it was evident that the courts may never side with the notorious Amityville murderer. After all, by 1978, Jay Anson's *The Amityville Horror* was a bestseller, so the entire country knew of the heinous crimes Butch had been convicted of, and about George and Kathy Lutz's so-called plight in the DeFeo house. It was now clear that Weber's insanity defense strategy had backfired.

BUTCH BATTLES WEBER

By the end of March 1980, Butch had decided it was time to part company with William Weber. Upon the advice of Roger Nonnewitz, he retained the services of attorney Jack Glazer to act on his behalf with regard to any future exploitation of his story. Butch claimed Weber was unwilling to leave because of his vested interest in the Amityville stories. Hence, it was Glazer's job to inform Weber that his services were no longer needed.

An excerpt from an April 10, 1980 letter to Glazer showed the lawyer's determination. Weber wrote, " . . . Mr. DeFeo's formal withdrawal of rights previously assigned to me is consented to, subject to existing commitments and present negotiations . . ."

Weber made sure he informed Butch and Glazer that he was still connected to Hans Holzer's *Murder in Amityville* project and the ongoing negotiations with Dr. Daniel Schwartz, Herman Race, and Frank D'Annibale to make the true DeFeo story, which meant no more fabricated demons or Indian chiefs.

Butch inevitably blamed Weber for his predicament, obviously forgetting his own greedy participation with the capitalization of his family's deaths. On February 27, 1988, Butch filed a lawsuit against his former attorney, citing that Weber's exploits deprived him of his right to due process.

By feigning insanity, contributing to a hoax, and pretending to be possessed by an evil spirit, Butch's plans for an early release through a successful appeal went unrealized.

"Before the trial, there was talk of Butch having to serve only 16-1/3 to 18 years," Geraldine explained, "but because he became so notorious, there was never any chance that the public would forget him or the Amityville story."

After his efforts with D'Annibale proved fruitless, William Weber ended his exploits with Amityville, except, of course, for the occasional TV interview. Considered by some to have been the devil's lawyer, Weber will be remembered most for his association with Butch. What is unclear, however, is whether he meant for this to overshadow the rest of his career and follow him the rest of his life.

DeFeo vs. Weber, nonetheless, provided Butch with the opportunity to provide corroborating affidavits from witnesses who knowingly perjured themselves in Butch's trial in order to comply with Weber's strategy.

Linnea and Roger Nonnewitz declared, "William Weber rehearsed me to testify only about things that were consistent with

SWORN AFFIDAVIT

STATE OF FLORIDA }
COUNTY OF

I WILLIAM DAVIDGE, being duly sworn deposes and says:

1. I am affiant and make this affidavit voluntarily and freely regarding Dawn De'Feo and Ronald De'Feo Jr.

2. I am 33 years of age, I reside at:

3. That I was the boyfriend of Dawn De'Feo and I am a friend of Ronald De'Feo Jr. and I was friends with the rest of the De'Feo family.

4. That I have direct knowledge about Dawn De'Feo, as she was in love with me and wanted to come to Florida to live with me, but her mother, Louse De'Feo and father Ronald De'Feo Sr., forbid her from doing so, which led up to hostile incidents between Dawn and her mother and father over all this, and Dawn was determined to come to Florida, no matter what.

5. I have direct knowledge that Dawn De'Feo was using drugs, L.S.D., and mescaline from time to time, and about Dawn's bad temper, which got out of hand on occasions.

6. I have direct knowledge of Dawn's hatred towards her mother and father, and how Dawn's only use for "Butch" (Ronald De'Feo, Jr.), was to use him, as "Butch" (Ronnie Jr.), gave Dawn money that she requested from him. "Butch", Ronnie Jr., even gave me William Davidge, money to take Dawn to her High School Prom, but Dawn,s only use for "Butch", Ronnie Jr., was to use him.

7. I have direct knowledge of Dawn's attitude right up to the begining of November 1974, as per my phone conversations with her from Florida to Amityville.

Wherefore, the above is true and correct to the best of this affiants personal knowledge.

WILLIAM DAVIDGE

Sworn to before me this
24 day of July 1990

THEODORE YURACK
NOTARY PUBLIC, State of New York
#4751630
Qualified in Suffolk County

Affidavit from Billy Davidge attesting to Dawn's out-of-control behavior.

STATE OF PENNA)
)SS:
COUNTY OF BERKS)

I, Linnea Nonnewitz, being duly sworn, deposes and says:

    1. I am the above named affiant and make this affidavit freely and voluntarily attesting to facts regarding Ronald DeFeo and his criminal defense counsel under Suffolk County criminal indictment #1251/74 in the State of New York.

    2. I am approximately 53 years of age, and reside at ██████████

    3. I am familiar with Ronald DeFeo and have been a long time friend of the family.

    4. I was approached by Ronald DeFeo's defense lawyer, William Weber to testify at the trial, at which Weber attempted to rehearse me to testify to facts which were not true in reference to state, "Ronnie beat the children up".

    5. I refused to testify incorrectly at the DeFeo trial.

    6. While Ronnie was incarcerated pending trial, I use to visit him, and prior to trial he telephoned me and told me that he did not want to pursue an insanity defense at the trial, and asked me to telephone William Weber and advise him that Ronald DeFeo did not want to try any insanity defenses at trial.

    WHEREFORE, the foregoing is true and correct to the best of your affiant's knowledge.

Linnea Nonnewitz

Sworn to before me this 28th day of June, 19 88

Notary Public

ARTHUR J. HERB, NOTARY PUBLIC
BOYERTOWN BOROUGH, BERKS COUNTY
MY COMMISSION EXPIRES SEPT. 18, 1990

Affidavit from Linnea Nonnewitz

Recovery of DeFeo evidence from Brooklyn sewer (above). Agrement between Butch DeFeo and William Weber (below), enabling exploitation of the DeFeo tragedy.

```
                                    Clinton Correctional
                                        Facility
                                    Box B
                                    Dannemora, New York 12929
                                    February 27, 1976

William E. Weber, Esq.
Mars & Burton, P.C.
38 Oak Street
Patchogue, New York 11772

Dear Bill:

            This letter will serve to assign to you
any and all right, title and interest I may have
in and to any of my rights in connection with the
publication or any disclosure of the events which
occurred in November of 1974 relative to my family
and any and all circumstances surrounding such
events, up to and including the present time.

            It is understood that you may publish with-
out any further consent from me any and all such facts,
circumstances and other information you may have and
that I hereby specifically waive any and all privileges
in that regard.

            In the event that such publication is made
which shall result in the receipt of revenues from
any source in which you are connected, I will receive
a royalty payment as follows:

      1)   Five (5%) Per Cent of the first
           One Million And 00/100 ($1,000,000.00)
           Dollars in gross receipts;

      2)   Four (4%) Per Cent of the second
           One Million And 00/100 ($1,000,000.00);
           and

      3)   Three (3%) Per Cent of the revenues
           thereafter received.
```

his insanity defense . . . Mr. Weber would not allow me to testify about Ronald Jr. and the members of his family the way I wanted to as I had direct knowledge about incidents and things that occurred in the DeFeo home by the entire DeFeo family."

In their affidavits, both of the Nonnewitzes further brought out that Detective Rafferty had come to their home in Amityville looking for a .38-caliber handgun, the same caliber of bullet Louise DeFeo was shot with.

Frank Davidge, in his affidavit, wrote, "I was directed, through Weber, to describe Ronald DeFeo as insane by testifying to acts to support the defense of insanity. The acts described were purposely directed to me while testifying by Weber's cross-examination at the DeFeo trial, in an attempt to place DeFeo in a mental hospital, and exonerate DeFeo from all criminal acts alleged in the indictment and proceedings."

Likewise, Charles Tewksbury's read, "Weber had me make up incidents, and he took a horseplay incident and made it appear DeFeo was insane, advising me it would help DeFeo.

"Weber prohibited me to testify the truth, where I could of testified to facts that would have changed the verdict. Weber insisted on pursuing an insanity defense, and cross-examined me to make DeFeo appear insane so he would be committed to a mental hospital."

Once more, Barry Springer, unable to testify at the original trial, stated, "I advised Weber that Ronald DeFeo was not crazy nor insane in any way. Weber then told me that he could not use me at the trial unless I testified his way.

"Weber also told me that if I testified for the defense and helped Ronnie that Ronald DeFeo would probably be out in a few years ahead, and be committed to a nut house, and have plenty of money when he was released from a mental institution."

During *DeFeo vs. Weber*, Butch also used Richard Romondoe, an obvious alias for Bobby Kelske. Butch's onetime best friend had cooperated with the police against him, failed to help Butch and used his knowledge about the Brigantes' criminal activities and their associations with several prominent crime families to fend off any reprisals from the Mob.

Richard Romondoe, the nonexistent brother of Geraldine DeFeo, stated in his affidavit that he and Butch were playing pool in the basement of the DeFeo home when Dawn went around killing everyone. In the fraudulent affidavit, the nonexistent Romondoe further stated that after Butch had killed Dawn, he disposed of the gun and cleaned up the house.

DeFeo vs. Weber based its merits on factual information, although Butch chose to omit the entire truth behind his family's murder, and concocted the Richard Romondoe character. Nonetheless, the suit was the first step in exposing the fallacies and injustices that had taken place in the original trial. Regardless, it failed to establish any federally recognized claim and was dismissed by the United States District Court.

THE 1992 HEARING

In 1992, Butch continued to allege that Weber had prevented him from presenting the true facts of his case to the jury during his trial, forced him to plead insanity, coerced many witnesses to testify falsely, did not allow Barry Springer to testify, and was motivated by financial prospects of a book and movie.

On June 22, 1992, Justice Stark, once again, presided over a preliminary hearing to determine if Butch's allegations held any merit. During the two days of testimony, Gerald Lotto, Butch's court-appointed attorney for the proceedings, called numerous witnesses to testify, including Roger and Linnea Nonnewitz, William Weber, William Davidge, John Carswell, Steven Hicks, Gerard Sullivan, Charles Tewksbury and, of course, Butch. During the hearing, Butch sat intently watching the proceedings, flashing an occasional smile.

Bobby Kelske refused to attend to testify on Butch's behalf or about his involvement with the murders. Geraldine DeFeo also refused to honor Lotto's subpoena because she knew Butch had every intention of using the fabricated Richard Romondoe story. She knew her testimony would only hurt Butch's newest attempt at justice since she refused to lie under oath and say she had a brother.

During the hearing, the various parties testified about their roles in the first trial. As in their previous affidavits, the Nonnewitzes and Butch's friends admitted under oath that Weber had forced them to testify falsely. William Davidge, Dawn's boyfriend in 1974, testified that he knew Dawn was enraged because her father would not let her go to Florida. Incredibly, Justice Stark failed to see how Davidge's testimony indicated Dawn had motive enough to want her family dead.

"There was corruption in this case from the first day," Lotto argued before Justice Stark. In addition to attacking Weber about his role with the Lutzes, Lotto pointed out that Dr. Howard Adelman had testified at Butch's trial that he believed there had been more than one killer.

Michael Ahearn represented the District Attorney's office during the proceedings and characterized Lotto as grandstanding. Obviously, Lotto's inability to present Romondoe, or prove he even existed, was a blow to his case. Weber, furthermore, denied any wrongdoing.

After the trial concluded, Butch felt that his court-appointed attorney did not have his best interests in mind. According to a letter written to Justice Stark on September 4, 1992, Butch argued that Lotto failed to mention that the contents of his parents' safe deposit box in a bank disproved the prosecution's robbery motive.

Butch also asked Justice Stark to continue the trial and compel Geraldine DeFeo to testify. In addition, Father James McNamara, who was prepared to testify on Butch's behalf, was told by the court that his testimony, which was about the condition of Butch's face prior to his arrest, was no longer relevant. Finally, according to Butch, the Nonnewitzes were never asked about the second gun.

Butch wrote, "It would have been revealed how Detective Dennis Rafferty and Detective G. Harrison went to the Nonnewitzes' home looking for jewelry and a gun, as this is part of the Nonnewitzes' affidavit, the moving papers in the 440 [motion]."

On January 6, 1993, Justice Stark issued his decision. It had

Chapter Twelve

taken so long because Butch had filed several other motions, including one to grant him DNA testing on the alleged bloodstained clothing found in the Brooklyn sewer.

Justice Stark decided that Butch's testimony had been "false and fabricated." He refused to believe that Butch was married prior to the murders even though several witnesses had made affidavits attesting to the fact.

Justice Stark also found William Weber to be truthful and credible, and did not believe that Weber forced Butch to use an insanity defense. This was in spite of the fact that an impartial federal judge, Judge Weinstein, who presided over the *Lutz vs. Weber* civil case, felt Weber had acted more like a literary agent than an attorney.

Overall, anything that refuted the original trial was disregarded, including the witnesses who had come forward and admitted they had perjured themselves at the original trial. Disappointingly, Butch's motion was denied.

Angry over Justice Stark's ruling, Geraldine explained, "Justice Stark refused to accept that Weber had ordered any witnesses to perjure themselves during Butch's trial. In 1992, these individuals came forward and were prepared to accept a perjury charge. Stark was oblivious to this and upheld their original testimony, overlooking the facts of the case."

In a letter to Geraldine DeFeo, Butch insisted, "The Department of Justice should be brought into this as this time the judge and D.A.'s lies cannot be overlooked."

Butch's request for an investigation was turned down, so Justice Stark's rulings against him stood.

DNA: THE IMPARTIAL WITNESS

Since the 1980s, DNA testing has revolutionized the justice system, allowing for both prosecutors and police officers to find and prosecute the guilty while offering defense attorneys a chance to exonerate their clients. On the other hand, post-conviction DNA testing can either reinforce a guilty verdict or be an invaluable tool for gaining freedom for those wrongly convicted.

At first, many people were skeptical of this new science, but today there is a national movement for a universal testing standard.

On June 13, 2000, Eliot Spitzer, Attorney General for New York state, testified before the Senate Judiciary Committee in Washington, D.C., on how post-conviction DNA testing should be incorporated into the American criminal justice system.

"With DNA testing, we can determine whether a particular patch of blood, hair, or a semen sample belongs to a specific individual," Spitzer said. "New York state is a leader in this area, having passed legislation granting a statutory right to post-conviction DNA testing almost six years ago."

Spitzer was referring to New York law §440.30, which was amended in 1994 to allow trial courts the authorization to grant post-conviction DNA testing. But before testing could be authorized, certain criteria had to be met.

First, evidence containing DNA had to have been secured in connection with the trial resulting in the verdict. Second, a probability must exist that the verdict would have been more favorable for the defendant if DNA testing had been conducted on such evidence and the results were admitted into the trial.

On Tuesday, December 19, 2000, then-Suffolk County District Attorney James M. Catterson Jr. announced a program to look at all convictions obtained prior to January 1, 1996 to determine if DNA testing would be appropriate. Catterson, a one-time opponent to DNA testing, reasoned that he now believed that such post-conviction testing was an essential part of the justice system, but only in certain circumstances to ensure no innocent person had been wrongly convicted.

Catterson announced, "Testing will go forward if DNA evidence exists, and if the defendant has consistently maintained his or her innocence. There's no point in going to the trouble of testing evidence if a defendant admitted the crime."

Yet Barry Scheck, co-director of the Innocence Project, an organization that provides free legal assistance to inmates who want to challenge their convictions through post-conviction DNA testing, challenged this faulty assumption the next day in *Newsday*. Although pleased with Catterson's change of heart, Scheck pointed out that there were cases in which inmates confessed or pleaded guilty just to avoid police brutality.

This can certainly be applied to Suffolk County, which has had numerous instances of police brutality, wrongful convictions, and an extraordinarily, if not suspiciously, high confession rate.

Believing DNA testing is the only means left to prove his innocence and right the grave wrongs inflicted upon him, Butch has bombarded the courts with a multitude of motions that have argued the relevance and need for post-conviction testing in his case.

THE BLOODY GARMENTS

After a prolonged interrogation, during which Butch insisted the police beat him, wouldn't let him use the restroom and deprived him of food and water, he finally gave in and told them about the items he had hurriedly discarded in the Brooklyn Sewer.

In the afternoon of November 14, 1974, detectives from the Suffolk County homicide division found these items in a sewer located on the corner of Seaview Avenue and East 96th Street across from a Shell gas station in Brooklyn.

The police, however, insisted that Butch's admission, which led them to the sewer, was unforced and given freely. According to the police, the items found consisted of eight spent rifle shell casings, two boxes of ammunition, a brown holster, a black rifle case, and a blue-and-white striped pillowcase that the police say contained a yellow towel, blue dungarees, a blue shirt, a pair of black socks, men's green underwear, and an identical pillowcase, which was empty.

The Suffolk County detectives had theorized that the alleged bloodstained clothing recovered from the sewer provided incontrovertible proof that Butch was guilty of the crime.

At Butch's trial, Detective Rafferty testified, "[Butch] then went into Allison's room and picked up the cartridge in her room. When picking it up, he got blood on his hands. He wiped the blood on his pants."

Assistant District Attorney Sullivan went even further in the grisly picture he painted of Butch and his reputed urgency to dump the incriminating clothing into the Brooklyn sewer.

He told the jury, "He [Butch] had to get down on his hands and knees and look for those things [spent shell casings] under furniture. He had to dip into a pool of his sister's blood spreading on the floor beneath her bed to get one of them. And when he wiped his hands off, and when he wiped his bloody fingers off on his pants, what did he proceed to do with his clothes? When he removed his clothing, every bit of his clothing, his underwear and his socks were found in that pillowcase."

Sullivan also referred to a photograph, which clearly showed the spent casings, the boxes of ammunition, the holster, and the rifle case lying outside the sewer. Off to the right of these items lay the two pillowcases, one allegedly full, while the other one was empty.

Detective Gerard Gozaloff testified during the DeFeo trial that he had not emptied the pillowcase or examined the contents at the Brooklyn sewer. Rather, he waited until he returned to the homicide squad. Because of this, William Weber alleged that the detectives commingled evidence. In other words, the detectives added the clothing that Butch was wearing at the time of his interrogation since it was stained with his blood.

Nevertheless, Sullivan insisted in his closing arguments that the full pillowcase contained the bloody clothing. "If you look at this photograph, members of the jury, and look at it closely when you retire to deliberate, you will see a blue garment in that pillowcase. And, if you will look, you will see the same characteristics on that blue garment. I am referring to the stitching that goes down the side of those dungarees that are on that garment in that photograph," Sullivan told the jury.

Sullivan's explanation did not change the defense's claim that the alleged clothing in the sewer was the same clothing that Butch had on during the police interrogation.

During his own summation, Weber blasted Sullivan, saying, "And the evidence that went into that sewer is not the way the

Chapter Twelve

police tell you about it. There is only one dressing [set] of clothing in this box [evidence box in courtroom]. There is only one pair of pants, one shirt, and one jacket. You heard them say they took the clothing from Ronnie at the precinct, and you heard them say that they took clothing out of the sewer. Where is it, Mr. Sullivan?"

"The blood on the clothing is mine," Butch has continued to insist to this day, "and DNA [testing] can prove this."

Indeed, there is ample evidence to support Butch's statement that the bloody clothing in the evidence box in the courtroom was not from the sewer but, instead, was the same clothing that he had on when he was detained by the Suffolk County Police.

In his report concerning the items found in the Brooklyn sewer, Detective Anthony Grieco, shield #394, wrote, "Upon returning to the Suffolk County Homicide squad office, the evidence was initialed by the defendant in the presence of Detective Gozaloff. The following clothing was then taken into custody by the assigned, off the person of the defendant, one pair brown shoes, one denim jacket (blue), one pair blue denim pants and one blue shirt."

At 7:00 p.m. on November 14, 1974, Butch was booked for the murders of his family. As Detective Grieco stated in his report, Butch's clothing was removed and was replaced with blue coveralls and a pair of sneakers. During this time, Suffolk County Police Laboratory technician Detective Sergeant Ernest Klug, shield #482, obtained a hair and blood sample from Butch.

It was not until 11:00 a.m., the next day, that any of the clothing was taken to the police laboratory. Initially, the clothing was listed as item #80, clothing of Ronald DeFeo Jr., and item #81, boots of Ronald DeFeo Jr. in the Suffolk County Police Laboratory's 32-page report. These reports, which were signed and certified by the various lab technicians responsible for the tests and the director of the laboratory itself, Lieutenant Vincent T. Sullivan, eventually singled out the articles of clothing that conveniently fit the police's theory about the DeFeo crimes.

Page 30 of the report contained the serology results for Item #80B, which was the denim jacket Butch was wearing during his interrogation. The results of the analysis performed by Detective

Nicholas Serverino, shield #576, read, "Gross examination revealed the presence of red stains inside each sleeve (near the cuff). Serological tests revealed these stains to be human blood, Type 'A.'"

Results for Item #80C, Butch's blue dungarees (jeans), read, "Gross examination revealed the presence of a stain on the right leg. Serological tests revealed this stain to be human blood, type 'A.'"

It should be noted that all of the DeFeos, except for Louise, had type "A" blood. Louise DeFeo, in contrast, had type "O" blood. Hence, the results neither proved it was not Butch's blood on the pants and in his denim jacket nor proved he had wiped Allison's blood on himself.

Gerard Sullivan, nevertheless, twisted the lab's findings to complete the gruesome assertions he had started about Butch. Sullivan informed the jury, "He [Butch] got into his shower, and he bathed himself and he cleaned himself and he washed away anything that could possibly connect him to this crime. And ask yourselves, members of the jury, at that point, was he also washing and scrubbing away the blood on his forearms, the same blood that had before that had dripped down the arms and stained the inside of the sleeves of his jacket?"

Hearing Sullivan's theory, Geraldine DeFeo retorted, "Butch is so meticulous and clean that he would never put on bloody clothing, let alone be stupid enough to get rid of one piece of incriminating clothing while wearing another."

The jacket Butch was wearing during his interrogation not only was stained with his blood, but also with a black smear. In fact, a similar black smear, Item #80H of the Suffolk County police laboratory reports, was found on the blue pillowcase later recovered from the Brooklyn sewer.

According to Butch, he had on his jacket when he disposed of the pillowcase evidence on the late afternoon of November 13. If this were true, then the smears may corroborate his claims since they can be tied together. After all, during the DeFeo trial, Lucy Burkin, an employee for Brigante Buick, testified that Butch's clothing earlier that day was as "clean as a whistle."

At trial, Weber pointed out that quite a bit of clothing was

Chapter Twelve

taken out of the DeFeo house by the police. So if there was any clothing in the pillowcase, then it is possible that the police planted it before later switching to Butch's clothes.

Geraldine said, "I was shown these large, puff-tent pants when I was questioned by the police. They said the pants were Butch's. Of course, I opened my big mouth and said they were nuts because Butch wore small pants. Dawn was the large one." According to Geraldine, the pants she was shown disappeared, never to be seen again.

But if clothing was located in the pillowcase, then what sort of condition would it have been in?

Under oath, Detective Gerard Gozaloff, one of the detectives credited with recovering the sewer evidence, said, "In the storm drain was a collection of leaves, which had formed a mat approximately four inches thick, and under that was approximately four feet of water."

Regarding this evidence, Detective Gozaloff testified that "all items were partially wet."

And Detective Nicholas Severino, the serologist responsible for testing the clothing, testified that the clothing was not tested until November 22, 1974, a full eight days after being discovered. Detective Severino, however, was unable to say, with any reasonable certainty, where these articles of clothing were for the eight days except to say they were somewhere in the lab.

What was unknown was if any alleged clothing found in the Brooklyn sewer, which according to testimony was wet and kept in a plastic bag for eight days prior to testing, would yield any scientific results. Therefore, I contacted a few medical examiners for their input. Ronald Singer, Laboratory Director of Tarrant County Medical Examiner's Crime Laboratory in Forth Worth, Texas, responded to my inquiry.

Singer said, "Let me point out that if there's one thing I've learned in almost 30 years in this business, it's that *anything* is possible. Having said that, your scenario combines all of the worst possible things that could happen to biological evidence—depending on how long the evidence was in the 'water and muck,' and assuming that it was submerged, it is likely that the water would have diluted any biological material present. Further, you run the risk of contamination from the 'muck' (depending on what its composition is).

"Next comes the plastic bag. Even in 1974, we knew that biologicals shouldn't be packaged in plastic because it traps the air and humidity inside, and promotes rot, which would make it difficult, at best, to get any information from the sample. Eight days, wet, sealed in a plastic bag should do the job very well, I'd think."

Whatever the case was, it is safe to say that it is doubtful that the clothing that wound up as evidence against Butch came from the sewer. Rather, it was taken off him after his brutal interrogation.

Furthermore, there is no mention of a yellow towel in any of the 32 pages of the "official" Suffolk County Police Laboratory's reports, nor was there any mention of other debris, such as a Pall Mall cigarette wrapper clearly visible in the crime-scene photos of the sewer drain. In the end, it was just further proof of shoddy police work.

POST-CONVICTION MOTIONS

Since 1990, Butch has made several post-conviction motions to the courts in order to gain approval for DNA testing on the clothes in question. Although Butch's motions raised several points in favor of how the DNA testing fulfilled the new evidence requirement under New York law, Justice Thomas Stark, who presided over the earlier motions, disagreed.

In his November 24, 1992 decision against Butch's 1992 appeal, Justice Stark wrote, "I have also examined that portion of the trial transcript containing Assistant District Attorney Sullivan's summation to the jury, and nowhere in his summation did Mr. Sullivan argue or contend that the blood stains of People's Exhibit #101 [the blue jeans allegedly found in the sewer] and People's Exhibit #110 [the dungaree jacket] was that of any of the murder victims.

"Defendant's claim that the police somehow 'switched' the blue jeans found in the storm drain and the dungaree jacket worn by him on November 14, 1974, is rebutted by the record, both garments being put into evidence at the trial.

"Should DNA testing of both garments determine that they were stained by defendant's blood, this would have no bearing on defendant's claims in this proceeding.

"If defendant contends that he was wearing both garments at the time of his interrogation, and that blood stains were the result of physical force by the police, he failed to raise the claim during his pre-trial suppression hearing . . ."

Accordingly, Butch's motion was denied.

Angered over the denial, Butch responded, "Justice Stark's decision of November 24, 1992 is a lie as the pre-trial transcripts verify that Stark lied again to try and justify his decision and keep me from the DNA testing."

Butch's statements are justified because the key points that Justice Stark made against the DNA testing are, at best, simply inaccurate, and, at worst, fabricated.

First, it was Justice Stark's opinion that Butch did not raise the issue of the bloody clothes during the hearing. From page 888 to page 925 of Butch's preliminary hearing testimony, Prosecutor Sullivan asked several questions pertaining to Butch's allegations of police brutality.

Wanting a time estimate about one episode when Butch was beaten, Sullivan asked, "Now, what is your best estimate as to the total length of time these men were in here beating you up before they left the room?"

Butch, unsure, asked, "The whole beating with the phone book and all?"

Justice Stark responded, "The phone book and the paper bag over your head, how long did the whole incident take place?"

Butch replied, "Ten or 15 minutes."

On page 924, Sullivan asked Butch, "Were you bleeding at that time?"

"My lips were bleeding. Lip was bleeding. It was cut," Butch replied.

"Profusely?"

"I don't recall. It was bleeding an awful lot."

"Was the bleeding inside or outside?"

"No, outside."

"The outside was?"

"Yes, sir. It was like a cut, you know."

"Did you taste the blood, or was it—?"

"I saw it. Some of it, you know, some of it went on the floor. I think a little went on my jacket, may have gone on my jacket."

Moreover, page 888 showed that Sullivan asked, "Mr. DeFeo, did there come a time when certain items were taken from you while you were in the homicide squad?"

"Yes, sir, they took my clothes," Butch answered.

"And what clothes were they?"

"Blue dungaree jacket, blue work shirt, blue pair of dungarees, and a pair of boots, brown boots."

Justice Stark in his denial against DNA testing obviously felt this line of questioning, and Butch's answers, were insufficient alone to tie the bloodied clothing with the alleged beatings.

Regarding Justice Stark's opinion that both sets of garments were put into evidence at the trial, Weber cleverly pointed out in front of the jury that only one set of garments were in evidence at the trial because the other set never existed.

But the most preposterous statement issued by Justice Stark in his three-page decision was that Sullivan never argued in his summation that the blood on the clothing was that of the victims. Justice Stark either ignored or overlooked the fact that on Page 6725 of Butch's trial transcript, during the prosecution's closing arguments, Gerard Sullivan, in fact, boldly stated the blood on Butch's pants and dungaree jacket was that of his sister's.

Throughout the years, Butch's other motions have repeatedly been denied on similar grounds, the most recent one being on September 29, 2000, in which Judge John Mullin denied it. In a simple half-page decision, Judge Mullin reasoned that the testing would not constitute newly discovered evidence, and if the results had been admitted at trial that the verdict would have remained the same.

Feeling Judge Mullin did not take the motion seriously, Butch commented in a letter to Geraldine, saying, "Judge Mullin is nuts, as the DNA testing would impeach Rafferty's oral statement I wiped a shell casing of blood on my pants from a pool of Allison's blood. No one wants me out, so they keep making up stories, but the transcripts speak for themselves. It has nothing to do with being innocent. They cannot give me a new trial."

It is almost inconceivable that two well-educated and respected judges would proclaim that evidence pointing to police brutality, and which would subsequently unravel the entire criminal case against Butch DeFeo, had little relevance.

Likewise, it is quite evident from Suffolk County's track record, especially during the era of the DeFeo murders, that a confession most likely was forcibly coerced from Butch. It stands to reason that nothing elicited from Butch during this time, including the sewer evidence, could have been used against him for his indictment or trial. If Butch had not been beaten into submission and had the right to an attorney during his prolonged interrogation, the homicide detectives would have had to rely upon investigative methods to answer the perplexing questions, and not a suspect's falsified confession.

If, however, the DNA testing were conducted on the bloodied clothing and it was proved that the blood on the garments was Butch's, then it would substantiate his claims and force the higher courts to step in and not just simply turn a blind eye. It is obvious from the ludicrous arguments used to prevent the testing that the Suffolk County justice system does not want Butch to have this chance.

Another fact that supports Butch's request for DNA testing is that the justice system would not be burdened with the costs of the tests. In 1992, Angela Brigante, Butch's grandmother, set aside $10,000 for the DNA testing. Yet the courts continued to deny Butch's request.

In his address to the Senate Judiciary Committee, the Attorney General of New York, Eliot Spitzer, said, "Our experience demon-

Butch DeFeo gets inducted into prison life (top).

Butch DeFeo's 1979 prison ID (middle).

Geraldine DeFeo (right).

Chapter Twelve

strates that post-conviction DNA testing can bolster the integrity of our judicial system without unduly burdening our criminal justice resources."

Obviously, not all of New York's courts share this opinion, particularly when it applies to notorious murderers like Butch DeFeo. Yet if Butch were ever granted the right to perform post-conviction DNA testing, it is not inconceivable that the evidence would somehow become "lost" or destroyed.

From the onset of Joseph Yeswoit's 911 call, the police moved quickly in its efforts to solve the DeFeo murders, even going as far as to fabricate evidence against Butch, who was but one of the guilty parties. Following suit, the District Attorney's office moved quickly to indict and convict Butch even though the experts said one man could never have committed this crime alone. So Butch became an easy target for a corrupt justice system.

The courts have already shown they are not interested in the facts of the case because they have continuously disregarded the other guilty parties, the forensic evidence, and just plain common sense.

In addition, the system displayed an unwillingness to provide Butch's attorneys with an equal chance to possess the necessary documentation for a quality defense. This left only one recourse: plead insanity and hope for mercy.

Chapter Thirteen
Life Incarcerated

IMMEDIATELY AFTER JUSTICE Stark imposed his sentence on Butch on December 4, 1975, Butch was transferred to Ossining State Correctional Facility, now known as Sing Sing Prison, for induction into the New York State Department of Corrections. Butch's manicured beard and shoulder-length hair were cut off, making him resemble a grunt in boot camp.

After completing his induction, Butch was transferred to Clinton Correctional Facility on December 19, 1975. Butch, now known as inmate #75A4053, was considered a security risk and categorized as being "high-profile."

High-profile status meant that every visitor, telephone call, piece of mail sent and received by Butch, would first be scrutinized by the facility. The notoriety he gained from the Amityville books and movies, however, prolonged his high-profile status. It was not until the late 1980s that this status was relaxed.

The reality of his fate sank in after Butch was transferred from

Chapter Thirteen

the Suffolk County Jail in Riverhead, Long Island, to Ossining. For Butch, this painfully meant giving up coveted freedoms like clamming on his boat, driving 95 miles per hour on the Long Island Beltway, drinking at Henry's Bar, or being the father and husband he had always wanted to be.

For the first few years, Butch had problems adjusting to prison life. Always having a bit of a problem with authority figures, Butch viewed the prison guards in a negative light, and he routinely got written up for offenses ranging from having sharpened knives in the prison yard to being intoxicated. However, that all changed when his showering privileges were reduced to one 10-minute shower a week.

"Butch did an about-face when the facility's adjustment board punished him by restricting the number of showers he could take," Geraldine DeFeo explained. "Right then and there, Butch decided to be a model prisoner."

Since conforming, Butch has routinely been on honor block, a separate wing in the facility that grants model inmates special privileges. Butch had become quite the opposite of the antisocial individual described by Gerard Sullivan.

Aside from the positive incidents while incarcerated, Butch has also gotten himself into trouble. One such incident occurred in December 1983 at Auburn Correctional Facility over a female corrections officer, whom Butch had begun having an affair with. Another inmate, who was jealous over the relationship, planted a bag of heroin underneath Butch's bunk. When the bag was discovered, Butch was sent to solitary confinement for five days.

Afterward, Butch, in his usual manner, sued the facility for $1,000, claiming he had become a raving maniac from the ordeal. Despite what seemed to be a frivolous lawsuit, State Court Judge Thomas Lowery awarded Butch $300 for the mental anguish he had suffered. After the ruling, the incident was stricken from Butch's record, and his honor-block privileges were restored.

When Butch was arrested on November 14, 1974, he weighed 180 pounds and, according to Geraldine, was a bit chubby. By the early 1980s, though, Butch had lost all of his unwanted body fat from working out. While incarcerated, Butch began a daily workout routine that consisted of lifting heavy weights and performing calisthenics. "Butch would often be challenged by younger guys who were much bigger than him," Geraldine said. "But he would routinely lift more weight then they could."

With his health failing by the late 1990s, Butch had a medical hold placed on him. Although he hoped to be transferred from Green Haven Correctional Facility, a placed he dubbed "a gladiator camp," his medical hold prevented the transfer. And he has subsequently sued the facility several times because it has willfully destroyed his property and caused him serious bodily injury.

Apparently while living in Amityville with his parents, Butch contracted Hepatitis C. Over the last 25 years, the disease has routinely resurfaced and has caused extensive damage to his kidneys and liver.

Accordingly, Butch's condition can be considered terminal, and his physical appearance shows it. He suffers from yellow jaundice, a yellowing of the skin, and has lost an extensive amount of weight.

DOING TIME WITH BUTCH

"Part of me died the day Butch was sentenced." Geraldine recalled. "The dreams we shared for the future have always been left unfulfilled.

"But my pain worsened after the Lutzes began all their stories. After that, when I visited Butch, the other wives and girlfriends would point and whisper, 'That's the devil's wife.'

"Even the guards joined in on the fun. On one occasion after I finished a visit with Butch, I walked out to find a guard spray painting a demonic tail on the hood of my car.

"The ridicule I could handle. But what got to me was what people were saying about Butch. He was my husband and a good father to my children. He was no child killer or demon like people dubbed him. Everywhere I went, Amityville popped up; I couldn't get away from it.

"Once at a K-mart, I was in line when these two women in

front of me started commenting on what a monster Butch was. This eventually took its toll on me, as I began needing more and more drugs and alcohol just to get through the day.

"Everyone was gone: Butch, Allison, all of them. My hopes and dreams died on November 13, 1974. So I couldn't bear life if I wasn't high on something. And I would spend most of my free time near Butch, crying from the start of the visit to the end. Butch couldn't stand seeing me like that, so in 1977 he filed for divorce. No matter how much he still loved me, he wanted me to be free."

Over the next two years, following the divorce, Geraldine picked up the shattered pieces of her life. After she sobered up, she restarted her singing career. When she was not singing, she was either attending law school or trying to be a better mother.

But in 1980, Geraldine found herself in legal troubles that eventually got her incarcerated for a period of 14 months. She claimed that Butch DeFeo had become so bitter after her departure from his life that he lashed out at her, setting her up to be prosecuted for passing bad checks. Because Geraldine had refused to go along with one of Butch's schemes, Butch had the Brigante stocks frozen, which Geraldine had used as collateral for living expenses, unknowingly writing bad checks. So if this is true, then why have anything more to do with Butch?

Although Geraldine had divorced Butch, she claimed that she remained close to Michael Brigante Sr., who she alleged had called in every contact he knew to ensure that she and her children were hidden from the mess of Amityville and the media circus that followed. Because of his friendship with Carlo Gambino and his connection to the Colombos, not to mention Geraldine's own ties to the Genovese family, Butch and Geraldine's marriage license and divorce papers miraculously disappeared.

In return for the anonymity he provided, Brigante requested a favor. Knowing he could trust Geraldine as one of the few people who would never betray or capitalize on his grandson, Brigante asked Geraldine to remain available for Butch. "Big Mike told me that Butch was a bum, but explained his continued devotion to his grandson by reminding me that blood was thicker than water,"

Geraldine said. "He told me that he loved Butch but that he never forgot that Butch had killed his beloved daughter Louise."

Honoring the request, Geraldine has remained Butch's friend and confidante to this day.

In 1985, Michael Brigante Sr. died, and Geraldine was left with the responsibility of breaking the news to Butch. Geraldine recalled, "The facility cleared out one of its visiting rooms before they brought down Butch because they had no idea how he would react. When Butch heard the news, he just buried his face in his arms and wept silently."

Brigante knew the full details of the murders and lived through the worst years of the Amityville hoax. Although his love for Butch was undying, Brigante was forced to remain silent. With his own skeletons in the closet, Brigante could not publicly lash out at the Suffolk County criminal justice system or the participants of the hoax. This tactic was continued up to Michael Brigante Jr.'s death in the late 1980s and Angela Brigante's death in 2000.

The death of his grandfather proved a turning point for Butch. While Brigante was alive, he had always told Butch in his brash, hoarse voice, "The truth will set you free."

With his court battles intensifying in the late 1980s, Butch wanted to remarry Geraldine for the simple fact that he wanted her to testify on his behalf. However, it was not until 1989 that United States District Court Judge Neal McCurn reversed the New York State law forbidding inmates who had life sentences to marry, or remarry in Butch's case.

The agreement was that she would have to stay married only until the end of his appeal. So in 1993, after all of Butch's legal motions were finished, Geraldine and Butch were once again divorced. Despite the fact that Butch had been officially divorced from Geraldine only a few months, he married his most recent wife, Barbara, on April 27, 1994. Butch's third marriage, however, would not last, either.

In October 1999, divorce papers were filed by Barbara, alleging a lack of intimate affection. In a suit against his ex-wife, Butch alleged that Barbara married him only to gain the rights and profits from his story. Thus, he sought over $750,000 in damages, even though Barbara vehemently denied Butch's absurd claims.

Just a few short months after his divorce, Butch wrote Geraldine to ask her to come back to him. He claimed that he still loved her. Choosing to remain only his friend and confidante, Geraldine passed on another try at marriage with him. Butch was not pleased and threatened to denounce her as a fraud.

But it was while he was married to Geraldine in 1989 that Butch developed another friendship with Abigail [pseudonym]. In a five-page affidavit attesting to the truthfulness of her claims, Abigail wrote, "Some time in either 1989 or 1990, I came across a book written by Gerard Sullivan, who wrote *High Hopes*. I had been somewhat fascinated with the actual murder case since I read the book written by Jay Anson, who wrote *The Amityville Horror*. When I read *High Hopes*, I decided to get in touch with Ronnie and see if he would answer some questions I had.

"I never really ever expected an answer, and I was surprised when I received a letter back from him soon afterwards. It was a short letter, asking how old I was (over 18?) and was pretty general in nature. He didn't really answer the questions I asked, except to say that it [the murders] didn't go down the way everyone thought.

"Soon after establishing our correspondence, Ronnie asked me for my phone number, which I gave him. In the first phone call, he stated he was married, and had a daughter. I expressed surprise, as there was never any mention of this in *High Hopes*. He said that he knew that, but he was, indeed, married. He told me that he got married way back in 1973 (or 1974, I don't recall for sure). He told me his wife's name—Geraldine—as well as his daughter's. He had expressed fatherly pride for [Shea Marie]; that she was a good girl who looked a lot like his sister Dawn. I asked if she ever came to visit him and he said, yes, he had seen her a few times and he was still in touch with her.

"It wasn't long after that that he was complaining about wanting to divorce Geraldine, and she was giving him a "hard time" about it. He made statements about having had several "marriages" with her (renewal vows) and that complicated things a bit. He said

Ric Osuna

State of New York - Department of Correctional Services

GREEN HAVEN CORRECTIONAL FACILITY

FAMILY SERVICES OFFICE

INTERDEPARTMENTAL COMMUNICATION

TO: DEFEO, Ronald #75-A-4053   B-1-116
FROM: V. Blaetz, Senior Correction Counselor, Family Services
SUBJECT: *MARRIAGE REQUEST*
DATE: 2 November 2000

RE: Ms. Geraldine 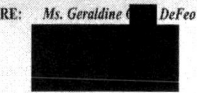 DeFeo

This will acknowledge receipt this date of your letter requesting permission to marry the above-noted woman.

Please be advised that we have not yet received a letter from your fiancée. Until such time as her letter is received, we cannot place you on the waiting list for marriage licensing.

We will hold your letter until we receive your fiancée's request. When we receive your fiancée's letter from the Superintendent, we will place your name in the earliest available opening on the licensing list, and you will be informed of your tentative licensing date. Be advised that there is a lengthy wait for licensing; we are currently scheduling couples for the *FEBRUARY 2001* licensing. Be further advised that your position on the waiting list will be determined by when your fiancée's letter is received in this office; *any delay in the receipt of her letter MAY result in a later licensing date!*

Questions concerning the marriage process should be directed to my office in writing.

NOTE: If you have failed to provide us with the name and/or address of your fiancée, it is YOUR responsibility to inform her of the need for her to submit a letter of request!

VB:sah
xc: Fiancée (where address provided)
      File

Butch's request to prison officials to remarry Geraldine, who quickly refused a third try at marriage.

that they had gotten married in three separate states: New Jersey, New York and Pennsylvania.

"He was talking about getting married to me. While I was fond of him, there was never a possibility that I would actually marry him. It just wasn't what I wanted in life. I felt bad for him, but knew it just wasn't really a possibility."

BUTCH'S DOWNFALL

As a child, Butch was taught that money and material possessions—the more pretentious, the better—were a necessity in life. More important, they afforded bragging rights, another essential in the DeFeo world. Even while incarcerated, Butch has remained faithful to his upbringing even if that meant capitalizing on the deaths of his own family.

Being behind bars has not stopped Butch from sleeping on silk sheets or having monogrammed towels. Tailored shirts and pants, custom-made for Butch following prison guidelines, routinely arrived from the outside. Of course, Butch demanded that his clothes have sharp creases and be wrinkle-free, including his silk underwear.

Butch's bravado did not stop there. Explaining the burdensome affair of visiting Butch, Geraldine said, "I was Mrs. DeFeo, so I had to look the part. I was expected to arrive with layers of makeup and in the expensive clothes Butch had bought me. And God forbid if I forgot the gaudy rings he had given me."

According to Geraldine, it didn't matter if she brought Butch a cheesecake from Junior's, his favorite Brooklyn bakery, or Kentucky Fried Chicken with extra gravy, his favorite meal during visits, Butch would gripe the entire time if she did not dress as he had expected her to.

By touting his fame, and greasing the palm of a guard or two, Butch made sure that his wife was given priority when visiting. "Once I arrived at the facility, I'd be waved to the front of the line and escorted through the metal detector. It didn't matter that it buzzed when I went through. I was never strip-searched or asked to take off the copious amounts of jewelry I had on. This favoritism did not go over well with the other women waiting in the long line to see their own men," Geraldine said.

Even though Geraldine was hidden from view and given special accommodations when visiting Butch, all of that did not stop certain authorities in Suffolk County law enforcement from persecuting her. In fact, she described being arrested and hauled in on a number of occasions for questioning. Of course, no charges were ever filed. "They just wanted me to know that no matter where I went, they would find me," Geraldine said.

Commenting on this, Geraldine's daughter, Stacy, said, "The cops persecuted my mother for information. It seemed to me that they bothered her a lot. If they had Ronnie for the crime, then why find my mother every so often and ask her the same questions over and over about the murders? It bothered me that the cops could come up to my mother's house and drag all of us to Long Island to question us about Ronnie's friends. They all said the same thing: 'He had help.'"

* * *

Despite all his little luxuries, Butch has had his share of money troubles while in prison. Besides being betrayed by the Lutzes, Butch also has had to contend with problems associated with his parents' estate.

Even before the DeFeos were laid to rest and Butch had been formally charged, a dispute between the Brigantes and DeFeos regarding the DeFeo home had started. According to Butch, the person who acted most insensitively was his Aunt Phyllis, Big Ronnie's sister. Butch claimed his aunt wanted him convicted so he would forfeit his right to her brother's estate.

In a March 1990 legal motion, Butch wrote, "Phyllis Procita seen that Weber was paid also from the estates and maintained an active relationship, prior and during the trial, with the prosecutor, Gerard Sullivan. This, in itself, is prejudicial and cause for vacating the verdict and ordering a new trial. Weber was assigned under the county's assigned counsel program when Procita paid Weber from the estates, and was in a relationship with both Weber and the prosecutor. Procita wanted to see me go to jail to take over the estate monies and worked with Weber in obtaining a conviction against me."

Today, neither Phyllis nor Butch are on speaking terms. Geraldine reasoned, "It's no surprise that Aunt Phyllis wants nothing to do with Butch. He was horrid to her when she would visit him. Many times she would exit the visiting room shaken because of the lies Butch told her about the night of the crime."

The recorded value of the DeFeo estate, including 112 Ocean Avenue, was assessed at $286,994. It was not until December 8, 1978, more than four years after their children and grandchildren had been murdered, that the Brigantes and the DeFeos finally settled the estate. Both sets of parents received $67,338.70. The rest was consumed by bills the DeFeos had left, surrogate court taxes and, of course, attorneys' fees.

All except for Big Ronnie and Butch's, the life-size portraits, which hung on the staircase wall in the DeFeo home, went to Michael and Angela Brigante. Big Ronnie's family took his.

After Angela Brigante's death in July 2000, the portraits that hung in her home were cut out of their frames, rolled-up, and placed inside her casket. It is reported that Big Ronnie and Butch's portrait was accidentally destroyed in a fire. Today, color photographs are all that remain of the haunting images that have immortalized the DeFeos and have come to symbolize a great American tragedy.

According to the estate's final accounting, more than $1,100 in cash was accounted for on December 23, 1974, at least $650 of which came from the master bedroom. Additionally, at Columbia Federal Savings and Loan in Amityville, Big Ronnie and Louise had a joint savings account containing more than $7,200. This does not include more than $3,300 in savings and bonds that were in the names of their children, including Butch. Nor does it include more than $10,000 worth of jewelry that Big Ronnie and Louise had stored in a bank's safe deposit box.

Despite all of this, Prosecutor Gerard Sullivan alleged that

Butch's motives for the crime were over money and valuables stored in the DeFeo house. Regardless, the jury believed the robbery motive proposed by Sullivan and convicted Butch.

In November 1993, at the age of 51, Gerard Sullivan died from a massive stroke. According to *Newsday*, Sullivan was most famous for being the prosecutor in the DeFeo trial. Commenting on Sullivan's career, the article explained how Sullivan wanted the case because he could not begin to understand Butch DeFeo's motive.

Responding to the article, Butch said, "Hey, no motive. Nice, huh? That's not what he said during the trial."

Regardless, the $20,000 Butch would need to appeal the conviction Sullivan had earned him would have to come from his parents' estate. Since he had consented to his grandfathers being the administrators on November 21, 1974, Butch had no control over its affairs. Butch, nevertheless, needed the money, or there would have been no appeal.

In a letter from William Weber dated April 9, 1976 to the Honorable John P. Cohalan of the appellate division, Weber outlined an agreement by which Butch could receive monies from his parents' estate; in return, he would forfeit any further claims to it.

One point requested Surrogate Court Judge Ernest Signorelli, the same judge who once presided over the DeFeo case and who would later disqualify himself, "to direct that a psychiatric examination be made of the defendant, Ronald DeFeo Jr., in order to determine his mental capacity in so far as executing a renunciation of all right, title, and interest in and to the estates of Ronald DeFeo and Louise DeFeo."

It is quite comical to think that for the estate proceedings, and for the purpose of getting paid, Weber was suggesting Butch was sane enough knowingly to waive his rights to his parents' estate. Yet Butch was appealing his conviction on the grounds of insanity.

Regardless, in August 1977, the surrogate court permitted Butch's motion, and he was awarded the $20,000 in return for renouncement of all of his rights. Of course, if Butch was found not guilty by reason of insanity, he would be able once again to contest the estate.

Nonetheless, on August 23, 1977, Weber was paid half his money, and collected the other $10,000 on August 11, 1978, several months after Butch's appeal had been filed and subsequently denied.

Butch would later name the surrogate court as a party in the suit he brought against Weber. Among the estate items, Butch also contested the sale of his Buick Electra, his diamond ring, his 19-foot Searay boat, and other various tools and pieces of furniture he had owned prior to his conviction.

According to his 1986 letter to attorney Hesterberg, Butch wrote, "What I am asking for is not the estate (that is to go to my wife and daughter both equally), but for the property's and monies that are legally mine, along with the interest that accrued over these past 12 years, which in itself is well over $20,000." The lawsuit, nonetheless, would eventually be dismissed.

Although Butch's statement seemed suspicious, he did have genuine love for Geraldine and his daughter, Shea Marie. The problems that plagued his relationship with them stemmed from his inability to express his love or to handle the anger he was feeling over his incarceration. However, the three do share some fond memories.

Geraldine recalled, "Shea Marie had wanted to follow her boyfriend to England, but did not have the money. Regardless of the expense, Butch sent her the money so she could go. It was his gift to her to make her happy."

Looking back on it, it was ironic for Butch to be faced with the same problem that plagued his own parents and which led to the destruction of his entire family, that, of course, being Dawn's insistence to be allowed to move to Florida to be with her boyfriend.

INTERVIEW WITH SHEA MARIE

On August 21, 1974, less than three months before the murders, Shea Marie DeFeo was born. Although shielded from the public since her father's trial, and even more so after the hoax began, Shea Marie has struggled with her own identity. Knowing all too well the ridicule Shea Marie would face in school, Geraldine did not tell her daughter about her true identity until she was old enough to understand. Even at that point, Geraldine told her only what she felt she needed to know.

According to Geraldine, it was a sentiment that Butch shared. "At first, Butch was happy that I brought his daughter to see him at Clinton Correctional. But a few visits later, he ordered me not to bring her back because he did not want his daughter exposed to the filth or degradation found there," Geraldine said.

I was fortunate enough to be granted an interview with Shea Marie. It was her first and, I am told, last public interview. Seeing her for the first time, I was amazed at how closely she resembled her aunt, Dawn DeFeo.

At the time I met Shea Marie, she was still coping with the absence of her father and the crimes he was alleged to have committed. At the time of our interview, she had just entered therapy to cope with the feelings and emotions she had buried since childhood. Worried for her own children's privacy, she requested I use a pseudonym to protect her family. In my opinion, her interview illustrates how innocent lives were devastated by the DeFeo murders and the subsequent hoax.

> Ric Osuna: Is this a difficult subject matter for you to talk about?
>
> Shea Marie: It is something that I am not too comfortable discussing because I didn't know my father until later in life. I handled the trauma of learning my real identity with drug and alcohol abuse.
>
> RO: How did you find out who your father was?
>
> SM: You get older, you get nosy and start going through things in rooms that you are not supposed to see. There, I found letters from him to my mom.

Chapter Thirteen

RO: How old were you at this time?

SM: Ten or 11. I'd hear things late at night. It was obvious something was going on because my mother had someone else in her life.

RO: After finding out who you were, how often did you correspond with your father?

SM: I didn't write too much, but I got a letter from him two to three times a week. He'd call late at night every three days or so. My mother would yell up to my room, "It's your father. It's the animal." That was her nickname for him. We'd talk about school, my boyfriend, stuff like that.

RO: How long did this go on?

SM: We did this for a while; then we finally met when I was about 12.

RO: What do you remember about visiting your father?

SM: I remember visiting him on a couple of occasions. I remember he tried to be friendly towards me. Of course, there was fear because of so much mystery surrounding him. I was very nervous because of all the hearsay. All the people staring at us in the visiting room did not make me feel any better.

RO: What were your thoughts when you met him?

SM: It was a real casual meeting. I never cried, "Daddy, I love you." I didn't know him. I just still can't understand that if he knew he was going to be a father, why didn't he make better choices? I haven't had a relationship with him in years.

RO: Have you ever gone by the DeFeo house?

SM: Yeah, I was real young, about four. My mother brought me there with my stepsisters. We couldn't go up to the house because someone was living there, but I remember thinking it was a nice house. I remember my mother walking around the yard and just staring intensely. Afterwards, I met Grandmother Brigante for the first time, and some of the other relatives. I think we all went to Jones Beach that day.

RO: Did your mother tell you anything specific about the house?

SM: She might have told us that this is the house that the murders happened at. Nothing much. My stepsisters knew the whole story because they lived with my father before it all went down.

RO: How much contact did you have with your grandmother?

SM: Grandma sent me money, cards, and nice letters. That was about the extent of it.

RO: Does your mother scoff at *The Amityville Horror*?

SM: My mother thinks the Lutzes are lunatics. I remember that when the movie came on TV, she would tell my sisters and me to go into the other room. As for me, I just wanted to ignore the whole thing. I am sure you can imagine why.

RO: Going back to your father, what did he tell you about the murders?

SM: He didn't talk about his youth. All he told me was that he loved his parents.

RO: You don't believe that your father acted alone?

SM: There is no way he could do it all by himself. I can believe he wanted to kill his father because he was such a bastard to Ron. Obviously, in hindsight, there was apparent signs of physical, mental, and emotional child abuse on my father. If he shot his father, then the man was in crisis. Of course, that does not excuse murder or condone it. In the end, he will have to stand before God to be judged. Now that I am older and thinking all this through, I feel sad because there was nobody my father could turn to. If the murders didn't happen, then I could have had my mother, father, and God knows how many brothers and sisters. A family.

RO: How do you feel about the murders?

SM: Any type of murder is abominable, no matter who deserved it, no matter what went wrong or if it was an accident. Allison must have felt safe with her big sister there telling her it would be okay. To keep a child lying down, a child you had comforted as a baby, and then kill them is cold-blooded.

RO: Do you resent your father?

SM: I don't know the man. When he made his choice, he may have done so either because he was depressed, stoned, or in a chaotic stupor. I have to pity him because he had nobody to turn to in a time of crisis.

RO: What do you want people to know about your father and that fateful night in November 1974?

SM: This isn't a soap opera. This is not a movie. This is about a man who grew up in a dysfunctional family, whose father treated him like a piece of shit. He lashed out in a fit of rage, trying to help his family, his brothers and sisters, and everything fell apart. He was a man just like everyone else.

THE VINDICTIVE BUTCH

If there is a word that best described Butch, it would have to be "enigmatic." He may have deserved to be sent to prison for the role he played in the murder of his parents, but so did his co-conspirators, which a corrupt justice system allowed to go free. At the core of the American justice system is the belief that every individual deserves the right to a fair trial. This is a right that Butch was never afforded. This injustice has unmistakably left Butch feeling bitter and angry. And at times, his anger is directed toward the only ones who are within Butch's reach: his friends, family and the people that try to help him.

Abigail explained Butch's bitterness, by saying, "Over the years I knew [Butch], the topic of conversation mostly centered on 'his case.' He ranted and raved about all the people who cheated him, including his wife and friends. He boasted about all the lawsuits he filed over every little thing. He boasted he sued friends and family—anyone who he thought hurt him. I remember him saying he had filed a lawsuit over his thinning hair! The prison wasn't giving him

Chapter Thirteen

Rogaine, so he wanted to sue to get it. He said, 'I'll get $10 million dollars out of that one!'

"He often talked about his father and Dawn, usually not in good terms. He might have mentioned his mother a couple of times, but never the kids. He ranted about the rest of the family, his grandparents, aunts, uncles, and so forth, who he felt had thrown him to the wolves. He said they were the worst—they got all the money, so they let him rot in prison. He ranted about his lawyers, the prosecution, the courts, Suffolk County, and so on.

"He often said what he wanted to do if and when he ever got out of prison. He wanted to go after the people who did him wrong. He was very, very bitter about many people who were involved in the case, and those who had since tried to help, but failed him. I tried to tell him that doing something like that would do him no good. He would only wind up back where he started from, or worse. There was just no getting through to him. One could not tell him to 'just get on with his life.' He did not want to hear that.

"The friendship was not all give and no take. He did give me a lot of encouragement to improve myself. He was a big cheerleader when I decided to go back to school to become a secretary. He encouraged me to develop a sense of independence from my parents, and to improve my diet. He could be a good friend when he wanted to be.

"Little by little, the letters had trickled down to nothing. I believe it was 1994 when I received a final Christmas card from him. In it, he wanted to wish me and my family a Merry Christmas and hoped all was well with me. That was the last contact I've had with him."

In his 1994 television interview for Christopher Berry-Dee's "The Serial Killers," Gerald Lotto said it best. "Ronnie is a creature of the system now. If he ever was a soft person, he isn't anymore."

Butch has often blamed his own attorneys for the constant defeats he has suffered in the courts, forgetting that the courts seem prejudiced to his fate. As a rule of thumb, when an attorney represents Butch, he has to expect to get a number of hateful and degrading letters. Many of Butch's past attorneys have recognized the injustices done to him, which have inspired them with a desire to right a wrong. Eventually, this inspiration dies out after the realization that the deck is stacked against Butch.

In no way do the injustices Butch has suffered from afford him the right to mistreat others. Even Angela Brigante received her fair share of hate mail from Butch. Geraldine explained, "One time Butch filled up two full pieces of paper with the words 'fuck you' on it because Angela refused to give into one of his requests. But a few weeks later, Butch sent her a birthday card like nothing had ever happened. That's Butch for you."

Sadly, on July 15, 2000, Green Haven Correctional Facility received notice that Angela Brigante had died. Butch, who is perceived by the Department of Corrections as not being an escape risk, pleaded with the facility to attend the funeral. The superintendent denied his request, stating, "A review of your criminal history and your status within this department was considered. Because of the nature of your crime, concerns for your family's safety and your safety, I decided to deny any request for a funeral visit."

Out of love for Butch, his grandmother placed $100,000 in a trust account for him before her death. While in prison, he would be able to receive a monthly stipend from the interest accrued. If he was ever released, he would get the full amount to start a new life. However, the one stipulation was that Butch not contest her will, which he later did. In fact, he unsuccessfully tried to have his own grandmother exhumed so he could get the portraits buried with her because he purportedly wanted to sell them.

BUTCH'S BID FOR PAROLE

A loophole in the law prior to 1978 allowed Butch to serve his six life sentences concurrently. On September 21, 1999, Butch had his first opportunity to go before the parole board. When asked to explain what happened on the night of November 13, 1974, Butch responded, "I will be truthful with you, really; there [are] certain parts of it that I cannot answer. What I can tell you is that I am not making excuses for anything. I loved my family very much, and I had a very serious drug problem. Like I said, I am not using that as an excuse."

Ironically, at his trial, police testimony proved that Butch DeFeo was not a big drug addict, but rather an occasional user. Butch, nevertheless, went on to explain that he was in the basement with a friend at the time of the murders, and identified Dawn, whom he subsequently killed, as the real killer.

As anticipated, the parole board subsequently denied his request, stating, "Your instant offense involved the murder of your parents and four siblings through the use of a rifle. It shows a total disregard for human life. You have gained little insight into your violent antisocial behavior while incarcerated. Discretionary release at this time is incompatible with the safety and welfare of society."

Privately, Butch has always maintained that Bobby Kelske had a hand in the murder of his family. Since his earlier efforts to tell the truth with Jacob Siegfried were thwarted by the Suffolk County criminal justice system, Butch has resigned himself to allow the mystery of what really happened the night his family died to be left unanswered. Butch once even claimed how today he can still hear the maniacal laughter of his sister Dawn, and how his dreams constantly send him back to that fateful night in November 1974.

"Big Ronnie always told Butch he would never amount to anything," Geraldine said. "But Amityville and all the speculation surrounding the murders made him infamous, proving, in Butch's mind, his father wrong."

Unlike Butch, however, Bobby Kelske refused to comment, even on his death bed, about the DeFeo murders. And on January 1, 2001, Kelske lost his long bout with cancer and met death showing little remorse or concern for Butch. But before his death, Kelske told a relative that it was ironic how he had beaten the cops and the Mob, only to die from cancer.

In one breath, Butch said he tried not to hold any grudges, but in another, he said, "I hope he died a slow, painful death and choked on his own blood."

Kelske was only 50 years old, and according to family members, never able to get past that fateful night in November 1974.

Although Bobby Kelske claimed to Butch that he did not kill the children and felt Dawn was anything but serious in her threats to do so, the way he took off running before Butch opened Allison's door indicated Bobby Kelske knew more about the children's deaths than he originally let on. It is quite possible that Bobby Kelske looked on in astonishment as Dawn killed her younger siblings.

In September 2001, Butch DeFeo again was scheduled to go before the parole board. This time, however, the hearing was postponed for six months because of Butch's pending appeal. Regardless, in the interests of justice, I wrote to the parole board.

Among the many things I addressed in my letter, I wanted the board to seek out the truth. I wrote, "I am writing you because I have seen evidence to prove that an injustice has been committed in the State of New York. Therefore, you should take it upon yourselves to read the trial transcripts, research the police evidence, statements from witnesses, forensic evidence, etc. Find, for yourselves, the truth about the case. This way you can come to a fair and impartial decision about inmate #75A4053's bid for freedom."

In addition, I asked the Attorney General of the State New York, Eliot Spitzer, to re-examine the DeFeo murders. I wrote, "Since Mr. DeFeo has yet to receive a fair and impartial trial, I feel that it is in the best interest of justice if your office takes an active role in re-examining the entire case, and those originally responsible for the criminal investigation, who are guilty of breaking the law."

As expected, my requests for a new investigation went unnoticed.

AFTERWORD

AFTER FINISHING MY investigation and my ensuing book, I came to the conclusion that the old Butch DeFeo, the one prior to incarceration, was not the monster he was made out to be. For instance, Lucy Burkin testified at the DeFeo trial how Butch would often ask if she wanted a sandwich or a grape soda on warm days because he knew she liked it. Certainly, those were not the actions of a mindless killer. Of course, Butch DeFeo was, by far, no choir boy.

Still, the Butch DeFeo that currently sits in prison is understandably filled with anger and bitterness. Butch DeFeo might have been guilty, but so were the other parties involved. Obviously, he was never afforded a fair trial.

Incredibly, in November 2001, Thomas Spota was elected to be the new Suffolk County District Attorney. During his bid for election, Spota made it a point to stress he helped prosecute Butch DeFeo. Regarding Butch DeFeo's future legal motions, Spota's tenure should prove interesting, to say the least. As they say, the cat is now out of the bag.

So does Butch DeFeo deserve a second chance at freedom? More important, will he ever be afforded the opportunity?

Gerard Sullivan may have been right when he argued that the existence of accomplices does not exonerate Butch DeFeo from his own criminal liability. After all, he was still guilty of murder. More important, Butch also is guilty of placing his younger siblings, Marc, John and Allison, in harm's way, regardless of whether he participated in their murders.

Butch's guilt, however, does not justify the unlawful conduct of those presiding over the DeFeo case. With regards to Butch DeFeo, they have proven themselves to be prejudiced. And by their own actions, they have corrupted the same justice system they vowed to protect.

Butch DeFeo, nonetheless, has exhibited a real disregard for those around him, including suing his ex-wife and wanting to exhume the body of his grandmother. Over the years, he has also proved himself to be a habitual liar, willing to change his story whenever it suits him.

Take, for instance, his claims at his trial that he was insane. Yet later, to get the money from his parents' estate he needed for his appeal, he was sane. Furthermore, both of Butch DeFeo's ex-wives proved to me, as has Butch by his own actions, that Butch will turn on someone the minute his demands are not met.

On the surface, it would appear that Butch has never taken responsibility for the murder of his family. Outside of my interview with him, the closest I have seen Butch ever come to admitting, publicly, his real role in the murders was in a letter to one of the producers of The History Channel documentary. Butch wrote, "It was cold blooded murder. Period. No ghost. No demons. Just three people, in which I was one."

It would not surprise me if Butch, in his future parole hearings, blamed Dawn DeFeo and Bobby Kelske for the murders, forgetting, once more, to mention his own involvement.

Aside from that, there is one thing I am certain about, and that is the story he revealed to me was true. Of course, that does not mean that Butch DeFeo revealed to me the entire story. After all,

Afterword

there is still the matter of the seventh body.

If this was a seventh victim, then who was she and why was she in the DeFeo basement? If this was a DeFeo who was brought back to the crime scene, or later moved downstairs, then what purpose would the police have in doing this? In spite of these questions, too much independent corroboration exists to support the story Butch DeFeo chose to tell me. His reasons for revealing the truth, I was later told, were anything but admirable. As he had tried with other writers, Butch felt that he could extort money from me. But his plan backfired when Geraldine DeFeo refused to profit from this book by suing me for royalties.

One cannot simply disregard Geraldine DeFeo's testimony because records indicating her marriage to Butch DeFeo, prior to the murders, cannot be found. The records, according to Geraldine, were destroyed by some powerful figures. So who is to say she is not telling the truth?

In her defense are several affidavits that were presented in federal court by Butch DeFeo's friends that vouched for Geraldine's authenticity. There also are third-party accounts, such as Abigail, that support her story. Even Dawn's boyfriend, William Davidge, told me that Geraldine was around prior to the murders. And when I called Linnea Nonnewitz's daughter, one of the first things I was asked was "is Geraldine still with Butch?" Even Hans Holzer, who alleged that Butch was possessed by a dead Indian chief, admitted to me that he had knowledge that Geraldine and Butch were married prior to the murders.

So would a women who is perpetrating a fraud venture into the Suffolk County District Attorney's office or the Suffolk County Police Department proclaiming she was married to Butch prior to the murders? Would she request a U.S. district court judge to unseal a civil case because she was a DeFeo, as Geraldine did with Judge Jack B. Weinstein?

Ever since stepping forward, Geraldine has been ridiculed and labeled a fraud by those who want to perpetuate the Amityville hoax or feel threatened by her existence. Yet this woman has no motive to lie. She neither wants fame, money nor Butch out of jail. Of course, she would like to see the wrongs done in his case corrected. But she is the first one to admit that Butch's own mistreatment does not give him a license to hurt others.

If there is one thing certain in the Amityville case, it would be that anything is possible. Aside from the ludicrous claims of demonic pigs and green slime, the coverup of the DeFeo murders was unprecedented.

Still, if Geraldine's testimony was disregarded, then what is left? There is still the matter of Bobby Kelske's being implicated in the murders; the second gun and different caliber of bullet found in Louise DeFeo; the DeFeos' bodies being moved and the blood-stained floors; the undeniable Mob elements associated with this story; the Lutzes conspiring with William Weber to write a fictional ghost story; a judge who, according to the prosecution, was hand-picked; and a seventh body.

ACKNOWLEDGMENTS

ALTHOUGH I WOULD like to name each and every person who helped me in my quest for the truth, I find it impossible to do so. I would, however, like to say "thank you" to all of those (you know who you are) who contributed to this effort. I also want to extend my appreciation to Ronald Singer, Roxanne Kaplan, Joel Martin, Jerry Gates, Harvey Aronson, Roger Stacy, Christopher Berry-Dee and the Criminology Research Institute, Blaine Duncan, Rip Holly, the W. Burghardt Turner collection at the State University of New York at Stony Brook, *The National Law Journal*, and *Newsday* for their generosity. I would also like to single out Geraldine DeFeo for her trust, friendship, and assistance, and Jim Cypher, my literary agent, friend, and one amazing line editor.

I want to extend a "special thanks" to those individuals in Suffolk County law enforcement who assisted me in uncovering the real story. As I said earlier, you are a testament to the honest men and women in law enforcement. Some of you even risked your jobs, and possibly more, by aiding me. Although there were several "bad apples" in the various departments in 1974, I am happy to say that that does not appear the case now.

I also want to take this opportunity to acknowledge the DeFeo family themselves. After all, six human beings, three of them being innocent children, had to die to make this story possible.

Finally, I just thank God for the opportunity to report the truth to the public. Far too long has the devil gotten undue credit regarding the Amityville case. His reign is over; the truth has prevailed.

ENDNOTES

NOTES FOR "MURDER ON OCEAN AVENUE"

24 "You got to help me": Statement of William Scordamaglia, owner of Henry's Bar, taken by Amityville Police Officer Kenneth Greguski on November 13, 1974.
26 "built in 1925": Records of 112 Ocean Avenue, Town of Babylon, New York.
30 "covered in blood": "A Quiet Drink Turns Into An Invitation to Disaster," *Newsday*, November 14, 1974.
30 "Unsure of the address": Transcript of tape-recorded 911 call from November 13, 1974.
30 "Greguski, who had just gotten a sandwich": Bill Jensen, "Resident Evil," *The Long Island Voice*, October 27, 1999.
32 "Take it easy": Testimony of Officer Kenneth Greguski, *People vs. DeFeo*, 1251-74, p. 2373.

NOTES FOR "AN OPEN AND SHUT CASE"

33 "He was a lamb": *Newsday*, November 15, 1974.
34 "Once I started": Testimony of Dennis Rafferty, *People vs. DeFeo*, 1251-74, p. 3403.
36 "I shall not attempt": *Newsday*, November 19, 1974.

NOTES FOR "LIFE AS A DEFEO"

43 "And on June 28, 1965": As recorded in the official mortgage for 112 Ocean Avenue.
50 "Big Ronnie co-wrote a song": Joe Williams, "One is a Lonesome Number," (Roulette Birdland Records, 1963).
51 "close ties to . . . police benevolent societies": "Surviving Son Held in Slaying of Six," *Newsday*, November 15, 1974.
51 "Joseph Colombo Sr. assumed control": Peter Diapoulos and Steven Linakis, *The Sixth Family*, (New York: Bantam Books, 1976) p. 25-27.
52 "Joseph Brancato . . . part of a tough Colombo crew. . . . in Suffolk County": Ibid. p. 237.
53 "At his trial, Butch DeFeo...described": Testimony of Butch DeFeo, *People vs. DeFeo*, 1251-74, p. 5377.
61 "Big Ronnie kept most of his jewelry": Detailed accounting of jewelry can be obtained in the estate papers of Ronald and Louise DeFeo located in Riverhead, Suffolk County, New York.
63 "Dawn . . . used . . . LSD": Affidavit of William Davidge, July 24, 1990.
63 "not to take after his example.": Testimony of Grace Fagan, *People vs. DeFeo*, 1251-74.
65 "Butch even gave me money": Affidavit of William Davidge, July 24, 1990.
65 "A gifted athlete, Kelske . . .": Information taken from 1968 Amityville High School Yearbook.
66 "Irene Reichelt . . . said": Bill Jensen, "Resident Evil," *The Long Island Voice*, October 27, 1999.
66 "would drink and then get into fights": George Vecsey,

"Neighbors Recall DeFeos as 'Nice, Normal Family'," *The New York Times*, November 15, 1974.

NOTES FOR "ON THE ROAD TO DISASTER"

68 "It just went on and on.": Linda Whitmore, *Official Transcription of Ronald J. DeFeo Parole Hearing*, September 21, 1999.
74 "prosecutors wanted him to stand trial": "Examination of Colombo Ordered," *The New York Times*, April 1, 1972, p. L27.
74 "kept . . . surveillance": Morris Kaplan, "Alleged Colombo Aide Held in Bribery," *The New York Times*, November 11, 1972, p. L37.
76 "a claim of $2200.99": Records of Suffolk County Surrogate Court, *File on the Estate of Ronald DeFeo and Louise DeFeo*.
77 Description of canal victim: Gerard Sullivan and Harvey Aronson, *High Hopes: The Amityville Murders*, (New York: Coward, McCann, and Geoghegan, 1981), p. 155.
84 "Dawn's hatred toward": Affidavit of William Davidge, July 24, 1990.
85 "Lin, I am going to warn you": E-mail from Linnea Nonnewitz to Ric Osuna, August 25, 2000.
85 "Linnea believed the miracle" : Ibid.

NOTES FOR "IN THE SWEAT OF AN AUTUMN NIGHT"

97 "the weather report had called for wind": "Weather Report," *Newsday*, November 12-13, 1974.
99 "'Castle Keep' was playing on Channel 5": "TV Listings," *Newsday*, November 12, 1974.
112 "Vito D'Iorio arrived": Detective Edward Simmons, shield #312, *Statement of Vito D'Iorio*, November 13, 1974.

NOTES FOR "EXPOSING POLICE BRUTALITY"

121 "basically accurate and credible": Judge Thomas Stark, *People vs. DeFeo*, Indictment #1251-74, October 1, 1975, p. 1083.
122 "We demand prosecution": *Suffolk Street Papers*, November 1974.
131 "the handwriting was . . . Rafferty": Court of Appeals New York, *People vs. Maerling*, 46 N.Y. 2d 289, 385 N.E. 2d 1245, 1978 N.Y. LEXIS 2420, 413 N.Y.S. 2d 316, December 21, 1978.
131 "tied a piece of paper": Rafael Abramovitz, "When the Wrong Man Confesses," *The National Law Journal*, June 11, 1979.
131 "The prosecutor who served on the case": "Maerling Found Guilty," *Newsday*, November 3, 1973.
132 "he had been severely beaten": Ibid.
132 "Wallace's death . . . strangulation": Ibid.
132 "the accused has much": The Suffolk County Bar Association, *Report of the Civil Rights Committee on Allegations of Police Brutality in Suffolk County*, January 16, 1980, p. 4.
133 "The victims are usually poor", Ibid., p. 9.
134 "Judge Jack Weinstein . . . had to dismiss": Judge Jack B. Weinstein, *Coleman vs. Klein*, 73-C-1857, July 21, 1976.
136 "Stuart Namm": Thomas J. Maier, "The Old Namm Highly Praised Suffolk Law Enforcement; the New Namm is Sharply Critical," *Newsday*, January 26, 1988.
136 "The initial investigation": State of New York Commission of Investigation, *An Investigation of the Suffolk County District Attorney's Office and Police Department*, April 1989, p. 43.
136 "Eventually the jury acquitted": Judge Stuart Namm, *People vs. Corso*, Indictment #562-84, 129 Misc. 2d 590, 493 N.Y.S. 2d 520, 1985 N.Y. Misc. Lexis 2641, July 19, 1985.
137 "We had detectives": Thomas J. Maier, "The Old Namm Highly Praised Suffolk Law Enforcement; the New Namm is Sharply Critical," *Newsday*, January 26, 1988.
138 "a three-page written confession . . . in Detective Dennis Rafferty's handwriting": State of New York Commission of

Investigation, *An Investigation of the Suffolk County District Attorney's Office and Police Department*, April 1989, p. 32.
138 "led to a reprimand": Thomas J. Maier, "The Old Namm Highly Praised Suffolk Law Enforcement; the New Namm is Sharply Critical," *Newsday*, January 26, 1988.
140 "high-profile cases": State of New York Commission of Investigation, *An Investigation of the Suffolk County District Attorney's Office and Police Department*, April 1989, p. 54.
141 "Both Robert Genna": Ibid., p. 63.
142 "Every black guy": Ibid., p.66.
143 "bastard child": Robert E. Kessler, "A Scathing Report SIC Urges Special Prosecutor for Suffolk Law Officials," *Newsday*, April 25, 1989.
143 "In 1991, he was elected": "Suffolk County Judges Profiles," *The New York Law Journal Web site*, August 24, 1998.
143 "police officers like Theodore Adamchak": Paul Vitello, "Up Against the Blue Wall," *Newsday*, September 25, 1988.
144 "That kind of judging": Elizabeth Wasserman, "Accolades for Retired Judge, but Namm Would Rather be back on Bench," *Newsday*, January 28, 1993.
144 "As early as 1992": Katti Gray, "Cop Review Panel Urged, Hundreds of Complaints Cited by ACLU," *Newsday*, April 1, 1993.

NOTES FOR "DISSECTING THE FACTS"

147 "to Louise DeFeo's": "A Convict's Tale," *Newsday*, March 19, 1986.
147 "to disembodied voices": John G. Jones, *The Amityville Horror Two*, (New York: Warner Books, 1982), p. 7.
148 "recollection of Deborah Consentino": Testimony of Deborah Consentino, *People vs. DeFeo*, 1251-74, p. 2668.
150 "news footage from November 14, 1974": *NBC Interview of Suffolk County Chief of Detectives*, November 14, 1974.
151 "Between 11 p.m. and 12:25 a.m.": Officer Kenneth Greguski, shield #123, *Village of Amityville Complaint and Investigation*

Report #249, November 13, 1974.
151 "On the afternoon of November 14, 1974, Dr. Adelman": Testimony of Dr. Howard Adelman, *People vs. DeFeo*, 1251-74, p. 2650-2651.
151 "the probability would rule against": Neil S. Rosenfeld, "After the funeral, six murder counts," *Newsday*, November 19, 1974.
151 "Race . . . a first grade detective,": Hans Holzer, "Interview with Herman Race," *Murder in Amityville*, (New York: Tower Publications, 1979), p. 233.
152 "trial exhibit #35," Mark D. Cohen, *Respondent Brief to Appeal of Ronald J. DeFeo Jr.*, December 30, 1977, p. 70.
152 "Sullivan openly questioned": Gerard Sullivan and Harvey Aronson, *High Hopes: The Amityville Murders*, (New York: Coward, McCann, and Geoghegan, 1981), p. 349.
152 "Detective Howard Sommers": Detective Robert Reichert, *Suffolk County Supplemental Police Report*, 74-340868, November 14, 1974.
159 Description of Butch DeFeo's arrest for grand larceny: Suffolk County Police Department, *Criminal History of Ronald Joseph DeFeo Jr.*, November 15, 1974.
164 "was put back in bed": *People vs. DeFeo*, 1251-74, p. 2521.
166 "Herman Race had testified": Testimony of Herman Race, *People vs. DeFeo*, 1251-74, p. 1129.

NOTES FOR "GUILTY UNTIL PROVEN INNOCENT"

174 "Like an average good family": *Newsday*, November 14, 1974.
174 "final blessings on the deceased": Phone call with Father James McNamara by Ric Osuna, February 16, 2001.
174 "to vacate 112 Ocean Avenue": Testimony of Detective Gaspar Randazzo, *People vs. DeFeo*, 1251-74, p. 2881.
175 "Gozaloff told me": Testimony of Butch DeFeo, *People vs. DeFeo*, 1251-74, p. 778.
175 "Don't worry about it": Testimony of Robert Kelske, *People vs. DeFeo*, 1251-74, p. 4114.

175 "The police searched his trunk": Suffolk County Impound Report, November 14, 1974.

176 "represent him...critical hours": Testimony of Richard Wyssling *People vs. DeFeo*, 1251-74, p. 658.

177 "a reputed hitman": The Genovese crime family is one of the most powerful and feared crime families that ever existed. On September 9, 1934, Peter DeFeo, with George Smurra, Gus Frasca, Michele Miranda and Ernest Rupolo, shot and killed, upon the orders of Vito Genovese, Ferdinand Boccia, a lieutenant in the Genovese crime family. Referenced from Jay Robert Nash's *World Encyclopedia of Organized Crime*, (New York: Da Capo Press, 1993), p.185.

177 "Peter DeFeo was never convicted": *Newsday*, November 15, 1974.

177 "he would later learn...Mr. Lee": Testimony of Detective James Barylski, *People vs. DeFeo*, 1251-74, p. 440.

181-190 Butch's description of interrogation and brutality: Testimony of Butch DeFeo, *People vs. DeFeo*, 1251-74; Interview with Ric Osuna, November 30, 2000.

185 "D'Iorio's claims were later corroborated": Testimony of Lucy Burkin, *People vs. DeFeo*, 1251-74, p. 4571.

186 "they're taking me to a white house": Testimony of Butch DeFeo, *People vs. DeFeo*, 1251-74, p. 791.

187 "the white framed house": Gerard Sullivan and Harvey Aronson, *High Hopes: The Amityville Murders*, (New York: Coward, McCann, and Geoghegan, 1981), p. 47.

192 Description of interviews: *NBC News footage*, November 14, 1974.

193 "Butch was picked up at 7:30 a.m.": Detention Log regarding report #74-340868 for the evening of November 14, 1974 to the morning of November 15, 1974.

193 "he informed...Berry-Dee": Letter from Christopher Berry-Dee to Ric Osuna, May 30, 2002.

194 "Symmons . . . was once": Testimony of Leonard Symmons, *People vs. DeFeo*, 1251-74, p. 4323.

196 "Bobby knew we destroyed": Interview with Butch DeFeo by

Ric Osuna, November 30, 2000.

202 "In his motion, Siegfried requested:" Jacob Siegfried, *Notice of Motion*, January 15, 1975.

203 "on May 27, 1975": Gerard Sullivan and Harvey Aronson, *High Hopes: The Amityville Murders*, (New York: Coward, McCann, and Geoghegan, 1981), p. 95.

NOTES FOR "A LOSING STRATEGY"

205 "William Weber was assigned": Mark Cohen, *Brief of Respondent*, December 30, 1977, p. 38.

205 "received an inquiring phone call": Gerard Sullivan and Harvey Aronson, *High Hopes: The Amityville Murders*, (New York: Coward, McCann, and Geoghegan, 1981), p. 96.

205 "Weber . . . had supported": Hearing transcripts from *People vs. DeFeo*, 1251-74, July 29, 1975.

205 "I assigned him": Ibid.

206 "So on July 29, 1975": Ibid.

206 "Barry Springer said": Affidavit of Barry Springer, July 23, 1988.

206-208 Reference to Gerard Sullivan's Quotes: Gerard Sullivan and Harvey Aronson, *High Hopes: The Amityville Murders*, (New York: Coward, McCann, and Geoghegan, 1981), p. 84-95.

208 "Maria Dascole . . . Butch": Mark Cohen, *Brief of Respondent*, December 30, 1977, p. 36.

208 "Weber attempted to rehearse": Affidavit of Linnea Nonnewitz, July 28, 1988.

208 "Weber advised me": Affidavit of Barry Springer, July 23, 1988.

211 "brought up canal murder": Preliminary Hearing of *People vs. DeFeo*, 1251-74, p. 546.

212 "opposed Weber's new omnibus motion": Gerard Sullivan, *Affidavit in Opposition*, July 28, 1975.

212 "Judge Signorelli won": *The New York Times*, November 5, 1975, p. 23.

213 "But I had not finished maneuvering": Gerard Sullivan and

Harvey Aronson, *High Hopes: The Amityville Murders*, (New York: Coward, McCann, and Geoghegan, 1981), p. 106.
214 "Justice Thomas M. Stark had served": Ibid., 107.

NOTES FOR "IMPEACHING THE DEFEO TRIAL"

215 "Butch told Justice Stark": Testimony of Butch DeFeo, *People vs. DeFeo*, 1251-74, p. 781.
216 "being threatened with death": Ibid., p. 796
216 "grimaced noticeably": Ibid., 799.
218 "three-years' probation": Gerard Sullivan and Harvey Aronson, *High Hopes: The Amityville Murders*, (New York: Coward, McCann, and Geoghegan, 1981), p. 216.
218 Details of Post-Hearing Conference: *People vs. DeFeo*, 1251-74, p. 1112-1147.
221 "at 4:08 p.m.": *Summary of Verdict*.
224 "not while I was questioning him": Testimony of Detective Dennis Rafferty, *People vs. DeFeo*, 1251-74, p. 3422.
226 "had been ringing": Gerard Sullivan and Harvey Aronson, *High Hopes: The Amityville Murders*, (New York: Coward, McCann, and Geoghegan, 1981), p. 39.
230 "Keep your voice down": *People vs. DeFeo*, 1251-74, p. 4047.
231 "Kelske and another man": Gerard Sullivan and Harvey Aronson, *High Hopes: The Amityville Murders*, (New York: Coward, McCann, and Geoghegan, 1981), p. 151.
232 "that there was a great deal of money": Summation of Gerard Sullivan, *People vs. DeFeo*, 1251-74, p. 6742.
233 "At this time he asked me": Testimony of Detective Gerard Gozaloff, *People vs. DeFeo*, 1251-74, p. 3729.
233 "Detective Barylski said": Testimony of Detective James Barylski, *People vs. DeFeo*, 1251-74, p. 446.
234 "Donahue wore his school uniform": Gerard Sullivan and Harvey Aronson, *High Hopes: The Amityville Murders*, (New York: Coward, McCann, and Geoghegan, 1981), p. 327.
235 "Boys of that age": *People vs. DeFeo*, 1251-74, p. 6617.
236 "dirty cop": Summation of Gerard Sullivan, *People vs. DeFeo*,

1251-74, p. 6752.

238 "piece of scrap paper": Testimony of Melvin Berger, *People vs. DeFeo*, 1251-74, p. 3627.

242 "Once he said": Testimony of Phyllis Procita, *People vs. DeFeo*, 1251-74, pp. 3844-3845.

244 "during an interview . . . Hans Holzer": Hans Holzer, *Murder in Amityville*, (New York: Tower Publications, 1979), p. 259.

246 "I killed them all": Testimony of Butch DeFeo, *People vs. DeFeo*, 1251-74, p. 5195.

247 "John Kramer, a jailhouse snitch . . .": Gerard Sullivan and Harvey Aronson, *High Hopes: The Amityville Murders*, (New York: Coward, McCann, and Geoghegan, 1981), p. 126/347.

NOTES FOR "CAPITALIZING ON A TRAGEDY"

252 "The DeFeo slayings . . . bother us.": "A Dream House Became a Nightmare," *Newsday*, February 17, 1976.

252 "Get out!": Jay Anson, *The Amityville Horror*, (New Jersey: Prentice Hall, 1977), p. 17.

252 "Don't use it": Paul Hoffman, "Our Dream House was Haunted," *Good Housekeeping*, April 1977, p. 238.

256 "The next night, she began . . .": Paul Hoffman, "Our Dream House was Haunted," *Good Housekeeping*, April 1977, p. 240.

256 "the priest was suffering": Jay Anson, *The Amityville Horror*, (New Jersey: Prentice Hall, 1977), p. 41.

256 "Will you stop?": Alan Landsburg, "In Search of the Amityville Horror," October 1979.

257 "more than $80 million dollars": Internet Movie Database, *www.imdb.com*.

257 "the right to examine": Jacob Siegfried, *Notice of Motion*, Indictment #1251-74, January 15, 1975.

259 "in 1908, George's grandfather": "Obituary Eleanor Parry Lutz," *Newsday*, September 21, 1999.

261 "one of the first trips": A.J. Carter and Christopher Cook,

"DeFeo Home Abandoned; Buyer Calls It Haunted," *Newsday*, February 14, 1976.

261 "In late January 1976": *Lutz vs. Weber*, 78CV119, "Interrogatories answered by William Weber," November 21, 1978.

265 "tie them up": Pete Stevenson, "Was the book a setup?" *The Morning Call*, February 28, 1978.

265 "of 50 percent": Peter Lester, "The Amityville Horror Hype, Hoax and Heroine," *People*, September 17, 1979, p. 91.

266 "I faced George Lutz": E-mail from Linnea Nonnewitz to Ric Osuna, September 16, 2000.

266 "the book is a work of fiction": Pete Bowles, "Amityville Book Gets Bad Review," *Newsday*, September 12, 1979.

267 "serious ethical question": Pete Bowles, "Lutz Family Horror Suit is Rejected," *Newsday*, September 11, 1979.

268 "The Lutzes deliberately": Ibid.

268 "I don't believe Mr. Lutz": Ibid.

269 "as early as February": *Lutz vs. Weber*, 78CV119, "Defendants' Pre-Trial Memorandum," September 7, 1979, p. 11.

269 "bypassed the plaintiffs'": *Lutz vs. Weber*, 78CV119, "Defendants' Pre-Trial Memorandum," September 7, 1979, p. 12.

270 "substantial": Ibid.

270 "as early as . . . buy a $180,000 house": *Lutz vs. Weber*, 78CV119, "Interrogatories answered by George and Kathleen Lutz," October 27, 1978.

272 "Father Pecoraro stated": Pete Bowles, "Amityville Book Gets Bad Review," *Newsday*, September 12, 1979.

277 "an evil black shadow": Marvin Scott, "Channel 5 Broadcast of March 6, 1976 seance," March 1976.

277 "I was the [DeFeos'] housekeeper": E-mail from Linnea Nonnewitz to author dated Friday, August 25, 2000.

278 "televised interviews": Taken from excerpts of George and Kathy Lutz's appearance on "The Merv Griffin Show" and "Good Morning America" in 1979.

278 "They further added": Don Longo, "Occultists dissect 'Amity

Horror'," *The Amityville Record*, September 29, 1977; Dr. Stephen Kaplan and Roxanne Salch Kaplan, *The Amityville Horror Conspiracy*, (Laceyville: Belfrey Books, 1995), p. 32.

279 "They claimed . . . Shinnecock Indians": Ed and Lorraine Warren, *Blair Witch 2 Webcast*, October 18, 2000.

280 "The bed was not there": E-mail from Linnea Nonnewitz to Ric Osuna, March 31, 2001.

280 "Ed Warren insisted Butch . . . told police": Ed and Lorraine Warren, *Blair Witch 2 Webcast*, October 18, 2000.

280 "I didn't hear no voices": Testimony of Butch DeFeo, *People vs. DeFeo*, 1251-74, p. 5429.

280 "were in a state of phantomania": Warrens' official Web site, www.warrens.net.

284 "there never was a witch named John Ketcham": E-mail from Ketcham Genealogy Organization to author dated July 14, 2000.

284 "Because of marital problems": Hans Holzer, *Murder in Amityville*, (New York: Tower Publications, 1979), p. 286; Should also be noted that author confirmed the divorce through interviews with Amityville residents in June 1999.

286 Description of "Spectrum with Joel Martin" Radio Show Interview with William Weber: From *The Amityville Horror Conspiracy* by Stephen and Roxanne Kaplan, pp. 167-179. Reprinted by permission of the author and the publisher, Toad Hall Press, R R 2 Box 2090, Laceyville, PA 18623.

289 "One of the primary reasons": Pete Stevenson, "Was the book a setup?" *The Morning Call*, February 28, 1978.

290 "In a discussion about Witchcraft": From *The Amityville Horror Conspiracy* by Stephen and Roxanne Kaplan, p. 22. Reprinted by permission of the author and the publisher, Toad Hall Press, R R 2 Box 2090, Laceyville, PA 18623.

291 "On March 12, 1980, Anson died": "Deaths," *Philadelphia Daily News*, March 14, 1980.

292 "He was very adamant": E-mail from Roger Stacy to Ric Osuna, October 4, 2001.

292 "On December 31, 1974": Information obtained from public

record of mortgage between George and Elizabeth Lutz, January 15, 1974.

293 "On January 13, 1977, Hans Holzer": Hans Holzer, *Murder in Amityville*, (New York: Tower Publications, 1979), p. 149.

293 "Whoever lived in the DeFeo": Hans Holzer, "Ghost house was scene of six shocking murders before scared family fled," *National Examiner*, November 9, 1982.

NOTES FOR "IN THE PURSUIT OF JUSTICE"

303 "the way he was dodging": Testimony of Detective Dennis Rafferty, *People vs. DeFeo*, 1251-74, p. 3447.

304 "The jurors . . . erroneously," William Weber and Steven Sulsky, *Appellant's Brief and Appendix*, 1978, p. 54.

304 "had inappropriately taken the," Ibid., p. 63.

307 "Jack Glazer to act on his behalf," Letter from Jack Glazer, Esq., to Butch DeFeo, March 25, 1980.

314 "Justice Stark failed to see," Honorable Thomas Stark, *Memorandum and Decision*, January 6, 1993, p. 5.

316 "Testing will go forward," Andrew Smith "Catterson seeks review to aid wrongly convicted," *Newsday*, December 20, 2000.

317 "Detective Rafferty testified": Testimony of Detective Dennis Rafferty, *People vs. DeFeo*, 1251-74, p. 3401.

318 "He had to get down": Summation of Gerard Sullivan, *People vs. DeFeo*, 1251-74, p. 6725.

319 "The blood on the clothing is mine," Letter from Butch DeFeo to Geraldine DeFeo, October 10, 2000.

319 "obtained a hair and blood sample," *Suffolk County Police Laboratory Report Certified Copy #74-340868*, November 22, 1974, p. 7.

320 "He got into his shower": Summation of Gerard Sullivan, *People vs. DeFeo*, 1251-74, p. 6726.

320 "clean as a whistle": Testimony of Lucy Burkin, *People vs. DeFeo*, 1251-74, p. 4573.

321 "In the storm drain": Testimony of Detective Gerard Gozaloff,

People vs. DeFeo, 1251-74, p. 3711.
321 "all items were partially wet": Testimony of Detective Gerard Gozaloff, *People vs. DeFeo*, 1251-74, p. 3741.
321 "not tested until November 22": Testimony of Detective Nicholas Severino, *People vs. DeFeo*, 1251-74, p. 3949.
323 "Angered . . . Butch responded," Letter from Butch DeFeo to Geraldine DeFeo, October 10, 2000.

NOTES FOR "LIFE INCARCERATED"

329 "sharpened knives," Department of Corrections, *Official Charge Sheet of Inmate #75A4053*.
329 "raving maniac," United Press International, "Amityville Killer Wins Case In Jail," *Philadelphia Daily News*, October 3, 1984.
337 "The recorded value of the DeFeo estate," Records of Suffolk County Surrogate Court, *Final Accounting of the Estate of Ronald DeFeo and Louise DeFeo*.
338 "the Surrogate Court permitted Butch's motion," Records of Suffolk County Surrogate Court, *File on the Estate of Ronald DeFeo and Louise DeFeo*.
339 "Weber was paid," Ibid.
346 "I will be truthful with you," Linda Whitmore, *Official Transcription of Ronald J. DeFeo Parole Hearing*, September 21, 1999.

ABOUT THE AUTHOR

Author Ric Osuna is no stranger to the mystery and intrigue surrounding *The Amityville Horror*. Osuna, a Las Vegas-based writer, has received a number of acclamations from both expert criminologists and journalists for his research into the notorious Amityville murders.

Compelled to report the truth about the DeFeo murders and ensuing coverup that included turning the DeFeo home into a house of horror, Osuna acquired crime-scene photographs, trial transcripts, police reports, and other official documentation previously unavailable to the public over a period of three years. Despite receiving death threats and warnings, Osuna finished his book, *The Night the DeFeos Died*.

Osuna's professional experience includes serving as editor, senior writer, and consultant for several prominent luxury magazines. His production experiences range from research consultant to producing roles on various films and documentaries relating to Amityville. Osuna is also the founder of *The Amityville Murders* Web site, located at www.amityvillemurders.com.

Due to the huge surge of interest in his book, Osuna has participated in more than a dozen TV and radio shows across the nation, including A&E's *City Confidential* and The Travel Channel's *On Location* series. In addition, *The Night the DeFeos Died* has been the subject of several editorials in Internet-based and traditional publications, including the *New York Post* and the *Skeptical Inquirer*. Osuna was honored in January 2003, when Xlibris named him "Author of the Month." Most recently, Osuna was inducted into the prestigious *New Criminologist's* Hall of Fame.

Author Ric Osuna sits behind a large sampling of the documentation he uncovered during his three-year investigation into the Amityville case.

Made in the USA
Lexington, KY
15 September 2011